Praise for

The Risk-Based Approach to Combating Modern Slavery

by

Ehi Eric Esoimeme

"Having read and enjoyed previous excellent work from Ehi Eric Esoimeme, I was really curious to dig into his new book, *The Risk-Based Approach to Combating Modern Slavery* (2019). I found the book to be well-written, and its ability to serve as a comprehensive reference guide provides an abundance of information on the topic in a very well-structured manner. The book offers robust research and provides the reader with a deep understanding of the concepts of human trafficking and modern slavery, as well as some practical ideas and solutions on how to best apply a risk-based approach across every company's supply chain. A must read for those interested in the topic."

—Gregory Dellas, CAMS-Audit, FICA., Director, Wealth and Markets, Bank of Cyprus and Chair, ACAMS Cyprus Chapter

"From a risk management perspective, Ehi Eric Esoimeme's book offers comprehensive coverage for how a risk-based approach can be used to prevent modern slavery. His in-depth research into the various different forms of modern slavery seamlessly combines with his expertise in the topic to enable anyone who reads this book to understand the myriad ways in which we can effectively combat modern slavery. The book meets its purpose by explaining how to combat, trace, and disrupt modern slavery. As an AML and financial crime expert, the risk-based approach has become central in the effective implementation of crucial requirements in most sectors – and something that is not optional, but a prerequisite. Ehi

Eric Esoimeme's use of this approach will enable state authorities, institutions, and individuals to take into consideration and focus on its key areas to allow them to achieve overall efficaciousness. Additionally, and through the risk-based approach, when dealing with high-risk jurisdictions and complex financial transactions without clear economic or legal purpose, the book helps to generate awareness of the broader risks and particularities of modern-day slavery, ultimately enabling state authorities, institutions, and individuals to apply measures in an effective and efficient manner and extent, commensurate to the findings.

In line with his vast experience in risk and compliance, Ehi Eric Esoimeme offers guidance on suspicious activity monitoring and the identification of red flags applicable to modern-day slavery, so that state authorities and institutions can more easily determine and assess whether their current programs are covering recent trends, and new and existing red flags. The book gives an extensive review of current pieces of contemporary international slavery legislation for several countries and a review of international regulations, recommendations, objectives, and initiatives. The purpose of this information provides the scope on how to prevent, protect against, control, and provide a public response to the international menace that modern day slavery is. Ehi Eric Esoimeme seeks to curb the spread of modern-day slavery by providing crucial enforcement and legislation details that are commensurate with and up to date with the specific governing bodies. This data serves to inform and restrict the modern-day slavery risks to the general public and prevent international human trafficking and trade.

Contemporary organisations and individuals should read Ehi's book because it provides a critical assessment based on existing evidence and has an explicitly-stated rationale on modern day slavery prevention. His analysis should engage significant intellectual debates in institutions of higher learning. Ehi's skill combination of governance, risk and compliance, and technical insight, along with his high level of conscientiousness in his previous works enables me to highly recommend this book."

—Maureen Mutua, Senior Partner, AML and Financial Crime, Eden Management Consultants (United Arab Emirates)

"In Russia, slavery is not spoken of, but it does exist. People are kidnapped and made to work in remote places in Caucasus like Dagestan, for a very long time. And many of them die in captivity. Yet, this subject remains a taboo in Russia, and it infuriates me because the authorities know and abet such crimes at local and federal levels. This cancer should be stopped from growing.

Ehi Eric Esoimeme has done us an important service by helping us compare risk mitigation strategies to determine the best approach to preventing despicable acts of slavery. It is not just that people get trapped in forced labour; it is because many of them die there, abandoned and hopeless to be rescued in this digital age. Examining and exposing forms of coercion and practices similar to human trafficking, along with what institutions play a muted role in that is of importance. Child labour still remains a curse that institutions grow comfortably tolerant of, regardless of how numerous the cases become. Describing who and what body of legislation are meant to reduce this scourge will help focus all efforts needed to eradicate this crime."

—Anatoly Yakorev, Director, Center for Business Ethics & Compliance (Moscow, Russian Federation)

THE RISK-BASED APPROACH TO COMBATING

MODERN SLAVERY

EHI ERIC ESOIMEME

DSC Publications Ltd.

ISBN-10: 978-2787-91-4
ISBN-13: 978-978-2787-91-0
Published by DSC Publications Ltd.
No. 2, Dapo Bode Thomas Street,
Off Thorburn Street, Via Montgomery/Commercial Avenue.

To God Almighty for his sufficient grace and mercies throughout my life and for giving me the inspiration, strength, and motivation to write this important book.

ACKNOWLEDGEMENTS

I take this opportunity to express my deep sense of gratitude to Mr. Ian Ross for his continuous bouts of encouragement and support and for contributing the foreword to this book.

I must also express my sincere gratitude to Gregory Dellas, CAMS-Audit, FICA., Director, Wealth and Markets, Bank of Cyprus and Chair, ACAMS Cyprus Chapter; Maureen Mutua, Senior Partner, AML and Financial Crime, Eden Management Consultants (United Arab Emirates); and Anatoly Yakorev, Director, Center for Business Ethics & Compliance (Moscow, Russian Federation) for taking time out of their tremendously busy lives to review the content of this book. I am heartened by their absolute endorsement of this publication.

I express my sincere appreciation to my mother, Dr. Angela Esoimeme, for her unwavering support, encouragement, and supreme patience. I consider myself particularly fortunate to have her as my mother. She created an environment of homely peace and tranquility, while I strove to ensure that this publication was of unequaled excellence.

TABLE OF CONTENTS

FOREWORD

Over recent years, a key focus of my reading has been the works and publications of Ehi Eric Esoimeme.

"The Risk-Based Approach to Combating Modern Slavery" (2019) is another exemplary piece of work from Mr. Esoimeme. It is, as all his other publications are, thoroughly researched and built upon a sound theoretical foundation. However, to say that Eric's work is informative wouldn't provide the credit it deserves. Better put would be to describe it as 'revealing,' because amongst the morass of narratives and policies, implausibilities, complexities, and twists that one associates with throughout the text, Eric brings a coherence that is often missing. For the discerning reader, knowledge gaps are addressed, and yet again, the work takes us into areas of innovation and creates sound workable perspectives for us.

It is again an immense pleasure to support the fine work of Ehi Eric Esoimeme, who brings such a vitality to the cause of combating money laundering and human slavery.

Ian Ross

Director: Financial Crime Risk & Training. Detecta E.U.S.

PREFACE

The 2018 Global Slavery Index by the International Labour Organization (ILO) and the Walk Free Foundation, in partnership with the International Organization for Migration (IOM), maintains that there are still 40.3 million slaves trapped in modern slavery worldwide. Of the 40.3 million enslaved worldwide, 24.9 million people are trapped in forced labour, while 15.4 million are forced into marriages. The Index maintains that modern day slavery is most prevalent in Africa (with 9.24 million slaves and an average vulnerability score of 62/100), followed by the Asia and the Pacific region. According to the Index, Eritrea, Burundi, and Central African Republic were the countries with the highest prevalence of modern slavery within the region; however, Nigeria and the Democratic Republic of the Congo led with the highest absolute numbers and accounted for over one-quarter (26.3 percent) of the region's victims. The Index notes that it is not possible to survey countries that are experiencing ongoing conflict, such as Libya, South Sudan, and parts of Nigeria. Furthermore, this absence of data leaves us with understated estimates of modern slavery within these countries.

The Index has also reported that there are considerably more slaves in the developed world than once thought, highlighting the fact that western consumerism often drives slavery in the developing world. Currently, the United States is thought to have 400,000 slaves, which is higher than previously believed, while the United Kingdom is thought to have 136,000 slaves, almost 12x higher than previous estimates.

The following research question seeks to determine how the above problem can be solved:

What must States do to eliminate forced labour, including human trafficking and related slavery-like practices?

The United Kingdom has taken major steps to eliminate forced labour. In 2015, the UK signed into law the **Modern Slavery Act. Section 54 of the Modern Slavery Act 2015** requires a commercial organisation to prepare a slavery and human trafficking statement for each financial year of the organisation's existence if its total turnover is not less than an amount prescribed by the Secretary of State. Regulations have set the total turnover threshold at £36m. The statement must identify the steps and initiatives already implemented during the financial year to ensure that modern slavery is not occurring in their supply chains and in their own organisation.

The Guidance issued under **section 54(9) of the Modern Slavery Act 2015 (Transparency in Supply Chains etc. A practical guide)** requires businesses to adopt a risk management process to their compliance programs. The process encompasses identifying modern slavery/human right risks in areas where they operate or host supply chain(s), and then prioritising those risks to ensure that they are well-addressed. Appropriate resources are needed to monitor these risk assessment strategies in terms of their efficacy. This means that the assessments should be able to identify the risks and issues, properly assess their level of importance, and ensure that appropriate remedies are in place.

Many organisations are already implementing measures that can properly identify, assess, and effectively mitigate the modern slavery risks in their supply chain(s). Tesco, for example, has started using the country risk ratings from the Food Network of Ethical Trade (FNET) to help identify areas of highest risk and inform its prioritisation. According to the 2017/18 Modern Slavery Statement of Tesco PLC, the greatest risks of modern slavery exist for workers who are not permanently employed. For example, these workers could be individuals in cleaning and security roles. In order to mitigate the aforementioned risks, Tesco works collaboratively with providers to help ensure that all temporary workers receive a reasonable number of paid hours each week and have the opportunity to transfer to permanent employment when vacancies arise.

Purpose of The Book

The focus of this book is on providing commercial organisations with a clear understanding of their due diligence obligations. The analytical approach adopted by this book ensures that readers will achieve the following:

i. Identify modern slavery and human rights risks where they have operations or supply chain(s).

ii. Assess the potential modern slavery and human rights risks of their supply chains.

iii. Determine how modern slavery and human rights issues can best be remediated or mitigated through measures like training and awareness, whistle-blowing mechanisms, and industry collaboration or improved internal purchasing practices.

iv. Measure the effectiveness of risk control measures.

Target Audience

The concepts in this book are aimed at commercial organisations and financial institutions, as well as undergraduate and postgraduate researchers.

Content of The Book

This book consists of 6 chapters, followed by a number of appendices that outline additional generally applicable material. The book incorporates a range of case studies that commercial organisations and business enterprises will, hopefully, find helpful in appreciating the overall context of, and obligations within, the anti-modern slavery framework.

The first chapter analyses the subject of modern slavery in relation to its definition, how it occurs, its macroeconomic impact, the international response to modern slavery, and in particular, how the United Kingdom has positioned its response to modern slavery.

Chapter two briefly analyses the approach that commercial organisations/business enterprises must adopt to combat modern slavery in their supply chain(s).

Chapter three gives an explicit explanation for how commercial organisations/business enterprises can assess each supplier's inherent modern slavery and human rights risks.

Chapter four describes the ways in which modern slavery and human rights issues can be adequately addressed by commercial organisations and business enterprises.

Chapter five expatiates on how money laundering and terrorist financing risks that involve proceeds of modern slavery can be addressed by financial institutions.

Chapter six gives an explicit explanation for how commercial organisations/business enterprises can measure the effectiveness of their internal ethics programme.

The Inspiration

I drew part of my inspiration to put together this outstanding book from one of my research papers: 'Using the Risk-Based Approach to Curb Modern Slavery in the Supply Chain: The Anglo American and Marks & Spencer Example.' I wrote the paper for the Journal of Financial Crime (the world's only quarterly, peer-reviewed journal designed to provide detailed analysis and insight on the latest issues in the law, regulation, and control of financial crime and related matters).

The paper broadened my interest in the area of modern slavery. It also enabled me to really understand the due diligence measures needed for assessing the inherent human rights risks in the supply chain, as well as the importance of risk control measures for the supply chain. The paper drove me to carry out more extensive research in this area, which eventually translated into the foundations of this book.

The book was also inspired by the efforts and commitment put in by the Lecturers in the **Department of Public Law, University of Lagos** to fight crime and defend the human rights of the people through public awareness and lectures.

Details of Competing Books, Either Published or In Preparation, And How This Book Distinguishes Itself From These:

Several books have been published on supply chain risk management. Notable amongst them are: Donald Waters, Supply Chain Risk Management: Vulnerability and Resilience in Logistics, Kogan Page; 2nd edition (3 Oct. 2011); John Manners-Bell, Supply Chain Risk Management: Understanding Emerging Threats to Global Supply Chains, Kogan Page; 2nd edition (3

Nov. 2017); Ken Sigler., Supply Chain Risk Management (Internal Audit and IT Audit), Routledge; 1st edition (20 Nov. 2017); and ManMohan S. Sodhi and Christopher S. Tang, Managing Supply Chain Risk (International Series in Operations Research & Management Science), Springer; 2012 edition (25 Feb. 2012).

Although the above-mentioned books examined a whole range of risks to supply chains, from traffic congestion to major environmental disasters, they did not specifically address the human right and modern slavery risk(s) that currently exist within supply chains throughout the world. This book analyses the risk assessment topic in line with **Section 54 of the United Kingdom Modern Slavery Act 2015**, and in line with human rights issues.

Internationally, this book would be the first comprehensive book on the assessment and mitigation of modern slavery and human rights risk(s) in the supply chain. This book would help commercial organisations and business enterprises with any problem regarding the application of the risk-based approach.

Business enterprises that implement the risk-based approach, in line with the guidance given in this book, will be well-placed to avoid the consequences of inappropriate de-risking behaviour.

I am aware that there are quite a number of reference guides provided by the United Nations, the Organisation for Economic Co-operation and Development (OECD), the United Kingdom Home Office, and the Ethical Trading Initiative (ETI) to assist firms with the implementation of the risk-based approach. However, it is important to note that those publications focus mainly on the risk assessment principles. More importantly, this book is particularly focused on both the principles and the practical aspect of its application.

This book is a must read for every professional specializing in the field of risk management in supply chains. It is also a must read for every individual who intends to know more about risk mitigation measures for modern slavery and human rights issues.

Ehi Eric Esoimeme Esq., Llb (Unilag), Bl, Ica (Manchester), Llm (Cardiff), PhD (in View) (Unilag)
Managing Associate at Deji Sasegbon and Co.
Deputy Editor in Chief of Dsc Publications Ltd.
Editorial Board Member at *Bilingual Publishing Company: Journal of Macro Management and Public Policies*
Editorial Board Member at *Science Publishing Group: International Journal of Law and Society*
Contributor at the *Journal of Money Laundering Control* (the world's only quarterly, peer-reviewed journal)
Contributor at the *Journal of Financial Crime*
Contributor at *Law Digest* (Africa's leading law journal)
Contributor at Kyc360 (the world's leading platform for anti-money laundering professionals)
Member of the Association of Certified Anti-Money Laundering Specialists (Acams)
Author of *Balancing Anti-Money Laundering/Counter-Terrorist Financing Requirements and Financial Inclusion: The Case of Telecommunications Companies*
Author of *Deterring and Detecting Money Laundering and Terrorist Financing*
Author of *The Risk-Based Approach to Combating Money Laundering and Terrorist Financing*
Author of *Banker-Customer Relationship: A Practical Legal Guide*
Author of approved scholarly papers (Ssrn) (Us)
Website: https://ehiericesoimeme.com/

ABOUT THE AUTHOR

Ehi Eric Esoimeme is the Deputy Editor in Chief of DSC Publications Ltd. His areas of expertise include, among others, risk assessment and risk management.

Ehi completed his undergraduate studies at the University of Lagos, postgraduate studies at Cardiff University, and his professional course on Money Laundering Law at the University of Manchester.

Ehi has authored more than 30 publications, including three books on Money Laundering Law/Banking Law. Ehi's second book, titled 'The Risk-Based Approach to Combating Money Laundering and Terrorist Financing,' became a bestseller on Amazon for banking law. Ehi's fourth book, titled 'Deterring and Detecting Money Laundering and Terrorist Financing: A Comparative Analysis of Anti–Money Laundering and Counterterrorism Financing Strategies,' has been well-received from both academic researchers and Anti-Money Laundering professionals as has garnered many recommendations by professionals in these fields.

Ehi was recently listed among the contributors for the new KYC360 website (the global financial crime and compliance knowledge hub powered by RiskScreen). Ehi Contributes articles, webinars, and podcasts to the website, and his most recent article, titled "Using anti-money laundering measures to curb pension fraud in Nigeria" has been endorsed by professionals in the anti-money laundering industry.

Ehi is a member of the industry's largest international network of financial crime detection and prevention professionals (ACAMS), and his Membership number is 1000157079. The membership provides Ehi with access to exclusive anti-money laundering publications, continuing education and training, networking, and professional growth.

TABLE OF CASES

REFERENCES ARE TO PARAGRAPH NUMBERS

COURT CASES/ADMINISTRATIVE CASES

CASE STUDIES

TABLES OF LEGISLATION

REFERENCES ARE TO PARAGRAPH NUMBERS

UNITED KINGDOM

PRIMARY LEGISLATION

Asylum and Immigration (Treatment of Claimants etc.) Act 2004 (AI (ToC) Act) as amended	1.4
Coroners and Justice Act 2009	1.4
Court of Session Act 1988	1.4
Criminal Finances Act 2017	5.5.3
Human Tissue Act 2004 (prohibition of commercial dealings in organs and restrictions on use of live donors)	1.4
Legal Aid, Sentencing and Punishment of Offenders Act 2012	1.4
Modern Slavery Act 2015	1.1.2, 1.4, 2.2.1, 3.1
Proceeds of Crime Act 2002 (as amended)	1.4, 5.5, 5.5.3, 5.5.4, 5.5.5, 5.5.6
Protection of Children's Act 1978 (indecent photographs of children)	1.4
Sexual Offences Act 2003	1.4
Terrorism Act	5.5.1

SECONDARY LEGISLATION

Financial Conglomerates and Other Financial Groups Regulations 2004	5.0
Money Laundering, Terrorist Financing and Transfer of Funds (Information on the Payer) Regulations 2017	5.0, 5.1, 5.2, 5.4, 5.6, 5.7

TERTIARY LEGISLATION

JMLSG, Prevention of money laundering/combating terrorist financing 2017 Revised Version, Guidance for the UK financial sector Part I, June 2017 (Amended December 2017)	5.1, 5.5.1, 5.5.2, 5.5.3, 5.6.
Joint Money Laundering Steering Group, Prevention of Money Laundering/Combating Terrorist Financing 2017 Revised Version, Guidance for the UK Financial Sector Part II: Sectoral Guidance, June 2017	5.0
Transparency in Supply Chains etc. A Practical Guide 2015 (Last Updated 2018)	1.0, 1.1.3, 1.4, 2.2.1, 2.2.2, 3.1, 3.2, 6.1

AUSTRALIA

PRIMARY LEGISLATION

Anti-Money Laundering and Counter-Terrorism Financing Rules Instrument 2007 (as amended)	5.1
Modern Slavery Act	4.4

CANADA

TERTIARY LEGISLATION

Officer of the Superintendent of Financial Institutions Canada Guideline: Deterring and Detecting Money Laundering and Terrorist Financing 2008	5.1

NIGERIA

SECONDARY LEGISLATION

CBN (Anti-Money Laundering and Combating the Financing of Terrorism in Banks and Other Financial Institutions in Nigeria) Regulations, 2013	5.1

TERTIARY LEGISLATION

Central Bank of Nigeria' Anti-Money Laundering/Combating the Financing of Terrorism (AML/CFT) Policy and Procedure Manual' 2018	5.6

SOUTH AFRICA

SECONDARY LEGISLATION

Financial Intelligence Centre Guidance Note 3A Guidance for accountable institutions on client identification and verification and related matters 2013	5.3
Money Laundering and Terrorist Financial Control Regulations, 2002 (as amended)	5.1

UNITED STATES

PRIMARY LEGISLATION

Bank Secrecy Act of 1970	5.5.6.2

SECONDARY LEGISLATION

TERTIARY LEGISLATION

TABLE OF INTERNATIONAL CONVENTIONS AND GUIDELINES

REFERENCES ARE TO PARAGRAPH NUMBERS

LIST OF ABBREVIATIONS

AML/CFT: Anti-Money Laundering/Countering the Financing of Terrorism

AMS: Anti-Modern Slavery

BHRRC: Business and Human Rights Resource Centre

BPGBF: Bali Process Business and Government Forum

BSA: Bank Secrecy Act

BSCI: Business Social Compliance Initiative

CCR-CSR: Centre for Child Rights and Corporate Social Responsibility

CCVI: Climate Change Vulnerability Index

CDD: Customer Due Diligence

CEO: Chief Executive Officer

CFR: Code of Federal Regulations

CGF: Consumer Goods Forum

CIP: Customer Identification Programme

CPS: Crown Prosecution Service

CSR: Corporate Social Responsibility

CTR: Currency Transaction Reports

DRC: Democratic Republic of the Congo

DWP: Department for Work and Pensions

ECDD: Enhanced Customer Due Diligence

ECHR: European Convention on Human Rights

EDD: Enhanced Due Diligence

EEA: European Economic Area

EMS: Environmental Management System

ESG: Environmental, Social and Governance (ESG)

ETI: Ethical Trading Initiative

EU: European Union

FATF: Financial Action Task Force

FDIC: Federal Deposit Insurance Corporation

FinCEN: Financial Crimes Enforcement Network

FIU: Financial Intelligence Unit

FLEX: Focus on Labour Exploitation

FNET: Food Network for Ethical Trade

FTSE: Financial Times Stock Exchange

GCC: Gulf Cooperation Council

GDP: Gross Domestic Product

GFR: Goods For Resale

GLAA: Gangmasters & Labour Abuse Authority

GSI: Global Slavery Index

HMRC: Her Majesty's Revenue and Customs

ICT: Information and Communications Technology

ID: Identity Document or Identification Document

IHRB: Institute for Human Rights and Business

ILAB: The Bureau of International Labor Affairs

ILO: International Labour Organisation

IMF: International Monetary Fund

IOM: International Organization for Migration (IOM)

IPEC: International Programme on the Elimination of Child Labour

ITUC: International Trade Union Confederation

JAC: Joint Audit Cooperation

JMLSG: Joint Money Laundering Steering Group

KPIs: Key Performance Indicators

KYC: Know Your Customer

KYCB: Know Your Customer's Business

KYE: Know Your Employee

KYS: Know Your Supplier

MD: Managing Director

MIS: Management Information Systems

ML/FT: Money Laundering and the Financing of Terrorism

MLRO: Money Laundering Reporting Officer

MSHTU: Modern Slavery Human Trafficking Unit

MSIs: Multi-stakeholder initiatives

MSRO: Modern Slavery Reporting Officer

NCA: National Crime Agency

NGOs: Non-governmental Organizations

NGPs: Next Generation Products

NKDB: Database Center for North Korean Human Rights

NSF: Non-sufficient funds

OECD: Organisation for Economic Co-operation and Development

OHS: Occupational Health and Safety

PEPs: Politically Exposed Persons

PNG: Papua New Guinea

POCA: Proceeds of Crime Act

RACC: Regional Audit and CSR committee

RBS: Risk Based Supervision

RCWS: Responsible Car Wash Scheme

RSP: Responsible Sourcing Policy

SAI: Social Accountability International

SAQ: Self-Assessment Questionnaire

SAR: Suspicious Activity Report

SEA Alliance: Seafood Ethics Action Alliance

SEC: Securities Exchange Commission

SIP: Supplier Identification Program

SMETA: SEDEX Members Ethical Trade Audit

SoBC: Standards of Business Conduct

STP: Sustainable Tobacco Programme

STR: Suspicious Transaction Report

TIN: Tax Identification Number

TIP: Trafficking in Persons

TVPA: Trafficking Victims Protection Act

TVPRA: Trafficking Victims Protection Reauthorization Act of 2005

U.S. Treasury: U.S. Department of the Treasury

UAE: United Arab Emirates

UN: United Nations

UNGPs: United Nations Guiding Principles on Business and Human Rights

UNILAG: University of Lagos

UNODC: United Nations Office on Drugs and Crime

US: United States of America

USC: U.S. Code

USDOL: U.S. Department of Labour

UVDB: Utilities Vendor Database

VPSHR: Voluntary Principles on Security and Human Rights

WHO: World Health Organization

CHAPTER 1

INTRODUCTION TO MODERN SLAVERY

Slavery, in accordance with **the 1926 Slavery Convention**, is the status or condition of a person over whom all or any of the powers attaching to the right of ownership are exercised. Since legal 'ownership' of a person is not possible, the key element of slavery is the behaviour on the part of the offender as if he/she did own the person, which deprives the victim of their freedom.[1] Slavery is prohibited under **Article 4 of the 1948 Universal Declaration of Human Rights**, which states: "No one shall be held in slavery or servitude: slavery and the slave trade shall be prohibited in all their forms". About 150 years after most countries banned slavery – Brazil was the last to abolish its participation in the transatlantic slave trade, in 1888 – millions of men, women and children are still enslaved. Slavery thrives on every continent and in almost every country.[2]

The recent **Global Estimates of Modern Slavery**, published by the International Labour Organization (ILO) and the Walk Free Foundation, in partnership with the International Organization for Migration (IOM), maintains that there are still 40.3 million slaves trapped in modern slavery worldwide. Of the 40.3 million

---

[1] Home Office (2015 but Updated in 2018), 'Transparency in Supply Chains etc. A practical guide', Available at: https://assets.publishing.service.gov.uk/government/uploads/system/uploads/attachment_data/file/649906/Transparency_in_Supply_Chains_A_Practical_Guide_2017.pdf (accessed 25 June 2019).

[2] The Guardian (2013), 'Modern-day slavery: an explainer', Available at: https://www.theguardian.com/global-development/2013/apr/03/modern-day-slavery-explainer (accessed 9 March 2018).

enslaved worldwide in 2016, 24.9 million people are trapped in forced labour, while 15.4 million are in forced marriages. Not surprisingly, women and girls continue to be vastly over-represented, making up 71% of victims. Modern slavery was most prevalent in Africa (7.6 per 1,000 people), followed by Asia and the Pacific (6.1 per 1,000) then Europe and Central Asia (3.9 per 1,000).[3]

Although it is not defined in law, "modern slavery" is used here as an umbrella term covering the various forms of coercion prohibited in international instruments on human rights and labour standards (e.g. **slavery, institutions and practices similar to slavery, forced labour, trafficking in persons and forced marriage**). Essentially, what all of these situations have in common is that that a person is being exploited or forced to marry and cannot refuse or leave because of threats, violence, coercion, deception and/or abuse of power.[4]

1.1 TYPES OF MODERN SLAVERY CRIME

There are several broad categories of exploitation linked to modern slavery:

1.1.1 FORCED OR COMPULSORY LABOUR

The term "forced or compulsory labour" is defined by the **International Labour Organization (ILO) Forced Labour Convention, 1930 (No. 29), Article 2.1**, as "all work or service which is exacted from any person under the menace of any penalty and for which the said person has not offered himself voluntarily".

[3] International Labour Office, Walk Free Foundation and International Organisation for Migration (2017), 'Global Estimates of Modern Slavery: forced labour and forced marriage', Available at: https://www.ilo.org/wcmsp5/groups/public/---dgreports/---dcomm/documents/publication/wcms_575479.pdf (accessed 24 April 2019).

[4] The Guardian (2013), 'Modern-day slavery: an explainer', Available at: https://www.theguardian.com/global-development/2013/apr/03/modern-day-slavery-explainer (accessed 9 March 2018).

It implies the use of deception or coercion, either by the state and public agencies, or by private individuals and enterprises, to force people to enter work or service against their will, to work in conditions they did not accept and to prevent them from leaving the job by using any form of punishment or threat of penalty.[5]

The **International Labour Organisation [ILO]** has identified six elements which individually or collectively can indicate forced labour. These are:

- Threats or actual physical harm;
- Restriction of movement and confinement to the workplace or to a limited area;
- Debt-bondage;
- Withholding of wages or excessive wage reductions that violate previously made agreements;
- Retention of passports and identity documents (the workers can neither leave nor prove their identity status);
- Threat of denunciation to the authorities regardless of whether the worker holds legal status in the UK or not.

1.1.2 CHILD LABOUR

Child labour is a much narrower concept and refers to children working in contravention of ILO standards contained in **Conventions 138 and 182**. This means all children below 12 years of age working in any economic activities, those aged between 12 and 14 engaged in more than light work, and all children engaged in the worst forms of child labour.[6] Drawing on the **1999**

[5] National Crime Agency (2018), 'Types of modern slavery crime', Available at: http://www.nationalcrimeagency.gov.uk/crime-threats/human-trafficking/types-of-human-trafficking (accessed 10 March 2018).

[6] The term "child labour" is often defined as work that deprives children of their childhood, their potential and their dignity, and that is harmful to physical and mental development. Whether or not particular forms of "work" can be called "child labour" depends on the child's age, the type and hours of work performed, the conditions under which it is performed and the

International Labour Conference Convention No.182, concerning the Prohibition and Immediate Action for the Elimination of the Worst Forms of Child Labour, the term "worst forms of child labour" comprises:

- All forms of slavery or practices similar to slavery, such as the sale and trafficking of children, debt bondage and serfdom and forced or compulsory labour, including forced or compulsory recruitment of children for use in armed conflict;
- The use, procuring or offering of a child for prostitution, for the production of pornography, or for pornographic performances;
- The use, procuring or offering of a child for illicit activities, in particular for the production and trafficking of drugs as defined in the relevant international treaties;
- Work which, by its nature or the circumstances in which it is carried out, is likely to harm the health, safety or morals of children.

1.1.3 HUMAN TRAFFICKING

Article 3, paragraph (a) of the Protocol to Prevent, Suppress and Punish Trafficking in Persons defines Trafficking in Persons as the recruitment, transportation, transfer, harbouring or receipt of persons, by means of the threat or use of force or other forms of coercion, of abduction, of fraud, of deception, of the abuse of

---

objectives pursued by individual countries. Children can be particularly vulnerable to exploitation, but child labour will not always constitute modern slavery. It will still be necessary to determine whether, based on the facts of the case, the children in question are being exploited in such a way as to constitute slavery, servitude and forced or compulsory labour or human trafficking. For example, it is possible for children to undertake some 'light work' which would not necessarily constitute modern slavery. 'Light work' is defined by article 7 of ILO Convention No. 138. Children do have particular vulnerabilities which should be considered when determining whether modern slavery is taking place. The Modern Slavery Act 2015 specifically recognises that it is not necessary for a child to have been forced, threatened or deceived into their situation for it to be defined as exploitation.

power or of a position of vulnerability or of the giving or receiving of payments or benefits to achieve the consent of a person having control over another person, for the purpose of exploitation. Exploitation shall include, at a minimum, the exploitation of the prostitution of others or other forms of sexual exploitation, forced labour or services, slavery or practices similar to slavery, servitude or the removal of organs.

An offence of human trafficking requires that a person arranges or facilitates the travel of another person with a view to that person being exploited. The offence can be committed even where the victim consents to the travel. This reflects the fact that a victim may be deceived by the promise of a better life or job or may be a child who is influenced to travel by an adult. In addition, the exploitation of the potential victim does not need to have taken place for the offence to be committed. It means that the arranging or facilitating of the movement of the individual was with a view to exploiting them for sexual exploitation or non-sexual exploitation.[7]

1.1.4 SEXUAL EXPLOITATION

Sexual exploitation involves any non-consensual or abusive sexual acts performed without a victim's permission. This includes prostitution, escort work and pornography. Women, men and children of both sexes can be victims. Many will have been deceived with promises of a better life and then controlled through violence and abuse. It is also possible to exploit a person who consensually engages in providing sexual services.[8]

---

[7] Home Office (2015 but Updated in 2018), 'Transparency in Supply Chains etc. A practical guide', Available at: https://assets.publishing.service.gov.uk/government/uploads/system/uploads/attachment_data/file/649906/Transparency_in_Supply_Chains_A_Practical_Guide_2017.pdf (accessed 25 June 2019).

[8] National Crime Agency (2018), 'Types of modern slavery crime', Available at: http://www.nationalcrimeagency.gov.uk/crime-threats/human-trafficking/types-of-human-trafficking (accessed 10 March 2018).

1.1.5 FORCED MARRIAGE

"Forced marriage" refers to situations where persons have been forced to marry without their consent. A marriage can be forced through a range of different mechanisms, including physical, emotional or financial duress; deception by family members, the spouse or others; or the use of force or threats or severe pressure. **The 1956 United Nations Convention on slavery and slavery-like practices** covers various mechanisms of forced marriage, as institutions and practices similar to slavery.[9]

1.1.6 DOMESTIC SERVITUDE

Domestic servitude involves the victim being forced to work in private households. Their movement will often be restricted and they will be forced to perform household tasks such as child care and house-keeping over long hours and for little if any pay. Victims will lead very isolated lives and have little or no unsupervised freedom. Their own privacy and comfort will be minimal, often sleeping on a mattress on the floor in an open part of the house.

In rare circumstances where victims receive a wage it will be heavily reduced, as they are charged for food and accommodation.[10]

1.1.7 ORGAN HARVESTING

Organ harvesting involves trafficking people in order to use their internal organs for transplant. The illegal trade is dominated by demand for kidneys. These are the only major organs that can be

---

[9] International Labour Organization, Walk Free Foundation and International Organization for Migration (2017), 'Global estimates of modern slavery: forced labour and forced marriage', Available at: http://www.alliance87.org/global_estimates_of_modern_slavery-forced_labour_and_forced_marriage.pdf (accessed 10 March 2018).

[10] National Crime Agency (2018), 'Types of modern slavery crime', Available at: http://www.nationalcrimeagency.gov.uk/crime-threats/human-trafficking/types-of-human-trafficking (accessed 10 March 2018).

wholly transplanted with relatively few risks to the life of the donor.[11]

1.2 INTERNATIONAL LABOUR ORGANISATION'S RESPONSE TO MODERN SLAVERY

Responsibility for setting international labour standards is given by the international community to the **International Labour Organisation (ILO)** which was established for this purpose.[12] The **International Labour Organisation's** Governing Body has identified eight conventions as "fundamental", covering subjects that are considered as fundamental principles and rights at work: freedom of association and the effective recognition of the right to collective bargaining; the elimination of all forms of forced or compulsory labour; the effective abolition of child labour; and the elimination of discrimination in respect of employment and occupation. These principles are also covered in the **ILO's Declaration on Fundamental Principles and Rights at Work (1998)**. There are currently over 1,367 ratifications of these conventions, representing 91,4% of the possible number of ratifications. A further 129 ratifications are still required to meet the objective of universal ratification of all the fundamental.

The eight fundamental Conventions are:

I. Freedom of Association and Protection of the Right to Organise Convention, 1948 (No. 87)

[11] National Crime Agency (2018), 'Types of modern slavery crime', Available at: http://www.nationalcrimeagency.gov.uk/crime-threats/human-trafficking/types-of-human-trafficking (accessed 10 March 2018).

[12] Ethical Trading Initiative (2018), 'The ETI Base Code', Available at: https://www.ethicaltrade.org/sites/default/files/shared_resources/ETI%20Base%20Code%20%28English%29.pdf (accessed 28 June 2019).

Convention No. 87 is about the right that all workers and employers, without distinction, shall have to establish and to join organizations of their own choosing without previous authorization. The objective is "to protect the autonomy and independence of workers' and employers' organizations in relation to the public authorities, in their establishment and in their functioning and dissolution."

II. Right to Organise and Collective Bargaining Convention, 1949 (No. 98)

This **Convention** provides workers organisations and employers' organisations with the right to self-determination and the right to form and join federations. It further provides for protection of organisations from state interference and embodies the principle of free and voluntary negotiations.

III. Forced Labour Convention, 1930 (No. 29)

This **Convention** requires the suppression of forced or compulsory labour in all its forms. Forced labour is 'all work or service which is exacted from any person under the menace of any penalty and for which the said person has not offered himself voluntarily.' The ILO Committee of Experts has held that this definition is sufficiently wide to cover debt-bondage.

In June 2014, governments, employers and workers at the ILO International Labour Conference (ILC) decided to give new impetus to the global fight against forced labour, including trafficking in persons and slavery-like practices.

They voted overwhelmingly to adopt a **Protocol and a Recommendation which supplement the Forced Labour Convention, 1930 (No. 29)**, and complement existing international instruments by providing specific guidance on effective measures to be taken to eliminate all forms of forced labour.

The **Protocol to the Forced Labour Convention, 1930**, is a new, legally-binding instrument that requires States to take measures regarding prevention, protection and remedy in giving effect to the Convention's obligation to suppress forced labour. It supplements the **Forced Labour Convention, 1930 (No. 29)**, so only ILO member States that have ratified the **Convention** can ratify the **Protocol**. The **Convention** itself remains open for ratification.

IV. Abolition of Forced Labour Convention, 1957 (No. 105)

This **Convention** prohibits the use of any form of forced or compulsory labour - including work following a criminal conviction - as a means of:

I. Political coercion or education, or punishment for the expression of political or ideological views,
II. Workforce mobilisation for purposes of economic development,
III. Labour discipline,
IV. Punishment for participation in strikes, or
V. Racial, social, national or religious discrimination.

V. Minimum Age Convention, 1973 (No. 138)

Convention 138 was developed to regulate child labour by setting a minimum age for admission to employment that the signatories are to respect. This **Convention** came into force on 19 June 1976. The minimum working age was set at 15 years (13 years for light work). For dangerous work, the **Convention** set the bar for admission to employment at 18 years (16 years under certain conditions). The **Convention** allows developing countries, whose economy and educational facilities are insufficiently developed, to temporarily set the minimum age for admission to employment at 14 years. This decision must be thoroughly justified.

VI. Worst Forms of Child Labour Convention, 1999 (No. 182)

Convention 182 outlines the 5 worst forms of labour that must be eradicated in order to step up the fight against child labour. They are as follows:

1. Slavery or similar practices, such as the sale or trade of children or the use of children in debt bondage or serfdom;
2. Obligatory or forced work, including the compulsory recruitment of children for use in armed conflicts;
3. The recruitment, use or offer of a child for involvement in prostitution, pornographic material or pornographic shows;
4. The use, recruitment or offer of a child for illicit activities, notably in the production or trafficking of drugs, as defined in the specific international treaties;
5. Work which, by its very nature or the conditions in which it is undertaken, is likely to jeopardise the health, safety or morality of children.

The **International Programme on the Elimination of Child Labour (IPEC)**, created by the ILO in 1992, supports the State members in implementing the necessary measures to eliminate these worst forms of work. The IPEC equally outlines child labour violation cases where support can be given to child victims and tailored solutions provided to each situation.[13]

[13] Humanium (2019), 'Convention 182 on The Worst Forms of Child Labour, 1999', Available at: https://www.humanium.org/en/child-labour-convention/ (accessed 25 June 2019).

VII. Equal Remuneration Convention, 1951 (No. 100)

THE CONVENTION DEFINES equal remuneration for work of equal value as remuneration established without discrimination of sex. This principle may be applied by means of national laws or regulations, legal machinery for wage determination, collective agreements or a combination of these various means. One of the means specified for assisting in giving effect to the Convention is the objective appraisal of jobs on the basis of the work performed.

VIII. Discrimination (Employment and Occupation) Convention, 1958 (No. 111)

THE CONVENTION ASSIGNS to each State which ratified it the fundamental aim of promoting equality of opportunity and treatment by declaring and pursuing a national policy aimed at eliminating all forms of discrimination in respect of employment and occupation.

CASE STUDY 1.1: INDICATORS OF SLAVERY, SERVITUDE AND FORCED OR COMPULSORY LABOUR

There are a number of factors which may indicate that an individual is being held in servitude or is being subjected to forced or compulsory labour. The essential elements are those of coercion or deception, which may be demonstrated in a number of ways.

The kind of behaviour that would normally of itself be evidence of coercion includes but is not limited to:

- Violence or threats of violence by the employer or the employer's representative;
- Threats against the worker's family;

- Threats to expose the worker to the authorities (for example because of the worker's immigration status or offences they may have committed in the past);
- The person's documents, such as a passport or other identification, being withheld by the employer;
- Restriction of movement;
- Debt bondage;
- Withholding of wages.

Other indicators of forced labour include but are not limited to:

- The worker being given false information about the law and their employment rights;
- Excessive working hours imposed by the employer;
- Hazardous working conditions imposed by the employer;
- Not being provided with safety equipment and clothing, and/or being charged for the provision of equipment essential to perform the work;
- Unwarranted and perhaps unexplained deductions from wages;
- The employer intentionally not paying the full tax or national insurance contributions
- Poor accommodation provided by the employer, for example accommodation that is overcrowded, is not licensed as a "House of Multiple Occupation" by Local Authorities, or does not have any necessary gas and electricity safety certificates;
- Intentionally poor or misleading information about the nature of the employment, for example about the location or nature of the work;
- The person being isolated from contact with others;
- Money having been exchanged with other employers/traffickers for the person's services in an

arrangement which has not been agreed with the person concerned or which is not reflected in his payment.

1.3 UNITED NATIONS OFFICE ON DRUGS AND CRIME (UNODC)'S RESPONSE TO MODERN SLAVERY

The **United Nations Office on Drugs and Crime (UNODC)** offers practical help to States, not only helping to draft laws and create comprehensive national anti-trafficking strategies but also assisting with resources to implement them. States receive specialized assistance including the development of local capacity and expertise, as well as practical tools to encourage cross-border cooperation in investigations and prosecutions.

The adoption in 2000 by the United Nations General Assembly of the **Protocol to Prevent, Suppress and Punish Trafficking in Persons, Especially Women and Children** marked a significant milestone in international efforts to stop the trade in people. As the guardian of the Protocol, UNODC addresses human trafficking issues through its Global Programme against Trafficking in Persons. A vast majority of States have now signed and ratified the Protocol. But translating it into reality remains problematic. Very few criminals are convicted and most victims are probably never identified or assisted.[14]

1.4 UNITED KINGDOM'S RESPONSE TO MODERN SLAVERY

The United Kingdom is leading the way in the fight against modern slavery. In 2015, the UK government passed the **Modern Slavery Act**, the first piece of UK legislation focusing on the

[14] United Nations Office on Drugs and Crime (2019), 'Human Trafficking', Available at: https://www.unodc.org/unodc/en/human-trafficking/what-is-human-trafficking.html (accessed 9 July 2019).

prevention and prosecution of modern slavery and the protection of victims.[15] Key statutory provisions are excerpted below:

Slavery, Servitude, Forced and Compulsory Labour - Section 1 of the UK Modern Slavery Act, 2015

1. A person commits an offence if:

    1. the person holds another person in slavery or servitude and the circumstances are such that the person knows or ought to know that the other person is held in slavery or servitude, or

    2. the person requires another person to perform forced or compulsory labour and the circumstances are such that the person knows or ought to know that the other person is being required to perform forced or compulsory labour.

2. In subsection (1) the references to holding a person in slavery or servitude or requiring a person to perform forced or compulsory labour are to be construed in accordance with **Article 4 of the Human Rights Convention** (which prohibits a person from being held in slavery or servitude or being required to perform forced or compulsory labour).

3. In determining whether a person is being held in slavery or servitude or required to perform forced or compulsory labour, regard may be had to all the circumstances.

4. For example, regards may be had -

---

[15] The Guardian (2015), 'The UK's new slavery laws explained: what do they mean for business?', Available at: https://www.theguardian.com/sustainable-business/2015/dec/14/modern-slavery-act-explained-business-responsibility-supply-chain (accessed 24 April 2019).

1. to any of the person's personal circumstances (such as the person being a child, the person's family relationships, and any mental or physical illness) which may make the person more vulnerable than other persons;

2. to any work or services provided by the person, including work or services provided in circumstances which constitute exploitation within s. 3(3) to (6) of the Act (for human trafficking for exploitation)

5. The consent of a person (whether adult or child) to any of the acts alleged to constitute holding the person in slavery or servitude, or requiring the person to perform forced or compulsory labour, does not preclude a determination that the person is being held in slavery or servitude or required to perform forced or compulsory labour.

Points to prove –

- Holds another person in slavery or servitude
- Knows or ought to know that the person is so held
- Requires another person to perform forced or compulsory labour
- Knows or ought to know that the person is being required to perform forced or compulsory labour.

A person guilty of an offence under this section is liable: on summary conviction, to imprisonment for term not exceeding 12 months or a fine or both; and on conviction on indictment, to imprisonment for life.

In this section, **"Human Rights Convention"** means the Convention for the Protection of Human Rights and Fundamental Freedoms agreed by the Council of Europe at Rome on 4 November 1950. **Article 4** states that no one shall be held in slavery or servitude and no one shall be required to perform forced or compulsory labour. The definition of each element of the offence is described below.

This offence can be used in cases where the victim has been exploited in accordance with the **European Convention on Human Rights (ECHR)** definition but was not trafficked, or the trafficking element cannot be proved to the criminal standard. The offence under **s. 1 Modern Slavery Act 2015** has been extended to cover all forms of exploitation relevant to human trafficking. This means that prosecutors should consider any work or services provided in circumstances amounting to exploitation within the meaning of **s.3 of the Act.** This may include, for example, children involved in pickpocketing or begging. However, the circumstances must still be interpreted in accordance with **Article 4 ECHR.**

For offences of Slavery, Servitude, Forced and Compulsory Labour which occurred before 31 July 2015, the following legislation should be used: **Section 71 of the Coroners and Justice Act 2009.**

Exceptions to the offence

Article 4(3) of the ECHR sets out exceptions (below) which are applicable to this offence. For the purpose of this offence the term "forced or compulsory labour" shall not include the following exceptions:

- any work required to be done in the ordinary course of detention imposed according to the provisions of **Article 5**

of this Convention or during conditional release from such detention;

- any service of a military character or, in case of conscientious objectors in countries where they are recognised, service exacted instead of compulsory military service;
- any service exacted in case of an emergency or calamity threatening the life or well-being of the community;
- any work or service which forms part of normal civic obligations. This might include obligations to conduct free medical examinations or participate in medical emergency service.

Whilst there is a range of pre-existing legislation which could cover behaviour relating to servitude and forced or compulsory labour, such as offences of false imprisonment, fraud, blackmail and assault, this offence allows prosecutors to present the full extent of the behaviour, rather than relying on these offences which may not fully reflect the nature of the offending.

Notwithstanding this, prosecutors should also consider charging specific offences in addition to the offence where appropriate (for example where the person has been physically assaulted while subjected to forced labour).

Elements of the offence

Slavery, servitude and forced or compulsory labour are not specifically defined in the Act. In interpreting the offence therefore, police, prosecutors and the courts will need to have regard to existing case-law on **Article 4 ECHR** and international conventions to find guidance defining the parameters of each of the terms. A brief synopsis of the terms follows.

Slavery or Servitude

Slavery is described as the status or condition of a person over whom any or all of the powers attaching the right of ownership are exercised. In essence, characteristics of ownership need to be present for a state of slavery to exist.

Servitude is a linked but much broader term than slavery. In ***Siliadin v. France* [2005] EHRLR 660 (paragraph 123)**, the ECHR reaffirmed that servitude "prohibits a particularly serious form of denial of freedom. It includes, in addition to the obligation to provide certain services to another, the obligation on the "serf" to live on the other's property and the impossibility of changing his status". The evidence showed the applicant, an alien who arrived in France at the age of sixteen, had worked for several years for the respondents carrying out household tasks and looking after their three, and subsequently four, children for seven days a week, from 7 am to 10 pm, without receiving any remuneration. She was obliged to follow instructions regarding her working hours and the work to be done, and was not free to come and go as she pleased, though she was allowed out on her own with permission of her employers. The Court unanimously held that there has been a violation of **Article 4 of the Convention**.

Forced or compulsory labour

The ECHR, in **the case of *Van der Mussele* 8919/80**, affirmed that the **International Labour Organisation (ILO) conventions** were the starting point for interpreting Article 4. The conventions defined forced or compulsory labour as being "all work or service which is exacted from any person under the menace of any penalty and for which the said person has not offered himself voluntarily".

Domestic case law

The case of ***William Connors and others* [2013] EWCA Crim 324** offers some further guidance on the distinction between these 3 elements. This case involved a family who, cajoled, bullied and through deception, recruited vulnerable men to work for them. The men worked long hours in very poor conditions 7 days a week, whilst being subjected to violence, threats and abuse. A manifestation of this control was that many of the victims were deprived of the will to leave; others were too demoralised to do so. All five defendants were convicted of a single count of conspiracy to require a person to perform forced or compulsory labour. During the course of the trial, the judge directed the jury to acquit the defendants of conspiracy to hold a person in slavery or servitude. The trial judge had commented that in order for servitude to be established, a court must find that it was impossible for the workers to change their status.[16]

Arranging or facilitating the travel of another person with a view to exploitation - Section 2 of the UK Modern Slavery Act, 2015

1. A person commits an offence if the person arranges or facilitates the travel of another person (V) with a view to V being exploited.

2. It is irrelevant whether the victim consents to the travel (whether V is an adult or child).

3. A person may in particular arrange or facilitate V's travel by recruiting V, transporting or transferring V, harbouring or receiving V, or transferring or exchanging control over V.

---

[16] The Crown Prosecution Service (2017), 'Human Trafficking, Smuggling and Slavery', Available at: http://www.cps.gov.uk/legal/h_to_k/human_trafficking_and_smuggling/ (accessed 8 August 2017).

4. A person arranges or a person arranges or facilitates V's travel with a view to V being exploited only if

    (a) the person intends to exploit V in any part of the world during or after travel; or

    (b) the person knows or ought to know that another person is likely to exploit V in any part of the world during or after travel.

5. Travel is defined as:

    (a) Arriving in, or entering, any country

    (b) Departing from any country, or

    (c) Travelling within any country.

6. A person who is a United Kingdom (UK) national commits an offence regardless of where the arranging or facilitating takes place, or where the travel takes place.

7. A person who is not a UK national commits an offence if any part of the arranging or facilitating takes place in the UK, or the travel consists of arrival or entry into, departure from, or travel within the UK.

Section 3 defines the meaning of exploitation for the purposes of **section 2**. A person is exploited only if one or more of the following apply:

2. Slavery servitude and forced or compulsory labour, where a person is the victim of an offence under **section 1 Modern Slavery Act 2015** (see Slavery, Servitude, Forced and Compulsory Labour below).

3. Sexual exploitation, which involves the commission of an offence under

    - **Section 1(1)(a) of the Protection of Children's Act 1978 (indecent photographs of children),** or

    - **Part 1 Sexual Offences Act 2003**

which would involve the commission of such an offence if it were done in England and Wales.

4. Removal of organs in circumstances where a person is encouraged required or expected to do anything which involves the commission of an offence under **section 32 or 33 of the Human Tissue Act 2004** (prohibition of commercial dealings in organs and restrictions on use of live donors).

5. Securing services etc. by force, threats or deception, where the person is subjected to force, threats or deception designed to induce him or her -

    (a) to provide services of any kind,

    (b) to provide another person with benefits of any kind, or

    (c) to enable another person to acquire benefits of any kind.

6. Securing services etc. from children and vulnerable persons in circumstances where another person uses or attempts to use the person for a purpose within **section (5) (a), (b) or (c)**, having chosen him or her for that purpose on the grounds that -

(a) he or she is a child, is mentally or physically ill or disabled, or has a family relationship with a particular person, and

(b) an adult, or a person without the illness, disability, or family relationship, would be likely to refuse to be used for that purpose.

Under **sections 3(5) and 3(6)** "benefits" is defined as any advantage derived by the trafficker, which could include financial gain, profit, personal benefit or privilege as well as state financial assistance.

Points to prove

- Arranges/facilitates travel for another person
- Arrival in/entry into the United Kingdom/another country
- Intending to do anything to or
- believing that another person is likely to do something in respect of that other person after the journey and in any part of the world which if done would have involved the commission of a relevant offence

This is an either-way offence and on summary conviction is subject to twelve months' imprisonment and/or unlimited fine. On conviction on indictment, it is life imprisonment. The offence is also a "lifestyle offence" for the purposes of the **Proceeds of Crime Act 2002.** As the offence is likely to lead to a significant sentence on conviction all cases should be tried in the Crown Court.

Committing an offence with intent to commit an offence under section 2 of the Act -Section 4 of the UK Modern Slavery Act, 2015

Section 4 creates an offence of committing any offence with the intention to commit an offence of human trafficking under **section 2.** This includes an offence committed by aiding, abetting, counselling or procuring an offence under **section 2**. The offence will also capture activity such as supplying false documents to be used to facilitate trafficking. The offence is drawn widely enough to encompass any offence committed by aiding, abetting, counselling or procuring an offence of trafficking.

This is an either-way offence and on summary conviction is subject to twelve months' imprisonment and/or unlimited fine. On conviction on indictment, the maximum sentence is ten years' imprisonment. However, where the offence involves false imprisonment or kidnapping, it is life imprisonment.

For offences of trafficking for sexual exploitation which occurred before 31 July 2015, but after 13 April 2013, the following legislation should be used: **Trafficking people for sexual exploitation - section 59A Sexual Offences Act 2003**.

For offences of trafficking for sexual exploitation which occurred before 13 April 2013, the following legislation should be used: **Trafficking into the UK for sexual exploitation - section 57, 58 and 59 Sexual Offences Act 2003**.

For offences of trafficking for all other forms of exploitation (non-sexual exploitation) which occurred before 31 July 2015, the following legislation should be used: **Trafficking people for labour and other exploitation - section 4 of the Asylum and Immigration (Treatment of Claimants etc.) Act 2004 (AI (ToC) Act) as amended.**

In circumstances where the victim was not trafficked, or the trafficking element cannot be proved to the criminal standard, prosecutors should consider the offence of "holding another person in slavery or servitude" or "requiring them to perform forced or compulsory labour" under **section 1 Modern Slavery Act 2015** or, if before 31 July 2015, **section 71 of the Coroners and Justice Act 2009**.

Slavery and trafficking prevention orders on sentencing - Section 14 of the UK's Modern Slavery Act, 2015

This section empowers a Court to make a slavery and trafficking prevention order against a person ("the Defendant") where it deals with the Defendant in respect of—

(a) A conviction for a slavery or human trafficking offence,

(b) A finding that the defendant is not guilty of a slavery or human trafficking offence by reason of insanity, or

(c) A finding that the defendant is under a disability and has done the act charged against the defendant in respect of a slavery or human trafficking offence.

The Court may make the order only if it is satisfied that—

(a) There is a risk that the defendant may commit a slavery or human trafficking offence, and

(b) It is necessary to make the order for the purpose of protecting persons generally, or particular persons, from the physical or psychological harm which would be likely to occur if the defendant committed such an offence.

Transparency in supply chains etc - Section 54 of the UK Modern Slavery Act 2015

This section requires that any commercial organisation in any sector, which supplies goods or services, and carries on a business or part of a business in the UK, and is above a specified total turnover, must produce a slavery and human trafficking statement for each financial year of the organisation. For the purposes of this requirement, 'supply chain' has its everyday meaning.[17] Regulations have set the total turnover threshold at £36m.[18] The statement must set out what steps they have taken during the financial year to ensure that modern slavery is not occurring in their supply chains and in their own organisation.[19]

Section 54 of the UK Modern Slavery Act 2015 contains language that permits UK Companies who are subject to the UK Modern Slavery Act, to some degree, to apply a risk-based approach to their Anti-Modern Slavery programmes.[20] **Section 54(5) of the UK Modern Slavery Act 2015** is to the effect that an organisation's slavery and human trafficking statement may include information about –

a. The organisation's structure, its business and its supply chains;

b. Its policies in relation to slavery and human trafficking;

c. Its due diligence processes in relation to slavery and human trafficking in its business and supply chains;

---

[17] A supply chain is the entire process of making and selling commercial goods, including every stage from the supply of materials and the manufacture of the goods through to their distribution and sale. (Source: Collins English Dictionary 2019). Many of the products we buy and use every day were made by people in slavery. There is evidence of slavery in different stages of supply chains from the production of raw materials, for example cocoa, cotton, or fishing, to manufacturing every-day goods such as mobile phones or garments and even at the final stage, when the product reaches the market. For more on the slavery risks associated with a supply chain, see Anti-Slavery International (2019), 'Slavery in supply chains', Available at: https://www.antislavery.org/slavery-today/slavery-in-global-supply-chains/ (accessed 20 July, 2019).

[18] The UK Modern Slavery Act 2015 (Transparency in Supply Chains) Regulations 2015, regulation 2.

[19] The UK Modern Slavery Act 2015, s. 54(4).

[20] Transparency in Supply Chains etc. A Practical Guide 2015 (Last Updated 2018), paras. 1.8, 1.9, 3.13, 5.2, 5.5, 6.2.

d. The parts of its business and supply chains where there is a risk of slavery and human trafficking taking place, and the steps it has taken to assess and manage that risk;

e. Its effectiveness in ensuring that slavery and human trafficking is not taking place in its business or supply chains, measured against such performance indicators as it considers appropriate;

f. The training and capacity building about slavery and human trafficking available to its staff.

One key purpose of this measure is to prevent modern slavery in organisations and their supply chains. A means to achieve this is to increase transparency by ensuring the public, consumers, employees and investors know what steps an organisation is taking to tackle modern slavery. Those organisations already taking action can quickly and simply articulate the work already underway and planned. Organisations will need to build on what they are doing year on year. Their first statements may show how they are starting to act on the issue and their planned actions to investigate or collaborate with others to effect change.[21]

If a business fails to produce a slavery and human trafficking statement for a particular financial year the Secretary of State may seek an injunction through the High Court (or, in Scotland civil proceedings for specific performance of a statutory duty under **section 45 of the Court of Session Act 1988**) requiring the organisation to comply. If the organisation fails to comply with the injunction, they will be in contempt of a court order, which is punishable by an unlimited fine.[22]

The study by the Business and Human Rights Resource Centre (BHRRC), a monitoring group, found that while most of the

[21] Transparency in Supply Chains etc. A Practical Guide 2015 (Last Updated 2018), para. 1.5.
[22] Transparency in Supply Chains etc. A Practical Guide 2015 (Last Updated 2018), para. 2.6.

Financial Times Stock Exchange (FTSE) 100 largest companies listed on the London Stock Exchange complied with Section 54 of the UK Modern Slavery Act 2015, their statements were vague and lacked detail. "The vast majority of companies' reported efforts are wholly inadequate," its executive director Phil Bloomer said in a statement.[23]

Retailer Marks & Spencer performed best of the FTSE 100 firms, scoring 78 out of 100 points in the annual evaluation of the firms' statements.

Drinks company Diageo and supermarket chain Morrison ranked second and third, with 62 points each, but almost three out of four companies scored fewer than 40 points.

Chapters 2 to 6 of this book will critically analyse the risk assessment/risk mitigation strategies adopted by commercial organisations in the United Kingdom, to determine if the approaches adopted by the selected institutions are effective enough to curb modern slavery in their supply chain(s) or if there is need for reform. **The focus of the analysis will be on UK companies that scored 50 percent and above in the Business & Human Rights Resource Centre (BHRRC's) third annual assessment of transparency statements by the FTSE 100 Index, under the Modern Slavery Act.**

---

[23] Business and Human Rights Resource Centre (2018), 'third annual assessment of transparency statements by the FTSE 100 under the Modern Slavery Act', Available at: https://www.business-humanrights.org/en/ftse-100-the-uk-modern-slavery-act-from-disclosure-to-action (accessed 24 April 2019); Reuters (2018), 'Britain's top firms 'wholly inadequate' in tackling slavery, survey finds', Available at: https://www.reuters.com/article/us-britain-business-slavery/britains-top-firms-wholly-inadequate-in-tackling-slavery-survey-finds-idUSKCN1NO28Y or https://www.business-humanrights.org/sites/default/files/FTSE%20100%20Briefing%202018.pdf (accessed 24 April 2019).

The results from the analysis would assist institutions around the world to determine the best approach to preventing modern slavery.

CASE STUDY 1.2: MODERN SLAVERY HUMAN TRAFFICKING UNIT (MSHTU)

The **Modern Slavery Human Trafficking Unit (MSHTU)** is a multi-agency organisation led by the National Crime Agency (NCA) UK. Its role is to provide a central point of expertise, support and coordination for the UK's response to modern slavery and the trafficking of human beings.

MSHTU work in a coordinated way within the UK and internationally. MSHTU's work to combat modern slavery crimes involves a wide range of partners and stakeholders.

MSHTU's key responsibilities are to protect the public – safeguarding potential victims from such crimes and to target those who enable or facilitate crimes of modern slavery here in the UK.

In that respect, the MSHTU collaborate with partners including police forces, the Home Office and other government departments, the UK Border Force and UK Immigration Enforcement, the Gangmasters Labour Abuse Authority (GLAA), international agencies, non-governmental organisations (NGOs) and many charitable and voluntary expert groups.[24]

Preventing human trafficking

[24] National Crime Agency (2018), 'Modern Slavery Human Trafficking Unit (MSHTU)', Available at: http://www.nationalcrimeagency.gov.uk/about-us/what-we-do/specialist-capabilities/uk-human-trafficking-centre (accessed 10 March 2018).

The mainstay of the Modern Slavery Human Trafficking Unit's (MSHTU) work will always be supporting the victims of trafficking and bringing to justice those responsible. But preventing the crime is just as important. Prevention efforts are therefore a key component of the MSHTU's proactive strategy to reduce harm and protect victims of human trafficking.

Protecting victims of human trafficking

The MSHTU is a victim-focused organisation. The identification, recovery, support and, when appropriate, repatriation of human trafficking victims is at the core of everything it does.

Protection activity includes:

- Working closely with partners across the public, private and voluntary sectors to support the provision of a full care, end-to-end programme for the victims of human trafficking
- Providing expert Tactical Advisors who can offer real-time support and advice 24/7 on a variety of issues. These include tactical advice to police forces and Government agencies to support pre-planned operations, advice on the disruption and prosecution of identified offenders, and help in determining whether individuals may be trafficking victims.
- Providing a central collection point for the National Referral Mechanism (NRM) data, as one of the UK's two Competent Authorities.
- Recording, tracking and analysing all NRM referrals and the resulting decisions

- Playing an active role alongside partners in the UK Government partnership groups

MSHTU tactical advisors

The MSHTU's team of expert Tactical Advisors provides 24/7, UK wide, real-time support in all human trafficking matters. This includes advice to first responders such as key NGOs, police forces and Government agencies in pre-planned operations, live advice in reactive investigations, help with the disruption and prosecution of identified offenders, best evidence and operational practice, victim care, and the NRM. They have the necessary experience to establish whether an individual may be a trafficked victim.

Prosecution

The MSHTU works with the UK and international law enforcement agencies to pursue and prosecute those responsible for human trafficking. In doing this the centre:

- Collates, develops and shares innovative tactics, techniques, expertise and good practice;
- Develops high quality intelligence to help identify and fill knowledge gaps in the understanding of human trafficking crime;
- Draws on the wider resource afforded by being part of the National Crime Agency;
- Encourages and advises on the use of relevant legislation in holding traffickers to account;
- Provides support and advice to police forces and government agencies to help identify trafficking offences and potential victims;

- Plays a full role alongside the Police, the Gangmasters and Labour Abuse Authority, UK Border Force and the Home Office Immigration and Enforcement in the UK Human Trafficking Law Enforcement forums.

Compensation

In addition to the prosecution of traffickers as set out above, there is the option for victims to seek justice against their traffickers for the human rights and labour abuses they have endured by bringing a claim for financial compensation for the damage they have suffered.

There are four avenues through which a victim of trafficking might receive compensation:

1. Compensation Orders following criminal proceedings
2. Civil claims in the County Court or High Court
3. Employment claims in the Employment Tribunal
4. Criminal Injuries Compensation Authority claims

As a result of the **Legal Aid, Sentencing and Punishment of Offenders Act 2012** and the subsequent amendments brought in by the **Modern Slavery Act 2015**, legal aid is available for claims for damages, and claims under employment law as a result of the exploitation of an individual (Options 2 & 3 above).[25]

Further Information on how to make a claim:

[25] National Crime Agency (2018), 'Modern slavery and human trafficking: Prevention, protecting victims and prosecution of offenders', Available at: http://www.nationalcrimeagency.gov.uk/about-us/what-we-do/specialist-capabilities/uk-human-trafficking-centre/prevention-protecting-victims-and-prosecution (accessed 10 March 2018).

https://www.gov.uk/compensation-victims-modern-slavery-human-trafficking
https://www.gov.uk/government/organisations/criminal-injuries-compensation-authority

For further information on the Government's response to trafficking and modern slavery:
https://www.gov.uk/government/collections/modern-slavery-bill

CHAPTER 2

THE RISK-BASED APPROACH: AN OVERVIEW

Although any type of Supply Chain is potentially vulnerable to modern slavery, by the nature of their business, occupation, or anticipated transaction activity, certain suppliers may pose specific risks. At this stage of the risk assessment process, it is essential that business enterprises exercise judgment and neither define nor treat all members of a specific category as posing the same level of risk.[26]

Businesses will determine the due diligence requirements appropriate to each Supply Chain. This may include:

- A standard level of due diligence, to be applied to all suppliers.
- An increased level of due diligence in respect of those suppliers that are determined to be of higher risk. This may be the result of the supplier's business activity, ownership structure, anticipated or actual volume or types of business activities, including those activities involving higher risk countries or defined by applicable law or regulation as posing higher risk.

---

[26] Esoimeme, E.E. (2015), 'The Risk-Based Approach to Combating Money Laundering and Terrorist Financing', Eric Press; Available on Amazon: https://www.amazon.co.uk/Risk-Based-Combating-Laundering-Terrorist-Financing/dp/9789486030/ref=sr_1_2?ie=UTF8&qid=1437508453&sr=8-2&keywords=ehi+eric+esoimeme (accessed 25 April 2019).

- The standard level being reduced in recognized lower risk scenarios, such as where:

    o the Recruitment policy of the supplier is very sound and effective;

    o the Procurement policy of the supplier and incentives to combat modern slavery are very strong and effective;

    o the countries the Supplier sources its goods or services are low risk countries where modern forms of slavery are not prevalent;

    o Policies concerning access to remedy, compensation and justice for victims of modern slavery are very effective;

    o the supplier has an Employee Code of Conduct and a supplier Code of Conduct; and

    o Polices of the supplier that relate to staff training and increasing awareness of modern slavery are very good.

In assessing the Supply Chain risk, Businesses are required to consider other variables such as:

- **Country risks** – exposure may be greater in global supply chains in countries where protection against breaches of human rights are limited, particularly with regard to rights of foreign contract workers to retain their own ID and papers, and/or where work arrangement by agents is common, etc. High and Medium level risk assessment should be based on key indices such as the **United States Department of Justice**

Trafficking in Persons report,[27] United States Department of Labour's 2017 Findings on the Worst Forms of Child Labour,[28] Bureau of International Labour Affairs (ILAB) List of Goods Produced by Child Labour or Forced Labour,[29] the Walk Free Foundation Global Slavery Index,[30] the International

---

[27] The Trafficking in Persons (TIP) Report is the U.S. Government's principal diplomatic tool to engage foreign governments on human trafficking. It is also the world's most comprehensive resource of governmental anti-trafficking efforts and reflects the U.S. Government's commitment to global leadership on this key human rights and law enforcement issue. You can view the full report here https://www.state.gov/wp-content/uploads/2019/06/2019-Trafficking-in-Persons-Report.pdf You can access the summary of this report on Appendix 4.

[28] The Department of Labor's annual Findings on the Worst Forms of Child Labor focuses on the efforts of certain U.S. trade beneficiary countries and territories to eliminate the worst forms of child labor through legislation, enforcement mechanisms, policies and social programs. The Report serves as a resource to foreign governments, NGOs, academics and policymakers working on labor and human rights issues. It helps inform Congress and Executive Branch agencies that formulate labor and trade policy and is an important resource for the Department in assessing future technical assistance and research priorities as it seeks to combat child labor around the world. View the full report here: https://www.dol.gov/sites/dolgov/files/ILAB/legacy/files/ChildLaborReport_Book.pdf or the summary of this report on Appendix 5.

[29] ILAB maintains a list of goods and their source countries which it has reason to believe are produced by child labor or forced labor in violation of international standards, as required under the Trafficking Victims Protection Reauthorization Act (TVPRA) of 2005 and subsequent reauthorizations. As of September 20, 2018, the List of Goods Produced by Child Labor or Forced Labor comprises 148 goods from 76 countries. ILAB maintains the List primarily to raise public awareness about forced labor and child labor around the world and to promote efforts to combat them; it is not intended to be punitive, but rather to serve as a catalyst for more strategic and focused coordination and collaboration among those working to address these problems. Publication of the List has resulted in new opportunities for ILAB to engage with foreign governments to combat forced labor and child labor. It is also a valuable resource for researchers, advocacy organizations and companies wishing to carry out risk assessments and engage in due diligence on labor rights in their supply chains. You can access the full list here: https://www.dol.gov/sites/dolgov/files/ILAB/ListofGoods.pdf or the summary on Appendix 6.

[30] The Global Slavery Index provides a country by country ranking of the number of people in modern slavery, an analysis of the actions governments are taking to respond, and the factors that make people vulnerable. See Appendix 1 for an overview of the 2018 Global Slavery Index.

Trade Union Confederation (ITUC) Global Rights Index[31] **and Sedex.**[32]

- **Sector risks** – there are different risks and levels of risk in different sectors. For example, the risks and arrangements which generate bonded labour situations for workers in the extractives sector may differ to those causes in manufacturing. Risk assessment should be based on the **Global Slavery Index, the Bureau of International Labour Affairs (ILAB) List of Goods Produced by Child Labour or Forced Labour and Sedex Self-Assessment Questionnaire (SAQ).**
- **Transaction risks** – banks or financial institutions may be involved in facilitating financing from or supporting cases of modern slavery and bonded labour in operations or supply chains or through money laundering. To reduce the money laundering risks associated with High-risk suppliers, the Banks should adopt Customer Due Diligence measures, record keeping measures, transaction monitoring measures and reporting measures. Banks or financial institutions should apply a risk-based approach to their compliance programs. Adopting a risk-based approach implies the adoption of a risk management process for dealing with fraud and money laundering. This process encompasses recognising the existence of the risk at the Standard Due Diligence stage, undertaking an assessment of the risks at the Enhanced Due Diligence stage and developing

[31] International Trade Union Confederation (ITUC) Global Rights Index 2019 highlights intensified repression & violence against workers globally. An overview of the Index has been provided in Appendix 2. You can view the full index here: https://www.ituc-csi.org/IMG/pdf/2019-06-ituc-global-rights-index-2019-report-en-2.pdf

[32] One of the key tools that UK companies use to inform their responsible sourcing programmes is the Sedex Self-Assessment Questionnaire (SAQ). The SAQ is completed by Sedex Supplier (B) and Buyer/Supplier (AB) members when they register a new site. See Chapter 3 for more on this.

strategies to manage and mitigate the identified risks at the Enhanced on-going monitoring stage.[33] The **Financial Action Task Force (FATF) Recommendations** support the development and implementation of a risk-based approach to anti-money laundering and countering the financing of terrorism measures. This risk-based approach allows countries, within the framework of the FATF requirements, to adopt a more flexible set of measures, in order to target their resources more effectively and apply preventive measures that are commensurate to the nature of risks, in order to focus their efforts in the most effective way. Independent testing (audit) should review a Bank's risk assessment for reasonableness. Additionally, management should consider the staffing resources and the level of training necessary to promote adherence with these policies, procedures, and processes. For those suppliers that assume a higher-risk money laundering profile, management should provide a more robust anti-money laundering compliance program that specifically monitors and controls the higher risks that management and the board have accepted.[34]

- **Business partnership risks** – Different supplier relationships and business partnerships will all carry different levels of risks. In some cases, existing long-term partnerships will involve less risk because the

---

[33] Esoimeme, E.E. (2015), 'The Risk-Based Approach to Combating Money Laundering and Terrorist Financing', Eric Press; Available on Amazon: https://www.amazon.co.uk/Risk-Based-Combating-Laundering-Terrorist-Financing/dp/9789486030/ref=sr_1_2?ie=UTF8&qid=1437508453&sr=8-2&keywords=ehi+eric+esoimeme

[34] United States' Federal Financial Institutions Examination Council (2014), 'Bank Secrecy Act/Anti-Money Laundering Examination Manual', Available at: https://www.occ.treas.gov/publications/publications-by-type/other-publications-reports/ffiec-bsa-aml-examination-manual.pdf (accessed 10 January 2017).

organisation will have a better knowledge of their partner's operations and policies. However, a new partnership or business relationship may be equally low risk as long as proper due diligence is conducted.[35] **The company's systems should be adequate to manage the risks associated with new partnership or business relationship and the management should have the ability to implement their monitoring and reporting systems effectively.**

BOX 2.1: NEED FOR COMPANIES TO HAVE AN ELABORATE RISK ASSESSMENT PROGRAMME

Companies must conduct a risk assessment that incorporates all of a supplier's product and services. An operational and organizational risk assessment is a vital part of a compliance program, as it permits companies to assess the particular risks posed by its business lines, practices, and clientele and establish appropriate controls to mitigate those risks. Failure to conduct an adequate risk assessment may leave a company ill-equipped to implement necessary risk management controls.

BOX 2.2: NEED FOR COMPANIES TO EFFECTIVELY RISK RATE SUPPLIERS

A company's written policies, procedures, and controls should effectively risk rate suppliers – either: HIGH, MEDIUM or LOW risk using the designated risk assessment matrix of the company. The Company's risk rating methodologies should be designed to evaluate suppliers based on specific supplier information and balanced consideration of all relevant factors, including country/jurisdictional risk, products and services provided, and nature of supplier profiles. Failure to

[35] Transparency in Supply Chains etc. A Practical Guide 2015 (Last Updated 2018), Annex E.

adequately risk rate suppliers may leave the Company ill-equipped to adequately monitor activities of high-risk suppliers. Companies should have up-to-date, accurate, and verified information on suppliers to enable it to conduct its annual risk assessment.

2.1 RISK ASSESSMENT

The steps a company takes for its supply chain depends on how it initially evaluates a supplier. The company must ask all but its lowest risk suppliers to complete its 'Sourcing with Human Dignity' questionnaire – which helps establish a high or medium risk of them falling below the standards set by a Company.

Risk profiling helps a company focus its efforts where they are most needed. For example, suppliers may present a higher risk of slavery or human trafficking because of where they're based or the type of product or service they provide. All medium risk suppliers must get a review. High risk suppliers must get a more detailed review to better understand the risk and put in steps to tackle it; this may mean visiting their sites.

Modern slavery risks are affected by various factors, including the strength of policies, laws and institutions to protect against modern slavery where the company operates. In areas of weaker governance, a company will find that the risk that it may be involved in modern slavery through its supply chain is greater. Using tools such as the Global Slavery Index a company will recognise the heightened risks of exposure to modern slavery in some emerging economies as well as that modern slavery may occur in developed markets.[36]

[36] The Global Slavery Index provides a country by country ranking of the number of people in modern slavery, an analysis of the actions governments are taking to respond, and the factors

To improve its understanding of the different modern slavery risks that a company may face in different locations as well as exposure to related issues such as broader human rights risks and corruption, the company can use tools including the Transparency International Corruption Perceptions Index[37] and Verisk Maplecroft Human Rights Indices.[38]

When a company is seeking more in-depth information on identified risks, country, industry and company specific resources such as the US Department of State's *Trafficking in Persons report*[39] and country narratives, KnowTheChain industry benchmarking[40] and the Modern Slavery Registry are also useful.[41]

---

that make people vulnerable. See Appendix 1 for an overview of the 2018 Global Slavery Index.

[37] The Corruption Perceptions index, which ranks 180 countries and territories by their perceived levels of public sector corruption according to experts and business people, uses a scale of 0 to 100, where 0 is highly corrupt and 100 is very clean. More than two-thirds of countries score below 50 on the 2018 Corruption Perceptions Index, with an average score of just 43. It reveals that the continued failure of most countries to significantly control corruption is contributing to a **crisis in democracy** around the world. While there are exceptions, the data shows that despite some progress, most countries are failing to make serious inroads against corruption. You can access the Corruption Perceptions Index 2018 via this link: https://www.transparency.org/cpi2018

[38] Recognised as the most robust and accurate in the market today, Verisk Maplecroft's data gives you an unparalleled 360° perspective of your global risk exposure and the issues impacting the long-term value of your investments, the security of your assets and personnel, and the sustainability of your operations and supply chains. See Appendix 3 for more on the Verisk Maplecroft Human Rights Risk Data and Indices.

[39] The 2019 U.S. Trafficking in Persons Report is contained in Appendix 4 of this book.

[40] KnowTheChain is a resource for companies and investors to understand and address forced labor risks within their global supply chains. Through benchmarking current corporate practices and providing practical resources that enable companies to operate more transparently and responsibly, KnowTheChain drives corporate action while also informing investor decisions. KnowTheChain is committed to helping companies make an impact in their efforts to address forced labor. You can view their website on https://knowthechain.org/

[41] The Modern Slavery Registry hosts modern slavery statements. This Registry is guided and supported by a governance committee which includes: Freedom Fund, Humanity United, Freedom United, Anti-Slavery International, the Ethical Trading Initiative, CORE Coalition, UNICEF UK, Focus on Labour Exploitation (FLEX), Trades Union Congress, UN Principles

For example, Rio Tinto PLC., makes use of the Modern Slavery Registry to view suppliers' and other business partners' modern slavery statements where available.

Some goods and services a company procures may be higher risk than others. Rio Tinto PLC., has assessed construction, shipping, cleaning, catering and other transport services to be among these because of a variety of factors including the use of sub-contracting, migrant workers and lower-skilled labour. In addition to identifying these sectors as higher risk as part of its initial supply chain risk mapping, Rio Tinto PLC., monitor expert analysis – such as research from governments, international institutions and think tanks – to ensure an up-to-date understanding of high-risk sectors.[42]

Each year **British Telecommunications PLC.,** do around 50 on-site audits of their higher risk suppliers. **British Telecommunications PLC.,** work together with them to address any problems they pick up.

British Telecommunications PLC., keep their processes under review. In 2014 **British Telecommunications** looked at their procurement processes as part of an overall human rights review of their business. **British Telecommunications** are implementing the review's recommendations, as well as looking again at their supply chain approach in light of the Modern Slavery Act.[43]

---

for Responsible Investment, and Oxfam GB. You can access the Modern Slavery Registry here: https://www.modernslaveryregistry.org/

[42] Rio Tinto PLC. (2018), 'Respecting Human Rights: Our Statement on Modern Slavery', Available at: https://www.riotinto.com/documents/RT_Slavery_and_human_trafficking_statement_2018.pdf (accessed 24 June 2019).

[43] British Telecommunications PLC. (2016), 'Modern Slavery Act Statement', Available at: https://www.btplc.com/Digitalimpactandsustainability/Humanrights/Modernslavery/ModernSlaverystatement.pdf (accessed 23 June 2019).

Because human rights situations are dynamic, assessments of human rights impacts should be undertaken at regular intervals: prior to a new activity or relationship; prior to major decisions or changes in the operation (e.g. market entry, product launch, policy change, or wider changes to the business); in response to or anticipation of changes in the operating environment (e.g. rising social tensions); and periodically throughout the life of an activity or relationship.[44] **Kingfisher PLC., for example, evaluates risk(s) on an ongoing basis using:**

——**Ethical risk matrix: Kingfisher PLC's** ethical risk matrix uses data from Maplecroft to help identify the high-risk product areas and countries in its goods for resale (GFR) supply chain.

Kingfisher PLC., are currently focused on risks in their direct supply chain, particularly labour risks among suppliers of finished goods for resale.

Kingfisher PLC., are also developing approaches to reducing risks in the wider supply chain including among raw materials suppliers.

——**Sedex: Kingfisher PLC.,** also use Sedex to help them assess risks in their goods for resale (GFR) supply chain. Sedex provides two indications of risk for each production site – an inherent risk (based on sector and country) and a self-assessment risk (based on a site's response to the Sedex risk assessment questionnaire).

Kingfisher PLC., aim for all suppliers of goods for resale to be using the Sedex platform by the end of 2020. Kingfisher PLC., made good progress in 2018 and around 1,900 suppliers, incorporating 2,600 factory sites, have now joined the Sedex

---

[44] United Nations (UN) 'Guiding Principles on Business and Human Rights' 2011, Principle 18 Commentary.

platform. This equates to around 66% of suppliers of goods for resale.[45]

CASE STUDY 2.1: ASSESSING THE RISK(S) OF MODERN SLAVERY (PART 1)

Tesco, PLC., assesses the potential human rights risks of its supply chains by considering the country of origin where it is sourcing products or raw materials from. In the Tesco UK stores and Central European businesses, Tesco uses the **Food Network for Ethical Trade (FNET)** risk ratings to inform their work, combined with their own understanding of labour rights and human rights risks in their key sourcing sectors.

In Thailand and Malaysia, **Tesco** uses a bespoke risk assessment, which takes into account the industry, the particular type of labour, internal recommendations, and supplier self-assessment.

At the next stage of its risk assessment, **Tesco** considers the type of work being carried out (mechanical vs. manual), as well as the type of labour (seasonal, permanent, agency).

Tesco also gathers intelligence surrounding new and emerging risks through their domestic team of sourcing specialists, in addition to the strong relationships that they've formed with local groups, non-governmental organisations (NGOs), and conventional organisations, such as the Ethical Trading Initiative, FNET, and the Consumer Goods Forum. Campaigners and activists can also play an important role in helping Tesco identify exactly where some of the biggest risks may lie. From there, Tesco

[45] Kingfisher PLC. (2018/19), 'Modern Slavery Act Transparency Statement', Available at: file:///C:/Users/user/Downloads/Kingfisher%20MSA%20Statement%202018%2019.pdf (accessed 23 June 2019).

collaborates with them and works closely to learn from their experiences wherever possible.

Tesco recognizes the important role played by investigative journalism in identifying current and emerging risks. This approach helps Tesco identify where the most salient and material risks exist within their supply chains. Tesco then seeks to mitigate the risks through a 'three pillar' approach – Improve, Transform, Advocate.[46]

CASE STUDY 2.2: ASSESSING THE RISK(S) OF MODERN SLAVERY (PART 2)

Barratt Developments, PLC., has reviewed their exposure and their risk of modern slavery across all aspects of their business, and they've focused their risk assessments on four key areas:

- Direct, agency, and temporary employment practices including temporary and agency employment. For example, at their sites or within their own factories in the UK.

- Subcontractor relationships, where Barratt Developments Plc consider employment and payment practices.

- Material suppliers, where Barratt Developments Plc assess risk based on geography, material or component type and its relationship with the supplier.

- IT Services.

Based on **Barratt Developments'** 2015/2016 risk assessment, they believe that the business has a low overall risk of modern slavery within their own operations and across their supply chain. **Barratt**

[46] Tesco PLC. (2018/19), 'Modern Slavery Statement', Available at: https://sustainability.tescoplc.com/media/476591/tesco-modern-slavery-statement_201819.pdf (accessed 24 June 2019).

Developments understands that however low the risk may be, the organization must be proactive in ensuring that its strategies address any residual risk, in addition to fostering a robust, aware, and vigilant workforce.[47]

BOX 2.3: UPDATING RISK ASSESSMENT

Companies shall verify suppliers' basic information regularly according to the level of the supplier or supply chain. Verification on suppliers or accounts with higher risk level should be carried out at least once per 6 months. Verification on suppliers with medium risk level should be carried out yearly while verification on suppliers with low risk should be carried out every two years.

BOX 2.4: ADJUSTING SUPPLIER RISK RATING WHERE THERE IS A DEVIATION IN A SUPPLIER'S BUSINESS ACTIVITY

A situation could occur where a supplier who sources its goods and services from low-risk countries might begin sourcing its goods and services from high-risk countries where modern forms of slavery are prevalent. Moreover, a situation could also occur where a supplier who is known to have a sound recruitment policy or procurement policy, could waver in their efforts to maintain such a policy. In such a situation like this, the company that hired the services of the supplier should change the supplier's risk rating from low-risk to high-risk. Failure to change the supplier's risk rating will undermine the purpose of conducting risk ratings and could pave the way for increasingly insufficient activity monitoring for suppliers. These instances could leave a

[47] Barratt Developments PLC. (2016), 'Modern Slavery and Human Trafficking Statement 2016', Available at: https://www.barrattdevelopments.co.uk/-/media/Files/B/Barratt-Developments/policies/2016/BARRATT-DEVELOPMENTS-PLC-MODERN-SLAVERY-AND-HUMAN-TRAFFICKING-STATEMENT-2016.pdf (accessed 22 June 2019).

company vulnerable to a high-risk supplier, and limit their ability to detect red flags and suspicious activity in the future.

2.2 RISK MITIGATION

Where issues have been identified in certain supply chains through investigations that were carried out at the Enhanced Due Diligence stage, Businesses must determine how such issues can best be remediated or mitigated through measures such as training and awareness, whistle-blowing mechanisms, and industry collaboration or improved purchasing practices internally.[48]

2.2.1 TRAINING AND AWARENESS

Businesses are required to provide their employees with business integrity training, and it is important that their employees receive appropriate and proportional training with regards to modern slavery and human rights risk(s) that were identified at the Enhanced Due Diligence Stage.[49]

A commercial organisation's commitment to having successful controls relies on both training and awareness. This requires an enterprise-wide effort to provide all relevant employees with at least general information on Modern Slavery laws, regulations and internal policies.

Training for global category management teams should focus on awareness of responsible sourcing risk and requirements for suppliers. Key items that should be emphasized include 1) the identification of key responsible sourcing risks (including human rights and modern slavery), 2) the due diligence approach and how

[48] Chapters 4 and 5 will address the risk mitigation measures in more detail.

[49] UK Modern Slavery Act 2015, s. 54(5)(f); Transparency in Supply Chains etc. A Practical Guide 2015 (Last Updated 2018), Annex E.

to integrate responsible sourcing requirements into supplier selection.

During 2017, Anglo American hosted more than 65 workshops in seven jurisdictions, in which 1,200 individuals received business integrity training. Furthermore, approximately 1,250 employees and contractors participated in online business integrity training.[50]

In 2017/18 in addition to one to one engagement sessions with key partners, the Global Social Compliance teams of Marks and Spencer had 1 day of specialist modern slavery training, North and South China M&S social compliance team attended the Ethical Trading Initiative (ETI) modern slavery training and modern slavery was a topic at International, retail and property Huddles and Hong Kong sourcing Office.

Capacity building of suppliers has remained a key focus for Marks and Spencer. Within Foods, where Marks and Spencer believe their risk is greatest, Marks and Spencer supported the scaling of Stronger Together Initiative to South Africa launching it at their joint December 2017 conference with Woolworths South Africa. Marks and Spencer also actively supported supplier modern slavery upskilling through multi retailer Spanish forum, the scaling of Food Network Ethical trade (FNET), supply chain events with Issara, Consumer Goods Forum (CGF) and Institute for Human Rights and Business (IHRB). At the suppliers' request Marks and Spencer updated Food Sustainability score card which over 95% food suppliers are engaged in with greater guidance on responsible recruitment and include a new pillar on extended Supply chains to increase greater focus on modern slavery risk at lower tiers. Marks and Spencer Clothing and Home

[50] Anglo American (2018), 'UK Modern Slavery Act: Statement for the financial year ending 31 December 2017', Available at: https://www.angloamerican.com/~/media/Files/A/Anglo-American-PLC-V2/documents/aa-plc-uk-modern-slavery-act-2017.pdf (accessed 24 April 2019).

team have continued to upskill UK suppliers via Fast Forward training sessions in the UK.[51]

2.2.2. WHISTLE-BLOWING

Businesses are required to have a whistle–blowing policy which shall be made known to employees, management, directors and other stakeholders such as contractors, shareholders, job applicants and the general public.[52] The policy should be disclosed in their web sites. It is the responsibility of the board to implement such a policy and to establish a whistle-blowing mechanism for reporting any illegal or unethical behavior.

Businesses shall establish whistleblowing procedures that encourage stakeholders by assurance of confidentiality, to report any unethical activity using, among others, a dedicated email or hotline to the company and the National Crime Agency.

The Head of Internal Audit shall review reported cases and recommend appropriate action to the Managing Director (MD)/Chief Executive Officer (CEO) and where issues affect Executive Management, such issues should be referred to the Board. The Board or CEO shall take appropriate action to redress the situation within a reasonable time. The Head of Internal Audit shall provide the Chairman of the Board Audit Committee with a summary of cases reported and the result of the investigation.

Anglo American has an independently managed 'Speak Up' facility which is a confidential and secure means for its employees, contractors, suppliers, business partners and other external stakeholders around the world to report concerns about conduct that is contrary to their values and integrity standards.

---

[51] Marks and Spencer Group PLC. (2018), 'Marks and Spencer: Modern Slavery Statement 2017/18', Available at: https://corporate.marksandspencer.com/documents/plan-a-our-approach/mns-modern-slavery-statement-june2018.pdf (accessed 24 April 2019).

[52] Transparency in Supply Chains etc. A Practical Guide 2015 (Last Updated 2018), Annex E.

Complaints can be submitted anonymously and are handled by a third party. Anglo American does not tolerate any form of retaliation against employees raising concerns in good faith.

During 2017, Anglo American received 225 alerts plus another 660 alerts related to a scam committed by a gang of fraudsters against suppliers and other companies – overall, no alerts were categorised as being related to modern slavery or human trafficking.

Marks and Spencer have a strong Whistleblowing Policy (aimed principally at their employees but also available to others working in their supply chain).

2.2.3 MULTI-STAKEHOLDER COLLABORATION AND ENGAGEMENT

Collaboration with external partners plays a key role in a company's approach to addressing human rights risk in their supply chains. The issues it faces are often complex and complicated, and its influence to leverage meaningful change can be limited. Engaging with their suppliers, competitors, non-governmental organizations (NGOs), charities, Trade Unions and multi-stakeholder initiatives (MSIs) help companies to maximise the resource and intelligence available to support their actions and forms a key part of their strategy.

CASE STUDY 2.3: ADDRESSING RISKS

In line with the **United Nations Guiding Principles on Business and Human Rights (UNGPs)**, **Diageo, PLC.**, identified three risks as particularly salient to its business:

- Labour rights, including the risk of child labour, specifically in agricultural supply networks.

- Labour standards for contract workers.

- Sexual harassment in the hospitality sector.

These issues are external risk factors in the places where **Diageo** operates. In addition, **Diageo** recognizes the challenges that these external risk factors pose within their value chain.

Having identified these risks, **Diageo** has developed a child protection programme for their work with smallholder farmers, where they have trained key functions and business partners on their local sourcing programme that spans seven countries in Africa in their effort to prevent child labour. **Diageo** has also developed initiatives aimed at preventing sexual harassment in the hospitality sector and as part of those initiatives, has gone on to launch a new Global Brand Promoter Standard, which establishes principles and guidelines to protect the rights of brand promoters.

Diageo has also created contractor standards guided by the **International Labour Organization's Declaration on Fundamental Principles and Rights to Work**, focused on promoting conditions in which people can work in freedom and safety.

In addition to the above, each market has produced an action plan to address its specific risks.

Furthermore, **Diageo, PLC.**, recognizes the specific risks that exist for women, as well as opportunities for their empowerment, both in agriculture and smallholder farming in Africa. In 2018, **Diageo** conducted research with CARE International UK, a global NGO, to better understand these issues, to identify new ways of working, and to design policies that improve farm work and better protect the rights of women on these farms. **Diageo** is now integrating their recommendations all throughout their local sourcing programme.

Because human rights issues are often systemic, **Diageo** also works with others to address them at scale. This includes further work with CARE International UK, with whom they have been collaborating with on a number of projects designed to combat sexual harassment of women in the hospitality sector, after initial work in Southeast Asia.[53]

[53] Diageo Plc (2018), 'Modern Slavery Act Statement', Available at: https://www.diageo.com/PR1346/aws/media/7282/74125_diageo_modern_slavery_act_2018-12-21_jy.pdf (accessed 24 June 2019).

CHAPTER 3

SUPPLY CHAIN DUE DILIGENCE

The starting point for Supply Chain Due Diligence is to assess each supplier's inherent human rights risk based on the type of supplier and the country where it operates. To do this, the business enterprise can use a series of **Verisk Maplecroft's human rights indices**, including the **2018 Global Slavery Index, funded by Forrest's Walk Free Foundation**. The business enterprise can then prioritise those suppliers identified as being exposed to the highest risks and ask them to complete a self-assessment questionnaire. The self-assessment questionnaire should be structured around the key areas of the company's supplier Code of Conduct and provide the company with information on the policies, procedures and practices the supplier has in place to effectively manage these risks.

Where the results of the self-assessment highlight minor areas for improvement, the commercial organisation/business enterprise should work with the supplier to develop corrective actions and agree on a timescale for material progress towards compliance.

Where the results reveal more significant issues, an on-site audit should be conducted by the company's independent auditor. This includes criteria on labour standards – with a specific section focusing on forced labour – as well as child labour, wages and hours, health and safety, environment and management systems.

In the event of serious and/or persistent non-compliance, or where suppliers fail to demonstrate a willingness to improve performance, the company reserves the right to terminate the business relationship.[54]

Human rights due diligence should be initiated as early as possible in the development of a new activity or relationship, given that human rights risks can be increased or mitigated already at the stage of structuring contracts or other agreements, and may be inherited through mergers or acquisitions.

Where business enterprises have large numbers of entities in their value chains it may be unreasonably difficult to conduct due diligence for adverse human rights impacts across them all. If so, business enterprises should identify general areas where the risk of adverse human rights impacts is most significant, whether due to certain suppliers' or clients' operating context, the particular operations, products or services involved, or other relevant considerations, and prioritize these for human rights due diligence.

Conducting appropriate human rights due diligence should help business enterprises address the risk of legal claims against them by showing that they took every reasonable step to avoid involvement with an alleged human rights abuse. However, business enterprises conducting such due diligence should not assume that, by itself, this will automatically and fully absolve

[54] British American Tobacco (2016), 'Modern Slavery Act Statement 2016', Available at: https://www.bat.com/group/sites/uk__9d9kcy.nsf/vwPagesWebLive/DOAK8P7C/$FILE/medMDAXGJD9.pdf?openelement (accessed 22 June 2019).

them from liability for causing or contributing to human rights abuses.[55]

CASE STUDY 3.1: BRITISH AMERICAN TOBACCO'S APPROACH TO HUMAN RIGHTS DUE DILIGENCE

British American Tobacco is one of the world's leading consumer goods companies. It employs more than 55,000 people worldwide, and operates 45 factories in 42 countries and offices all around the world. In 2017, **British American Tobacco Group** revenue was over £20 billion; British American Tobacco sold cigarettes in more than 200 markets and their Next Generation Products (NGPs) were available in 16 markets.[56]

British American Tobacco's supply chain consists of two discrete elements relating to agricultural and non-agricultural suppliers.

British American Tobacco, through their due diligence programme, discovered that their Agricultural supply chains are particularly vulnerable to a range of challenges, including climate change and water scarcity, increasing demand for land and natural resources, rural poverty and social inequality, child labour, and ageing farmer populations. Tobacco is no exception.

Based on careful assessment and the insights developed over many years, **British American Tobacco** believes that the greatest risk of modern slavery is in their tobacco leaf supply chain. At the same time, **British American Tobacco** acknowledges the potential – albeit lower – risk of modern slavery in their non-agricultural supply chain.

---

[55] United Nations (UN) 'Guiding Principles on Business and Human Rights' 2011, Principle 17 Commentary.

[56] British American Tobacco (2017), 'Modern Slavery Act Statement 2017', Available at: https://www.bat.com/group/sites/uk__9d9kcy.nsf/vwPagesWebLive/DO52AD7G/$FILE/medMDAWUNCY.pdf?openelement (accessed 22 June 2019).

British American Tobacco conducts due diligence on their tobacco leaf supply chain through the Sustainable Tobacco Programme (STP), which assesses and monitors suppliers' performance in meeting industry-wide standards.

The programme assesses the first-tier suppliers that **British American Tobacco** purchases their tobacco leaf from, some of which are **British American Tobacco**-owned companies. It checks if they have the appropriate systems, governance, and procedures in place to ensure high environmental and human rights standards on the farms they source from, in addition to providing the best quality tobacco leaf.

STP was developed in 2015 in collaboration with five other tobacco manufacturers to bring together best practice from across the industry.

Implementation began in June 2016, replacing **British American Tobacco's** Social Responsibility in Tobacco Production programme, which ran for more than 15 years (for which aggregated supplier scores were published annually at www.bat.com/srtpdata).

The programme is aligned to important external standards, such as those of the **International Labour Organisation (ILO),** and includes strengthened processes and more frequent on-site reviews. It is managed by AB Sustain, an independent supply chain management company, which is responsible for coordinating the annual self-assessments from suppliers across the industry, and also for conducting the on-site reviews, which each supplier undergoes on a three-year rolling basis.

The programme has 178 criteria under the key areas of crop, environment, people, and facilities. Suppliers must also show that they have good governance underpinning all four areas and are required to assess, identify, and mitigate any significant risks, which may affect their ability to meet the criteria.

The criteria include a number relating specifically to forced labour, covering the prevention of bond, debt and threat, freedom to leave employment, withholding of payments, retention of identity documents and valuables, and prison and compulsory labour.

Suppliers (including those supplying several tobacco companies) complete a comprehensive annual self-assessment. Independent onsite reviews will also be carried out every three years by AB Sustain, including an in-depth analysis of suppliers' policies, processes, and practices, as well as visits to the tobacco farms they source from.

British American Tobacco will use the results of the self-assessments and the on-site reviews to work collaboratively with suppliers to drive corrective action and improvements. In the event of any serious and/or persistent issues, or where suppliers fail to demonstrate a willingness to improve performance, **British American Tobacco** reserve the right to terminate the business relationship.[57]

BOX 3.1: COMPLIANCE OFFICER AND COMPLIANCE STAFF

A Commercial organisation should designate a person responsible for ensuring day-to-day compliance with supply chain due diligence requirements. Such person will be known as the Compliance Officer or the Modern Slavery Reporting Officer (MSRO).

---

[57] British American Tobacco (2016), 'Modern Slavery Act Statement 2016', Available at: https://www.bat.com/group/sites/uk__9d9kcy.nsf/vwPagesWebLive/DOAK8P7C/$FILE/medMDAXGJD9.pdf?openelement (accessed 22 June 2019).

Commercial organisations must ensure that the Compliance Officer or MSRO has sufficient authority and resources to administer an effective supply chain due diligence compliance program by defining a permanent Compliance department structure and to establish criteria regarding how the Compliance Officer's roles and responsibilities would successfully be performed.

Companies should avoid assigning the Compliance Officer/MSRO multiple non-risk management responsibilities that may make him or her unable to adequately fulfill his or her due diligence obligations. If such a thing happens, commercial organisations should designate an additional person to support the Compliance Officer or otherwise remedy the situation.

Commercial organisations should adequately staff the supply chain risk management compliance department at the Company with personnel that will support the Compliance Officer in ensuring day-to-day compliance with due diligence measures. The compliance department should not be understaffed, and the compliance team should be armed with the requisite knowledge and expertise to adequately perform their duties. Failure of a company to provide adequate numbers of appropriately trained personnel may limit the company's ability to initiate and complete reviews and file complete, accurate, and timely suspicious activity reports to the National Crime Agency.

3.1 STANDARD DUE DILIGENCE USING DESK-BASED RESEARCH AND SUPPLIER SELF-ASSESSMENT QUESTIONNAIRE

Businesses firstly need to research and identify risks where they have operations or supply chain(s) and then prioritise those risks.[58]

[58] UK Modern Slavery Act 2015, s. 54(5)(c); Transparency in Supply Chains etc. A Practical Guide 2015 (Last Updated 2018), Annex E.

Business enterprises may conduct standard due diligence using desk-based research and supplier self-assessment questionnaire.

Desk-based research will help business enterprises to identify suppliers who have been flagged high-risk by international bodies or suppliers who have been tagged by the media as high risk either because of where they operate or documentary/video evidence.

In 2017, National Grid PLC., completed a desktop risk assessment of their top 250 suppliers (global top 250 suppliers to the National Grid PLC., group based on spend) using recommended risk criteria which assessed: country of origin of the goods/service, brand association, supply chain complexity, levels of sub-contracting and category of spend. The desktop risk assessment identified suppliers who were high risk, medium risk and low risk. National Grid PLC., are engaging with those suppliers that have been identified as potentially high risk and will be working with them to complete a range of assessment questions to better understand what controls they have in place and to develop risk mitigation plans for any identified issues. If any issues or concerns are identified and the supplier is either unwilling or unable to make the required improvements, then National Grid PLC., would start a formal contract review process which could result in terminating the contract and removing the supplier from their approved supplier listing.

National Grid PLC., are developing a framework for their buyers so that the sustainability risk criteria, including modern slavery, can be embedded into the initial stages of the sourcing process and integrated into the selection criteria. Any risks identified will be reviewed through the contract management process.[59]

---

[59] National Grid PLC. (2018), 'Our Statement on Slavery and Human Trafficking 2018', Available at: https://www.nationalgrideso.com/sites/eso/files/documents/14842_NG_Modern_Slavery_A4_AW08_INT1%20%281%29.pdf (accessed 24 June 2019).

The supplier self-assessment questionnaire should be updated regularly to align closer with requirements set out in the Responsible Sourcing Standard for suppliers. The self-assessment questionnaires are designed to gauge compliance with the standard, identify potential responsible sourcing risks (which include human rights and modern slavery risks) and flag where further intervention is required, including the possibility of site-based audits.

British Telecommunications PLC., checks their potential suppliers before they enter into a contract with them. British Telecommunications PLC., starts by sending an ethical standards questionnaire to all potential new suppliers of higher and medium risk products and services. To decide if a product or service is high or medium risk British Telecommunications PLC., considers the country it is sourcing from, and the skill level of the labour force the supplier might use.

British Telecommunications PLC., sends the questionnaire either through its own procurement portal or from an independent, globally recognised tool called EcoVadis. EE (formerly Everything Everywhere) used EcoVadis in their business before they joined the British Telecommunications (BT) group and they are looking to use it more extensively throughout all their procurement.

Once **British Telecommunications PLC.,** gets responses back, **British Telecommunications PLC.,** will analyse those responses and generate a risk score – high, medium or low. This score determines what they do next; it could be as simple as a phone interview to clarify minor concerns or any issues they identified. Or they might arrange a more detailed on-site assessment with one of their procurement team. This will be discussed in more detail in the next section.

As well as assessments, **British Telecommunications PLC.,** assessors play a vital role in building close working relationships with their suppliers around the world, working with them to improve their products and services, and checking that they stick to their standards.

When checking for conflict minerals, **British Telecommunications PLC.,** makes use of the Conflict-Free Sourcing Initiative template to ask suppliers of applicable – including BT-branded - products, whether their products contain minerals that may have been sourced from the Democratic Republic of the Congo or neighbouring countries. This helps **British Telecommunications PLC.,** avoid minerals from these regions (mainly the 3TG metals: tin, tantalum, tungsten and gold), the mining of which can be used to fund wars and abuse human rights.[60]

Kingfisher PLC., an international home improvement company with 1,331 stores in 10 countries across Europe, Russia and Turkey, supported by a team of 77,300 colleagues, requires its suppliers to complete the EcoVadis questionnaire covering four themes – labour and human rights, environment, ethics and sustainable procurement. Their responses are reviewed by EcoVadis and a rating provided highlighting strengths, weaknesses and risk areas. Kingfisher PLC., have added the EcoVadis assessment as a requirement in its tender process and set a minimum score threshold which must be achieved within a year of the assessment. Kingfisher PLC., plans to contact 1,000 suppliers during 2019, including their top 400 suppliers that

---

[60] British Telecommunications PLC. (2016/17), 'Modern Slavery Act Statement', Available at: https://www.btplc.com/Digitalimpactandsustainability/Humanrights/Modernslavery/Modern-Slavery-Act-Statement-2017.pdf (accessed 23 June 2019).

account for 75% of their spend, asking them to complete the assessment.[61]

As at 30 June 2018 (the end of Financial Year 2018), 1,248 of **Diageo PLC's** supplier sites assessed as a potential risk had completed a SEDEX self-assessment questionnaire. Of the 486 supplier sites assessed as a potential high risk, 76% (370) were independently audited during the past three years against the SEDEX Members Ethical Trade Audit (SMETA) 4-pillar audit protocol or equivalent. This is an increase from 65% the previous year. Of these, 231 audits were commissioned by Diageo and 170 were accessed through SEDEX or AIM-PROGRESS.[62]

CASE STUDY 3.2: ECOVADIS QUESTIONNAIRE

The EcoVadis platform is designed to help companies better manage and communicate their Corporate Social Responsibility (CSR) performance in a clear and actionable way.

Benefits for the assessed companies:

- Understand your company's CSR performance with ratings on four themes (Environment, Labor & Human Rights, Ethics and Sustainable Procurement), including details of relevant strengths and improvement areas;

- Compare your company's CSR performance against industry and regional benchmarks;

- Share your company's CSR performance with multiple trading partners through the EcoVadis platform and instantly update your

---

[61] Kingfisher PLC. (2018/19), 'Modern Slavery Act Transparency Statement', Available at: file:///C:/Users/user/Downloads/Kingfisher%20MSA%20Statement%202018%2019.pdf (accessed 23 June 2019).

[62] Diageo PLC. (2018), 'Modern Slavery Act Statement', Available at: https://www.diageo.com/PR1346/aws/media/7282/74125_diageo_modern_slavery_act_2018-12-21_jy.pdf (accessed 24 June 2019).

network of any corrective actions and reassessments. The Premium and Corporate subscription plans offer access to a rich set of tools to share your company's CSR performance outside the network, such as the scorecard PDF, EcoVadis Rating Certificate, EcoVadis Medal, CSR Assessment Report, CSR Highlights and more;

- Take action on improvement areas and collaborate with your trading partners using the Corrective Action Plan feature;

- Embark on a continuous improvement journey with annual reassessments of your company's CSR performance.

Benefits for companies who request the assessments from their trading partners:

- Monitor the performance of your trading partners' CSR performance and manage risks;

- Promote transparency on CSR practices with reliable ratings and global benchmarks;

- Practical insight into the key sustainability issues which are applicable to different industries. **EcoVadis** industry risk profiles provide an overview of the industries' major regulations, strengths and improvement areas, key performance indicators (KPIs) and more;

- Identify high performers and encourage the continuous improvement of CSR practices across your network to drive innovation.[63]

[63] Ecovadis (2019), 'Benefits from the EcoVadis solution?', Available at: https://support.ecovadis.com/hc/en-us/articles/115002531387-Benefits-from-the-EcoVadis-solution- (accessed 19 July 2019).

CASE STUDY 3.3: SEDEX SELF-ASSESSMENT QUESTIONNAIRE

One of the key tools that UK companies use to inform their responsible sourcing programmes is the Sedex Self-Assessment Questionnaire (SAQ). The SAQ is completed by Sedex Supplier (B) and Buyer/Supplier (AB) members when they register a new site.

The SAQ collects data across four key pillars:

- **Labour standards**: includes questions on wages, working hours, children and young employees, freedom of association, non-discrimination, forced labour and human rights.
- **Health & safety**: includes questions on management, training, emergency and fire safety and worker health.
- **Environment**: includes questions on environmental management, waste, raw materials, water, energy and pollution.
- **Business ethics**: includes questions on bribery and corruption.

For Suppliers, the SAQ:

1. Helps you share information about your ethical practices with multiple customers – no duplication means it saves you time, money and resources.

2. Supports your learning about ethical standards and practices.

3. Aids you in finding strengths in your business practices and areas to improve.

4. Acts as a pre-audit tool, so you can share data with a prospective auditor prior to their inspection.

For Buyers, the SAQ:

1. Offers a wealth of useful information to assess suppliers on.

2. Helps you determine strengths and areas to improve in your supply chain.

3. Can be used to determine next steps and priority areas.

4. Flexes to fit the supplier, so you only get the information you really need.

5. Feeds data into the Sedex Risk Assessment Tool, to help you assess risk in your supply chain.

Sedex does not set policy or have its own code. The Sedex Self-Assessment Questionnaire is based on the following codes:

- **ETI Base Code: 2014** (Ethical Trading Initiative)
- **SA8000:2014** – Social Accountability (SAI – Social Accountability International)
- **ISO 14001:2015** – Environment Management System (International Organization for Standardization)
- **OHSAS 18001** – Occupational health and safety management system (Occupational Health & Safety Advisory Services).[64]

A. THE ETHICAL TRADING INITIATIVE (ETI) BASE CODE

The **Ethical Trading Initiative (ETI) Base Code** is founded on the **Conventions of the International Labour Organisation (ILO)** and is an internationally recognised code of good labour practice. It is viewed as a global reference standard and is widely used as a

[64] Sedex (2019), 'Self-Assessment Questionnaire', Available at: https://www.sedexglobal.com/our-services/saq/ (accessed 24 June 2019).

benchmark against which to conduct social audits and develop ethical trade action plans.

The provisions of the **Base Code** constitute minimum and not maximum standards. Companies applying this code are expected to comply with national and other applicable laws. Where the law and the Base Code address the same subject, companies are expected to apply the provision that affords the greater protection to workers.[65]

In addition to the **United Nations Guiding Principles on Business and Human Rights** along with other **International Principles and Codes** that Companies must adhere to and implement, a company's due diligence programme should also be based on the **ETI Base Code** which is reproduced below:

1. Employment is freely chosen

1.1 There is no forced, bonded or involuntary prison labour.

1.2 Workers are not required to lodge "deposits" or their identity papers with their employer and are free to leave their employer after reasonable notice.

2. Freedom of association and the right to collective bargaining are respected

2.1 Workers, without distinction, have the right to join or form trade unions of their own choosing and to bargain collectively.

2.2 The employer adopts an open attitude towards the activities of trade unions and their organisational activities.

[65] Ethical Trading Initiative (2018), 'The ETI Base Code', Available at: https://www.ethicaltrade.org/sites/default/files/shared_resources/ETI%20Base%20Code%20%28English%29.pdf (accessed 28 June 2019).

2.3 Workers representatives are not discriminated against and have access to carry out their representative functions in the workplace.

2.4 Where the right to freedom of association and collective bargaining is restricted under law, the employer facilitates, and does not hinder, the development of parallel means for independent and free association and bargaining.

3. Working conditions are safe and hygienic

3.1 A safe and hygienic working environment shall be provided, bearing in mind the prevailing knowledge of the industry and of any specific hazards. Adequate steps shall be taken to prevent accidents and injury to health arising out of, associated with, or occurring in the course of work, by minimising, so far as is reasonably practicable, the causes of hazards inherent in the working environment.

3.2 Workers shall receive regular and recorded health and safety training, and such training shall be repeated for new or reassigned workers.

3.3 Access to clean toilet facilities and to potable water, and, if appropriate, sanitary facilities for food storage shall be provided.

3.4 Accommodation, where provided, shall be clean, safe, and meet the basic needs of the workers.

3.5 The company observing the code shall assign responsibility for health and safety to a senior management representative.

4. Child labour shall not be used

4.1 There shall be no new recruitment of child labour.

4.2 Companies shall develop or participate in and contribute to policies and programmes which provide for the transition of any child found to be performing child labour to enable her or him to attend and remain in quality education until no longer a child; "child" and "child labour" being defined in the appendices.

4.3 Children and young persons under 18 shall not be employed at night or in hazardous conditions.

4.4 These policies and procedures shall conform to the provisions of the relevant ILO standards.

5. Living wages are paid

5.1 Wages and benefits paid for a standard working week meet, at a minimum, national legal standards or industry benchmark standards, whichever is higher. In any event wages should always be enough to meet basic needs and to provide some discretionary income.

5.2 All workers shall be provided with written and understandable Information about their employment conditions in respect to wages before they enter employment and about the particulars of their wages for the pay period concerned each time that they are paid.

5.3 Deductions from wages as a disciplinary measure shall not be permitted nor shall any deductions from wages not provided for by national law be permitted without the expressed permission of the worker concerned. All disciplinary measures should be recorded.

6. Working hours are not excessive

6.1 Working hours must comply with national laws, collective agreements, and the provisions of 6.2 to 6.6 below, whichever affords the greater protection for workers. Sub-clauses 6.2 to 6.6 are based on international labour standards.

6.2 Working hours, excluding overtime, shall be defined by contract, and shall not exceed 48 hours per week.

* International standards recommend the progressive reduction of normal hours of work, when appropriate, to 40 hours per week, without any reduction in workers' wages as hours are reduced.

6.3 All overtime shall be voluntary. Overtime shall be used responsibly, taking into account all the following: the extent, frequency and hours worked by individual workers and the workforce as a whole. It shall not be used to replace regular employment. Overtime shall always be compensated at a premium rate, which is recommended to be not less than 125% of the regular rate of pay.

6.4 The total hours worked in any seven-day period shall not exceed 60 hours, except where covered by clause 6.5 below.

6.5 Working hours may exceed 60 hours in any seven-day period only in exceptional circumstances where all of the following are met:

- this is allowed by national law;
- this is allowed by a collective agreement freely negotiated with a workers' organisation representing a significant portion of the workforce;
- appropriate safeguards are taken to protect the workers' health and safety; and
- the employer can demonstrate that exceptional circumstances apply such as unexpected production peaks, accidents or emergencies.

6.6 Workers shall be provided with at least one day off in every seven-day period or, where allowed by national law, two days off in every 14-day period.

7. No discrimination is practiced

7.1 There is no discrimination in hiring, compensation, access to training, promotion, termination or retirement based on race, caste, national origin, religion, age, disability, gender, marital status, sexual orientation, union membership or political affiliation.

8. Regular employment is provided

8.1 To every extent possible work performed must be on the basis of recognised employment relationship established through national law and practice.

8.2 Obligations to employees under labour or social security laws and regulations arising from the regular employment relationship shall not be avoided through the use of labour-only contracting, sub- contracting, or homeworking arrangements, or through apprenticeship schemes where there is no real intent to impart skills or provide regular employment, nor shall any such obligations be avoided through the excessive use of fixed-term contracts of employment.

9. No harsh or inhumane treatment is allowed

9.1 Physical abuse or discipline, the threat of physical abuse, sexual or other harassment and verbal abuse or other forms of intimidation shall be prohibited.[66]

B. SA8000:2014 – SOCIAL ACCOUNTABILITY (SAI – SOCIAL ACCOUNTABILITY INTERNATIONAL)

[66] Ethical Trading Initiative (2018), 'The ETI Base Code', Available at: https://www.ethicaltrade.org/sites/default/files/shared_resources/ETI%20Base%20Code%20%28English%29.pdf (accessed 28 June 2019).

Founded in 1997, **Social Accountability International (SAI)** is a global non-governmental organization advancing human rights at work. SAI's vision is of decent work everywhere – sustained by an understanding that socially responsible workplaces benefit business while securing fundamental human rights. SAI empowers workers and managers at all levels of businesses and supply chains, using its multi-industry SA8000® Standard, as well as Social Fingerprint®, TenSquared, and other training and capacity building programs. SAI is a leader in policy and implementation, working together with a diverse group of stakeholders, including brands, suppliers, governments, trade unions, non-profits, and academia.[67]

SA8000:2014 is the current version of the **SA8000®** Standard. It replaced **SA8000:2008** in June 2014. The most significant updates to the Standard as compared to **SA8000:2008** are explained here below:

- **Forced or Compulsory Labor**

All organizations certified to SA8000:2014 must now ensure that their workers are free from employment fees and costs.

- **Health and Safety**

All organizations certified to SA8000:2014 must have a Health and Safety Committee consisting of management representatives and workers, which is responsible for monitoring health and safety hazards.

- **Management System**

SA8000:2014 places increasing emphasis on the importance of a strong management system. A management system is a set of

---

[67] Social Accountability International (SAI) (2019), 'About SAI', Available at: http://www.sa-intl.org/index.cfm?fuseaction=Page.ViewPage&pageId=472 (accessed 15 July 2019).

policies, procedures, and processes that helps an organization integrate the requirements of the SA8000 Standard into its daily operations.[68]

C. ISO 14001:2015 – ENVIRONMENT MANAGEMENT SYSTEM (INTERNATIONAL ORGANIZATION FOR STANDARDIZATION)

International standards covering environmental management system (EMS) provide organizations with the elements of an EMS that can be integrated with other management functions to help them attain environmental and economic goals.[69]

ISO 14001:2015 specifies the requirements for an environmental management system that an organization can use to enhance its environmental performance. ISO 14001:2015 is intended for use by an organization seeking to manage its environmental responsibilities in a systematic manner that contributes to the environmental pillar of sustainability.

ISO 14001:2015 helps an organization achieve the intended outcomes of its environmental management system, which provide value for the environment, the organization itself and interested parties. Consistent with the organization's environmental policy, the intended outcomes of an environmental management system include:

- Enhancement of environmental performance;
- Fulfilment of compliance obligations;

[68] Social Accountability International (SAI) (2019), 'SA8000: 2014', Available at: http://www.sa-intl.org/index.cfm?fuseaction=Page.ViewPage&pageId=1711 (accessed 15 July 2019).

[69] Environmental Management Systems and ISO 14001: Federal Facilities Council Report No. 138 (1999)

• Achievement of environmental objectives.

ISO 14001:2015 is applicable to any organization, regardless of size, type and nature, and applies to the environmental aspects of its activities, products and services that the organization determines it can either control or influence considering a life cycle perspective. **ISO 14001:2015** does not state specific environmental performance criteria.

ISO 14001:2015 can be used in whole or in part to systematically improve environmental management. Claims of conformity to **ISO 14001:2015**, however, are not acceptable unless all its requirements are incorporated into an organization's environmental management system and fulfilled without exclusion.[70]

D. OHSAS 18001 – OCCUPATIONAL HEALTH AND SAFETY MANAGEMENT SYSTEM (OCCUPATIONAL HEALTH & SAFETY ADVISORY SERVICES

BS OHSAS 18001 is a framework for an occupational health and safety (ohs) management system and is a part of the **OHSAS 18000** (sometimes incorrectly identified as **ISO 18000**) series of standards, along with **OHSAS 18002**. It can help you put in place the policies, procedures and controls needed for your organization to achieve the best possible working conditions and workplace health and safety, aligned to internationally recognized best practice.

BS OHSAS 18001 has been replaced by **ISO 45001** the new international standard for occupational health and safety.

[70] International Organization for Standardization (2019), 'ISO 14001:2015: Environmental management systems -- Requirements with guidance for use', Available at: https://www.iso.org/standard/60857.html (accessed 15 July 2019).

Organizations who are already certified to **BS OHSAS 18001** will need to upgrade to **ISO 45001** by March 2021.[71]

CASE STUDY 3.4: PRE-QUALIFICATION QUESTIONS

For the majority of their UK procurement activities, **National Grid PLC.,** pre-qualifies their suppliers using a vendor registration system operated by Achilles called the Utilities Vendor Database (UVDB). The UVDB includes questions on slavery and human trafficking as part of the registration process and **National Grid PLC.,** is working closely with Achilles and other industry participants to enhance the pre-qualification questions relating to human rights. For certain high-risk categories, vendors are also required to take part in the Achilles Verify Process, which produces an evaluation rating and may result in further investigation. **National Grid PLC.,** continually reviews external media and use agency services to check for adverse reports, fines or sanctions against their direct suppliers and will act on anything that is highlighted via these processes.[72]

BOX 3.2: THE SUPPLIER IDENTIFICATION PROGRAM AND ITS ADVANTAGES

As part of its anti-modern slavery compliance program, a commercial organisation must implement a written Supplier Identification Program ("SIP") appropriate for its size and type of business. The program must include risk-based identity verification, recordkeeping, and retention procedures, as well as procedures to determine whether a supply chain is being used for

[71] The British Standards Institution (2019), 'BS OHSAS 18001', Available at: https://www.bsigroup.com/en-GB/ohsas-18001-occupational-health-and-safety/ (accessed 15 July 2019).

[72] National Grid PLC. (2018), 'Our Statement on Slavery and Human Trafficking 2018', Available at: https://www.nationalgrideso.com/sites/eso/files/documents/14842_NG_Modern_Slavery_A4_AW08_INT1%20%281%29.pdf (accessed 24 June 2019).

modern slavery activities and to take appropriate follow-up action if a supplier is designated as high risk. SIP helps a company determine the risks posed by a particular supplier, allowing the institution to ensure that it has the proper controls in place, including suspicious activity monitoring procedures, and to monitor and report on the risks of a particular supplier.

BOX 3.3: NEED FOR COMPANIES TO USE DIVERSE METHODS TO IDENTIFY HIGH RISK SUPPLY CHAINS

While the supplier self-assessment questionnaire is a good due diligence measure, it may not be able to deliver good results without the input of other risk assessment methods like desk-based research. For example, a supplier who is given a survey form to fill may decide to fill in false formation which may lead to the Company classifying the supplier as a medium risk or low risk supplier. This is why Marks and Spencer Group Plc makes use of diverse methods to identify high risk supply chains.

Companies should begin their risk identification/assessment process with a detailed mapping of supply chains and operations, and desk-based research before later going into supplier surveys, supplier engagement and discussions with expert stakeholders.[73] This measure will help to adequately identify the high-risk suppliers and it will make enhanced due diligence measures more effective.

3.2 ENHANCED DUE DILIGENCE USING THIRD PARTY AUDIT FIRMS AND OTHER DIVERSE METHODS

Having established different category of risk(s) at the standard due diligence stage, Organisations should then decide how identified

[73] Marks and Spencer Group PLC. (2018), 'Marks and Spencer: Modern Slavery Statement 2017/18', Available at: https://corporate.marksandspencer.com/documents/plan-a-our-approach/mns-modern-slavery-statement-june2018.pdf (accessed 24 April 2019).

risks can be investigated to determine the supply chain with the most relevant human rights issues.[74]

Businesses must apply Enhanced Due Diligence measures on a risk-sensitive basis in any situation which by its nature can present a higher risk of modern slavery. As part of this, a commercial organisation may conclude, through desk-based research and self-assessments, that certain suppliers qualify as possible high-risk suppliers. In this situation, the selected suppliers must undergo site-based audits. These audits are conducted by independent, third party audit firms. It is acknowledged that participation in the audits can have a material cost implication for host community suppliers and in these cases, Businesses are advised to subsidise the costs related to the audit.

Audits have a role to play in helping companies assess risk and implement improvement action. Audits provide the additional benefit of engaging suppliers in the conversation around ethical trading and modern slavery (in many cases for the first time). They lead to dialogue on how these challenging issues can be addressed, especially in countries where this may be contrary to historical employment practices.

Each year British Telecommunications PLC., do around 50 on-site audits of their higher risk suppliers. British Telecommunications work together with them to address any problems they pick up.[75]

Marks and Spencer have adopted sound enhanced due diligence measures. During late 2017, the Property and Retail teams of Marks and Spencer commissioned a 3rd Party Provider (Ergon) to carry out a more detailed risk assessment for the products and

[74] Transparency in Supply Chains etc. A Practical Guide 2015 (Last Updated 2018), Annex E.

[75] British Telecommunications PLC. (2016), 'Modern Slavery Act Statement', Available at: https://www.btplc.com/Digitalimpactandsustainability/Humanrights/Modernslavery/ModernSlaverystatement.pdf (accessed 23 June 2019).

services in their areas. Products and services were mapped by country where the most relevant human rights issues were scoped, this then produced a risk assessment that ranked risks by sourcing countries. Areas of focus were identified and next steps/ mitigating actions were recommended and fed back to Property and Retail Human Rights Practitioners. The process included two workshops with contract managers which validated supplier results and acted as an upskilling session for 15 key stakeholders on Human Rights and Modern Slavery Risks.[76]

Marks and Spencer has made it a requirement that all new and existing direct Clothing and Home suppliers, all new and existing direct Food suppliers (plus a subset of Food raw material suppliers deemed to be high risk), and all Property suppliers in high risk countries have due diligence checks in place in the form of ethical audits, conducted by third parties on behalf of Marks and Spencer. These audits assess compliance with the Marks and Spencer Global Sourcing Principles and are, amongst other things, intended to identify any Modern Slavery practices. If issues are identified, appropriate investigative and remedial actions are taken.

During 2017-18, ethical audits identified 28 non-compliances under the heading 'employment is freely chosen', this included recruitment fees, deposits for protective equipment, deposits to agency and labour providers, mandatory overtime, and restricted toilet breaks. In all instances, Marks and Spencer verified evidence of suppliers putting corrective actions in place, or are working with suppliers to achieve this.

Having recognised the limitation of mainstream ethical audits to identify Modern Slavery issues, and to have effective Modern Slavery due diligence, **Marks and Spencer** went further to adopt a

[76] Marks and Spencer Group PLC. (2018), 'Marks and Spencer: Modern Slavery Statement 2017/18', Available at: https://corporate.marksandspencer.com/documents/plan-a-our-approach/mns-modern-slavery-statement-june2018.pdf (accessed 24 April 2019).

range of other methodologies, as appropriate for the nature of their supply chain. In the past year, Marks and Spencer's due diligence has included:

- **Bespoke due diligence audits with leading forced labour experts, including the Gangmasters & Labour Abuse Authority (GLAA): Where a previous assessment, intelligence or whistleblower highlights a higher risk in relation to a Human Rights issue Marks and Spencer use specialists to tailor the investigation to increase the likelihood of uncovering the evidence. E.g. 2017/18 use of Fast Forward and GLAA with Car wash providers.**
- **Marks and Spencer team visits to high risk supply chains. E.g. 2017/18 visits to Italy, Thailand, India and China.**
- **Partnership approaches, including the scaling of new assessment tools such as Issara Responsible Recruitment Toolkit, described below, and roll out Stronger Together awareness training to South Africa.**
- **UK survey on prevalence of recruitment fees: During the year 2017, Marks and Spencer had undertaken research with a select number of suppliers and labour providers to further understand how growers and labour providers in the UK Fresh Produce industry undertake direct recruitment from origin countries and the costs incurred. Marks and Spencer have identified 11 types of recruitment channels that are used including recruitment days and open days, returnees and word of mouth. Possible costs incurred by workers have been identified as: travel, insurance, accommodation deposit, up front rental. Cases were highlighted in relation to labour providers where pastoral care, translation and support with transport were charged to workers.**[77]

---

[77] Marks and Spencer Group PLC. (2018), 'Marks and Spencer: Modern Slavery Statement 2017/18', Available at: https://corporate.marksandspencer.com/documents/plan-a-our-approach/mns-modern-slavery-statement-june2018.pdf (accessed 24 April 2019).

There were 1320 audits undertaken at sites linked to **Wm Morrison Supermarkets PLC.,** on the Sedex platform in 2017 using either the Sedex Members Ethical Trading Audit (Smeta) or Business Social Compliance Initiative (BSCI) methodology. The audit programme identified 11 active, tier one factories with non-compliances raised under the issue title of "Employment is Freely Chosen". The issues included misleading job advertisements, workers being charged for equipment, restrictions on workers movement and deductions from workers' pay.[78]

Businesses should also consider integrating 'anonymous worker surveys using mobiles' into part of their on-site audits programme as a means of ensuring that the worker voice is included. The survey sections related to modern slavery risks should be focused on working hours and overtime, as these are often proxy indicators for a broad range of other labour rights issues.

The anonymous surveys, which are run on behalf of **Vodafone Group Plc** by an independent third party, asked employees: "What do you think about your working hours, including your normal working hours and overtime?" Of the 1,693 who responded:

– 46% said "I am ok with the way they are now";

– 28% said "I have no opinion on this";

– 22% said "I want to work fewer hours"; and

– 5% said "I want to work more hours".

[78] Wm Morrison Supermarkets PLC. (2017/18), 'Modern Slavery Act Statement 2017/2018', Available at: https://www.morrisons-corporate.com/Documents/corporate2018/Morrisons_Modern-Slavery-Act-2018.pdf (accessed 5 May 2019).

The results of these surveys are integrated into Vodafone's on-site audit reports, and findings that require action are incorporated into the relevant suppliers' corrective action plans.[79]

BOX 3.4: NEED FOR A COMPANY TO TEST THE ACCURACY OF THE AUDITOR'S REPORT

Where a company is relying on a third-party audit firm for due diligence, the company should test the accuracy of the auditor's reports against the its own records and monitor the activities of the audit firm. This can be done through unannounced site visits and confidential reports from employees who use the whistleblowing system.

[79] Vodafone Group PLC. (2018-19), 'Slavery and Human Trafficking Statement', Available at: http://www.vodafone.co.uk/cs/groups/public/documents/webcontent/modernslaverydisclosure.pdf (accessed 24 June 2019).

CHAPTER 4

RISK CONTROL MEASURES FOR THE SUPPLY CHAIN

It is necessary for every company to base its human rights approach, including its modern slavery risk management, on the **United Nations (UN) Guiding Principles on Business and Human Rights (UNGPs)**. The **UNGPs** are the global standard for preventing and addressing adverse impacts on human rights by business. At a baseline, they help business to know and show that they are respecting all internationally recognised human rights across their own activities and business relationships.

The **UN Guiding Principles on Business and Human Rights** are grounded in recognition of:

(a) States' existing obligations to respect, protect and fulfil human rights and fundamental freedoms;

(b) The role of business enterprises as specialized organs of society performing specialized functions, required to comply with all applicable laws and to respect human rights;

(c) The need for rights and obligations to be matched to appropriate and effective remedies when breached.

The **UN Guiding Principles on Business and Human Rights** apply to all States and to all business enterprises, both transnational and others, regardless of their size, sector, location, ownership and structure.

According to **Principle 19 of the UN Guiding Principles on Business and Human Rights,** Business enterprises should integrate the findings from their impact assessments across relevant internal functions and processes, and take appropriate action. This will enable business enterprises to prevent and mitigate adverse human rights impacts.

Effective integration requires that:

(i) Responsibility for addressing such impacts is assigned to the appropriate level and function within the business enterprise;

(ii) Internal decision-making, budget allocations and oversight processes enable effective responses to such impacts.

Appropriate action will vary according to:

(i) Whether the business enterprise causes or contributes to an adverse impact, or whether it is involved solely because the impact is directly linked to its operations, products or services by a business relationship;

(ii) The extent of its leverage in addressing the adverse impact.

In assessing human rights impacts, business enterprises will have looked for both actual and potential adverse impacts. Potential impacts should be prevented or mitigated through the horizontal integration of findings across the business enterprise, while actual impacts—those that have already occurred – should be a subject for remediation **(Principle 22)**.[80]

[80] Principle 22 of the UN Guiding Principles on Business and Human Rights provides that Where business enterprises identify that they have caused or contributed to adverse impacts, they should provide for or cooperate in their remediation through legitimate processes.

Where a business enterprise causes or may cause an adverse human rights impact, it should take the necessary steps to cease or prevent the impact.

Where a business enterprise contributes or may contribute to an adverse human rights impact, it should take the necessary steps to cease or prevent its contribution and use its leverage to mitigate any remaining impact to the greatest extent possible. Leverage is considered to exist where the enterprise has the ability to effect change in the wrongful practices of an entity that causes a harm.

Where a business enterprise has not contributed to an adverse human rights impact, but that impact is nevertheless directly linked to its operations, products or services by its business relationship with another entity, the situation is more complex. Among the factors that will enter into the determination of the appropriate action in such situations are the enterprise's leverage over the entity concerned, how crucial the relationship is to the enterprise, the severity of the abuse, and whether terminating the relationship with the entity itself would have adverse human rights consequences.

The more complex the situation and its implications for human rights, the stronger is the case for the enterprise to draw on independent expert advice in deciding how to respond.

If the business enterprise has leverage to prevent or mitigate the adverse impact, it should exercise it. And if it lacks leverage there may be ways for the enterprise to increase it. Leverage may be increased by, for example, offering capacity-building or other incentives to the related entity, or collaborating with other actors.

There are situations in which the enterprise lacks the leverage to prevent or mitigate adverse impacts and is unable to increase its leverage. Here, the enterprise should consider ending the relationship, taking into account credible assessments of potential adverse human rights impacts of doing so.

Where the relationship is "crucial" to the enterprise, ending it raises further challenges. A relationship could be deemed as crucial if it provides a product or service that is essential to the enterprise's business, and for which no reasonable alternative source exists. Here the severity of the adverse human rights impact must also be considered: the more severe the abuse, the more quickly the enterprise will need to see change before it takes a decision on whether it should end the relationship. In any case, for as long as the abuse continues and the enterprise remains in the relationship, it should be able to demonstrate its own ongoing efforts to mitigate the impact and be prepared to accept any consequences – reputational, financial or legal – of the continuing connection.

BOX 4.1: DE-RISKING

De-risking refers to the phenomenon of commercial organisations terminating or restricting business relationships with suppliers or categories of suppliers to avoid, rather than manage, risk in line with the United Nations (UN) Guiding Principles on Business and Human Rights. Companies should avoid terminating business relationships with suppliers for the sole reason that the supplier or suppliers' source for goods in countries where modern forms of slavery are prevalent. Such an approach may force the supplier to lay off staff which in turn may result in the said employees looking to work in companies who may further exploit them, going by the fact that they have nowhere else to go or work, and that some of them may be

undocumented immigrants. So, if the business enterprise has leverage to prevent or mitigate the adverse human rights impact of the supply chain, it should exercise it. And if it lacks leverage there may be ways for the enterprise to increase it. Leverage may be increased by, for example, offering training, awareness and capacity-building or other incentives to the related entity, or collaborating with other actors. This approach is in line with Principle 19 of the UN Guiding Principles on Business and Human Rights.

"De-risking" should never be an excuse for a commercial organisation to avoid implementing a risk-based approach, in line with the UN Guiding Principles on Business and Human Rights. The UN Guiding Principles on Business and Human Rights only require commercial organisations to terminate business relationships, on a case-by-case basis, where the enterprise lacks the leverage to prevent or mitigate adverse human rights impacts and is unable to increase its leverage. This is fully in line with Principle 19 of the UN Guiding Principles on Business and Human Rights. What is not in line with Principle 19 of the UN Guiding Principles on Business and Human Rights is the wholesale cutting loose of entire classes of suppliers, without taking into account, seriously and comprehensively, their level of risk or risk mitigation measures for individual suppliers within a particular sector.

The risk-based approach should be the cornerstone of an effective anti-modern slavery system, and is essential to properly managing risks. The UN Guiding Principles on Business and Human Rights expect commercial organisations to identify, assess and understand their modern slavery and human rights risks and take commensurate measures in order to mitigate them. This does not imply a "zero failure" approach.

BOX 4.2: NEED FOR COMPANIES TO ADOPT EFFECTIVE KYE MEASURES THAT WILL AVERT SITUATIONS WHERE AN EMPLOYEE CONSPIRES WITH A SUPPLIER TO TRUNCATE RISK CONTROL MEASURES

All relationships between an organisation's suppliers, employees, and third-party service providers carry a level of risk; however, the risks posed by employees may ultimately be the greatest risk an organisation faces. This is because employees are responsible for ensuring day-to-day compliance with supply chain due diligence requirements and risk control measures. It is often said that *an organisation's greatest asset is its human capital;* and the *highest returns carry the greatest risk.* Where weak Know Your Employee (KYE) and internal control measures abound, corporate losses due to employee fraud and money laundering increases.[81]

It was recently reported in the news by the Crown Prosecution Service that an employee of Barclays Bank who acted as a "personal bank manager" to two money launderers was jailed for six years and four months for his role in a conspiracy to launder more than £2.5 million that had been stolen using malware.

Cyber-crime officials said London-based Jinal Pethad, 29, acted as the personal bank manager to money launderers Pavel Gincota and Ion Turcan, setting up 105 sham bank accounts using false ID documents.

Pethad managed the accounts to ensure that receipt of the stolen funds was not blocked by the bank's security processes and that the pair could freely transfer money between the accounts.

[81] SSA ZAIDI (2015), 'Banks need to follow Know Your Employees norms for robust internal AML control systems', Available at: https://www.moneylife.in/article/banks-need-to-follow-know-your-employees-norms-for-robust-internal-aml-control-systems/44095.html (accessed 15 February 2018).

Gincota and Turcan were jailed in October 2016 and Pethad was arrested the following month.

During a search of Pethad's home in Edgware, officials of the National Crime Agency (NCA) recovered more than £4,000 in cash, seven luxury watches and three mobile phones, all of which were used to communicate with Gincota.

Multiple text messages on one of the phones showed Gincota making arrangements to open new accounts and asking Pethad to change details, such as addresses and security information, on existing ones. Pethad pleaded guilty in the high court.

Jinal Pethad abused his position of trust at the bank to knowingly set up sham accounts for Gincota and Turcan, providing a vital service which enabled them to launder millions.

Using his knowledge of the financial system, he made sure the stolen money was not blocked before entering these accounts, and provided the pair with reports to evidence his efforts and maintain the criminal relationship.[82]

A strong KYE program may have prevented the above scenario.

A KYE program means that the institution has a program in place that allows it to understand an employee's background, conflicts of interest and susceptibility to money laundering complicity. Policies, procedures, internal controls, job descriptions, code of conduct/ethics, levels of authority, compliance with personnel

---

[82] Crown Prosecution Service (2017), 'Bank employee who created fake accounts to launder money is jailed', Available at: https://www.cps.gov.uk/cps/news/bank-employee-who-created-fake-accounts-launder-money-jailed (accessed 16 Februry 2018). **See also** Hindustantimes (2017), 'UK money-laundering: Indian-origin bank employee jailed', Available at: https://www.hindustantimes.com/world-news/uk-money-laundering-indian-origin-bank-employee-jailed/story-nYz94iQ1m9inoQbNrZ3beJ.html (accessed 16 February 2018).

laws and regulations, accountability, dual control, and other deterrents should be firmly in place.

The following procedures should be followed and strictly adhered to, in order to ensure the company recruits not only the best brains but equally people with good character, high ethical standing, honesty and integrity:

i. KYE information such as background information must be obtained prior to job interview, during job interview and just before offer of employment. Any serious gap observed must be documented and should form part of the basis for offer of employment.

ii. All prospective hires in the United Kingdom must be checked prior to offer of employment.

iii. After acceptance of offer, but before confirmation; background screening checks must be conducted to verify the identity of employees, viz:

iv. Certificates must be verified by awarding institutions; businesses must ensure that such credentials are sent to awarding institutions for confirmation along with scanned passport photograph of recipients.

v. Employee personal referees must be written and satisfactory report on character and suitability of employment obtained prior to confirmation of employee appointment.

vi. Former employer must be written and positive performance and character report obtained prior to confirmation.

vii. All information supplied by prospective employees must be verified during probation. Any change in such information, including marital status and additional qualifications obtained

during the period must be verified against appropriate documents and issuing institutions.

An on-going approach to screening should be considered for specific positions, as circumstances change, or for a comprehensive review of departmental staff over a period of time. Commercial organisations should have a policy that mandates that the lie detector test should be taken once in 5 years by all staff of the company. For Staff in very sensitive positions, the lie detector test should be taken every three years. This will enable the lie detector policy to be more effective.[83] Let us take for example, a person passes the lie detector test genuinely without any influence of corruption; there is still a possibility that the person may change over time. The temptation to follow current employees to collect bribes is very high. But if UK companies put a policy in place that mandates every employee working in the compliance department to take the lie detector test every five years starting from the first five years after recruitment, the cankerworm called corruption may be curbed effectively. Imagine if every compliance staff knew that they were going to be asked by an examiner, 5 years after working, to confirm if they ever collected bribe during the time they worked with the company, most employees will desist from taking bribes or engaging in corrupt acts. The above measure will ensure that current employees who are chosen as examiners for the lie detector tests are fit and proper persons for the job.

---

[83] A lie detector/polygraph test is very complex and depends heavily on the interaction between the examiner and the individual being tested, and requires that the examiner infer deception or truthfulness based on a comparison of the person's physiological responses to various questions. The quality of the questions asked depends in part on what information the examiner already has about the person being questioned. For more on the lie detector test, see Giannelli, P. C. (1985), 'Polygraph and Deception Tests', Faculty Publications. Paper 469. Available at: http://scholarlycommons.law.case.edu/faculty_publications/469 (accessed 4 June 2018).

4.1 TRAINING, AWARENESS AND CAPACITY BUILDING

A company's human rights training programme must include information on labour rights including modern slavery, and its training for security providers under the Voluntary Principles on Security and Human Rights (VPSHR) must include help identifying and reporting instances of forced labour and trafficking.

Rio Tinto PLC's site-level incident reporting procedure asks employees if a health, safety, environment, community or security incident has had human rights implications. Employees are then asked to say what human rights the incident may have impacted, including a specific prompt relating to labour rights where modern slavery related incidents may be included. Rio Tinto PLC., are building their employees' awareness of how best to engage with this tool, appreciating that recognition of what constitutes a human rights incident, including one related to modern slavery, could be improved.

4.1.1 TRAINING FOR COLLEAGUES

Businesses must ensure that all colleagues responsible for recruitment receive training on third-party labour exploitation.

Training for procurement and contract management professionals should be provided annually to refresh their knowledge and awareness on environmental sustainability and social and human rights issues, including modern slavery.

Training on a company's Code of Ethical Business Conduct must be made mandatory for all employees and should be refreshed on a continual basis.

Companies must develop the skills and knowledge of key frontline colleagues responsible for managing incidents in their business by collaborating with the Gangmasters and Labour Abuse Authority-led (GLAA) and Stronger Together to develop and deliver bespoke training.

Companies should further increase the capability of their Manufacturing and Logistics colleagues to manage incidents of modern slavery, forced labour and third-party exploitation.

It is necessary for companies to develop a e-learning module on slavery and human trafficking. The interactive module should be designed for all commercial teams, not just the technical functions where responsibility for these issues usually sits.

The training should ensure that all colleagues understand the issue and their role in combating this crime. The main training should take learners through a series of scenarios they might encounter in their day job. They need to decide if they are concerned about what they see and hear, and what follow up is required.

The training should be designed for the entire company. This allows for illustrative case studies to be switched for the ones that are relevant and understandable to a particular audience, whether it be the food side of its business or logistics and warehousing.

Establishing a Modern Slavery Working Group across the business and conducting a risk assessment helps commercial organisations to identify colleagues in areas that need support with more intensive in-person training, beyond e-learning.

In the year 2018 **J Sainsbury PLC.,** focused one of its training sessions on "vulnerable workers" as a follow-up to previous classroom training on modern slavery for its "Ethical Champions" who sit in each food product category. **J Sainsbury PLC.,** looked at how to identify these workers and take into account their vulnerabilities in the way they work. It is these vulnerable workers who are most at risk of becoming victims of modern slavery. The training was based on materials developed by specialist research organisation, Ergon, and on a similar session **J Sainsbury PLC.,** ran for one of their supplier workshops.

J Sainsbury PLC., has also developed new e-learning on broader ethical sourcing to complement training on modern slavery. It is also designed for a much wider set of colleagues than previously received classroom-based training to ensure **J Sainsbury PLC.,** are embedding responsible sourcing across the business.

The new e-learning modules are in addition to classroom training. Last year's classroom-based training that includes components on modern slavery continues as before. More than 150 **Sainsbury's Argos** colleagues have been trained on **J Sainsbury PLC.,** ethical standards, policies and processes. **J Sainsbury PLC's** Argos Asia team has five social audit specialists and all other team members have had lead auditor training to help suppliers and sites identify and remediate serious breaches of **J Sainsbury PLC.,** Code of Conduct.[84]

4.1.2 TRAINING FOR SUPPLIERS

Providing training and effective capacity building for suppliers is a key strategy in preventing slavery and human trafficking, and has been one of **J Sainsbury PLC's** focus areas to date.

[84] J Sainsbury PLC. (2017/18), 'Modern Slavery Statement', Available at: http://www.j-sainsbury.co.uk/-/media/Files/S/Sainsburys/documents/sainsburys-modern-slavery-report-2018.pdf (accessed 24 June 2019).

J Sainsbury PLC., continues to engage suppliers on modern slavery through discussions in regular ethical trade strategy meetings and targeted training, such as their **Gangmasters and Labour Abuse Authority-led (GLAA)** workshop on agency labour and extreme forms of labour exploitation. The **GLAA** also attended **J Sainsbury PLC's** annual Farming Conference again in the year 2017/18 to raise awareness of the issue among a key group of stakeholders. **J Sainsbury PLC's** direct suppliers that use agency labour are strongly encouraged to attend both the **GLAA** and Stronger Together workshops.[85]

CASE STUDY 4.1: MODERN SLAVERY TRAINING

In 2016, **British American Tobacco** delivered the following training that included specific content on human rights and modern slavery:

- Training webinars for **British American Tobacco's** Legal and External Affairs' employees on their Standards of Business Conduct and supplier Code of Conduct;

- A global roll out of new training and communications materials for all employees worldwide on **British American Tobacco's** Standards of Business Conduct, clarifying what they should do if they discover actions that conflict with their Standards;

- A series of workshops with **British American Tobacco-owned** and third-party tobacco leaf suppliers across the globe to introduce the Sustainable Tobacco Programme (STP) and their specific

[85] J Sainsbury PLC. (2017/18), 'Modern Slavery Statement', Available at: http://www.j-sainsbury.co.uk/~/media/Files/S/Sainsburys/documents/sainsburys-modern-slavery-report-2018.pdf (accessed 24 June 2019).

criteria on human rights and forced labour. They then delivered training to their teams and farmers; and

• Through their agricultural Extension Services, **British American Tobacco** provided training and capacity building on human rights issues for their farmers and members of local communities, attended by over 60,000 beneficiaries.

In 2017, **British American Tobacco** developed and rolled out a new human rights e-learning package to colleagues working within their Procurement and Legal and External Affairs functions.[86]

CASE STUDY 4.2: 'TEASER' TRAINING

British Telecommunications PLC., have introduced 'bite-sized' learning, where questions on modern slavery are emailed directly to employees. **British Telecommunications PLC.,** sent out an email reaching 27,000 employees asking them to answer a question by picking the right answer. It wasn't compulsory, and the primary aim of this type of training is to raise awareness.[87]

4.2 UNANNOUNCED SITE VISIT PROGRAMME

Monitoring the effectiveness of a company's actions to identify and prevent slavery and human trafficking is a challenge across the industry.

---

[86] British American Tobacco (2016), 'Modern Slavery Act Statement', Available at: https://www.bat.com/group/sites/uk__9d9kcy.nsf/vwPagesWebLive/DOAK8P7C/$FILE/medMDAXGJD9.pdf?openelement (accessed 25 June 2019).

[87] British Telecommunications PLC. (2017/18), 'Modern Slavery Act Transparency Statement', Available at: https://www.btplc.com/Thegroup/Ourcompany/Ourvalues/ModernSlaveryAct/Modern-Slavery-Act-Statement-2018.pdf (accessed 25 June 2019).

One way that a company can monitor improvement activity at manufacturing site level is through unannounced site visits.

Where a company has identified that a particular supplier is high-risk and requires monitoring, the company may evaluate that supplier's compliance with its Code of Ethical Purchasing through a detailed assessment that may involve an on-site audit.

The company may conduct some of these audits by themselves, sending appropriately qualified auditors from recognised audit firms, or the company's auditors, into the supplier's operations to examine working conditions on the ground and speak directly to employees on the factory floor or relevant worksite. A telecommunications company may conduct site audits under the **Joint Audit Cooperation (JAC)** initiative, an association of telecommunications operators established to improve ethical, labour and environmental standards in the **Information and Communications Technology (ICT)** supply chains.

Suppliers that are deemed not to comply with a company's standards as set out in its Code of Ethical Purchasing should be provided with a corrective action plan to address any areas for improvement and should be required to submit evidence that this has been completed. Corrective action plans through JAC are to be uploaded to a platform and reviewed on a quarterly basis by an independent provider, and ongoing monitoring should be carried out if and when grievances are raised.[88]

A review in August with representatives from Wm Morrison Supermarkets' global audit providers in Hong Kong highlighted

[88] Vodafone Group PLC. (2018-19), 'Slavery and Human Trafficking Statement', Available at: http://www.vodafone.co.uk/cs/groups/public/documents/webcontent/modernslaverydisclosure.pdf (accessed 24 June 2019).

concerns around the increasing use of consultants in China to prepare factories for audit, which may lead to changing employment records and coaching workers for interviews.

Morrison responded to these concerns with the establishment of an intelligence led, unannounced site visit programme delivered by Ethical Trading colleagues from their Hong Kong office. Wm Morrison Supermarkets aim to build on this in 2018 through targeted improvement visits and further use of sector and region-specific data.

4.3 ANONYMOUS WORKER SURVEYS USING MOBILES

Companies can also use mobile devices to gain insights into the views and experiences of some of their Tier 2 suppliers' employees, to understand the extent to which Tier 1 suppliers are mandating compliance of their suppliers to their Code of Ethical Purchasing. **Vodafone Group Plc** were the first telecoms operator in the world to use mobile worker surveys to enable employees to use their personal mobile phones to provide anonymous feedback on key aspects of their working conditions through the use of local-language surveys. Following **Vodafone,** other industry members from JAC have also adopted this solution, and collectively **Vodafone** have surveyed 12 factories in common employing 16,800 workers in China and India. **Vodafone** found that 10% of this workforce population responded to the anonymous mobile survey as part of their assessments.[89]

[89] Vodafone Group PLC. (2018-19), 'Slavery and Human Trafficking Statement', Available at: http://www.vodafone.co.uk/cs/groups/public/documents/webcontent/modernslaverydisclosure.pdf (accessed 24 June 2019).

4.4 COLLABORATIVE ACTION

Collaboration with external partners plays a key role in a company's approach to addressing human rights risk in their supply chains. The issues they face are often complex and complicated, and its influence to leverage meaningful change can be limited. Engaging with their suppliers, competitors, NGOs, charities, Trade Unions and multistakeholder initiatives (MSIs) help companies to maximise the resource and intelligence available to support their actions and forms a key part of their strategy.

In 2018, **Morrison Supermarkets Plc** worked with the following organisations on projects relevant to modern slavery:

I. Stronger Together:

• **Morrison Supermarkets PLC.,** is a founder sponsor of Stronger Together and provided further support for the initiative throughout 2018. **Morrison Supermarkets PLC's** suppliers continued to benefit from its funded training provision which was widened in 2018 to include a new programme based in South Africa. 62 workshops were held across the major fruit and wine growing regions and over 150 employees from **Morrisons** suppliers attended. In the UK **Morrison Supermarkets PLC.,** supported the development of new training courses and co-funded a pilot of the Stronger Together Operational Performance Assessments at five large suppliers.

II. Ethical Trading Initiative (ETI)

• **Morrison Supermarkets PLC.,** has been actively engaged with the ETI since 2015 and were confirmed as full members in 2018. ETI membership gives **Morrison Supermarkets PLC.,** the ability to join forces with other businesses, trade unions and civil society organisations to support wider advocacy and influence at government level in countries with systemic human rights issues. **Morrison Supermarkets PLC.,** are currently actively participating in and providing financial support for a number of ETI initiatives relevant to modern slavery and labour exploitation including:

- Good labour practices in Latin American horticulture

- Vulnerable migrant workers in Italy

- Human rights due diligence in Spain

- Thailand Working Group

III. Seafood Taskforce

- As a founder member of the Seafood Taskforce, **Morrison Supermarkets PLC.,** has continued to support the development of an industry approach to recruitment in the fishing sector by participating in their working group on Responsible Recruitment Oversight. **Morrison Supermarkets PLC.,** also contributed through supplier questionnaires to help build an understanding of existing recruitment practices across members over the past year, and used this information to shape the development of an aligned industry approach and support advocacy at national level.

IV. Gangmasters & Labour Abuse Authority (GLAA)

- **Morrison Supermarkets PLC.,** has a well-established relationship with the GLAA and continued to work closely with them throughout 2018. **Morrison Supermarkets PLC.,** holds regular meetings with the GLAA Compliance team and contributed to the development of the Retailer Protocol for Handling Reported Cases of Modern Slavery in the UK Supply Chain. The GLAA additionally provided support for investigations into suspected modern slavery incidents at Morrisons Manufacturing sites and assisted **Morrison Supermarkets PLC.,** with the creation of their bespoke process for incident management.

Morrison Supermarkets PLC., also commissioned the GLAA to deliver bespoke training workshops in 2018 to their Manufacturing, Loss Prevention and People teams, and funded dedicated modern slavery training for Daffodil growers in Cambridgeshire.

V. Seafood Ethics Action Alliance (SEA Alliance)

• **Morrison Supermarkets PLC.,** were founder members of the SEA Alliance in 2018, a collaboration of market facing companies with a stake in the UK seafood Sector established to share information on emerging issues, agree best practice solutions and provide a forum for pre-competitive action. The group is helping to inform and bring together supply chain actors and has already undertaken international advocacy on necessary instruments for vulnerable worker protection.

VI. Hope for Justice

• Following initial engagement in 2017, **Morrison Supermarkets PLC.,** formalised its relationship with Hope for Justice in 2018 and engaged them to undertake three modern slavery threat assessments at Morrisons Manufacturing and Logistics sites that had previously experienced potential incidents. Two of these assessments took place in 2018 with the third planned for May 2019. Both assessments have provided useful insight into the risks posed in the UK food industry and were complimentary of **Morrison Supermarkets PLC's** work to date. **Morrison Supermarkets PLC.,** site teams are implementing corrective action plans and **Morrison Supermarkets PLC.,** will formally review overall findings once the final assessment is complete.

VII. Food Network for Ethical Trade (FNET)

• In January 2019, **Morrison Supermarkets PLC.,** increased their support for suppliers in the lower tiers of their supply chain by joining the Food Network for Ethical Trade. FNET is a collaborative initiative which brings together major UK supermarkets and over 30 large UK food suppliers to improve human rights in global supply chains through a common approach to managing ethical trade. The initiative provides tools, support and guidance for **Morrison Supermarkets PLC.,** tier one suppliers to assess risk in their global ingredient supply chains and take ownership for driving improvement.

VIII. Responsible Car Wash Scheme (RCWS)

• **Morrison Supermarkets PLC.,** collaborated with their competitors, suppliers, and regulatory bodies including the GLAA and Environment Agency to formally establish the Responsible Car Wash Scheme (RCWS) in 2018. The scheme and associated code of practice seeks to ensure that all member car washes operate legally, treat workers fairly and respects the environment. All **Morrison Supermarkets PLC.,** operators are required to join, and **Morrison Supermarkets PLC.,** are active members of the RCWS Advisory Panel.

IX. Mekong Club

• Building on a commitment from their 2018 statement, **Morrison Supermarkets PLC.,** formalised their membership of the Hong Kong based anti-slavery partnership in June and are signatories to their "Business Pledge Against Modern Slavery". **Morrison**

Supermarkets PLC's Global Sourcing team in Hong Kong meets regularly to discuss improvements to their regional strategy and are developing a training programme for their colleagues and suppliers for implementation in 2019/20.

X. Centre for Child Rights and Corporate Social Responsibility (CCR-CSR)

• Following the discovery of an underage worker at one of their supplier's factories in China, **Morrison Supermarkets PLC.,** recently engaged with CCR-CSR to strengthen their approach to tackling child labour in the region and access their remediation services. **Morrison Supermarkets PLC.,** held meetings with their team in January 2019 and plan to formally join their working group of brands and retailers later in the year.

XI. Apparel and General Merchandise Public Private Protocol

• **Morrison Supermarkets PLC.,** has joined a number of major brands and retailers in becoming a signatory to The Apparel and General Merchandise Public and Private Protocol. This commits **Morrison Supermarkets PLC.,** to work together with enforcement bodies such as the **GLAA, Department for Work and Pensions (DWP), and Her Majesty's Revenue and Customs (HMRC)**, to tackle modern slavery in the UK Textiles Industry. **Morrison Supermarkets PLC.,** supports the work of the protocol to improve and increase the intelligence provided to enforcement bodies on instances of labour exploitation and illegal practices. This improved intelligence enables **Morrison Supermarkets PLC.,** to build a better understanding of patterns of illegal activity in UK textiles, while also highlighting those who display best practice.

XII. Indirect Procurement Human Rights Forum

• In 2018, **Morrison Supermarkets PLC.,** joined with nine other UK retailers and suppliers to establish the Indirect Procurement Human Rights Forum. This group works collaboratively to drive positive change and reinforce the human rights of workers in indirect procurement supply chains including security, cleaning, catering services, transport and waste management. Many of these sectors are recognised targets for exploiters due to the typical worker profile. This year the Forum focused on increasing transparency of indirect supply chains by improving the capability of the Sedex platform to share responsible sourcing information with customers. The group contributed to revisions of the current self-assessment questionnaire (SAQ), making it more relevant to service providers, ahead of their launch in the second half of 2019. **Morrison Supermarkets PLC.,** also developed a Minimum Standards for Labour Providers, outlining their shared expectations for suppliers of indirect labour. This includes measures to help prevent the occurrence of labour exploitation, modern slavery and human trafficking in their supply chains. **Morrison Supermarkets PLC.,** labour providers will be asked to demonstrate their commitment to meeting these standards on a regular basis.[90]

CASE STUDY 4.3: MULTI-STAKEHOLDER COLLABORATION AND ENGAGEMENT

Rio Tinto PLC., engages with peers, investors, civil society, workers' organisations and business partners on issues related to human rights including modern slavery. **Rio Tinto** encourages government efforts, especially in countries in which they have a

[90] Wm Morrison Supermarkets PLC. (2018/2019), 'Modern Slavery Act Statement', Available at: https://www.morrisons-corporate.com/globalassets/corporatesite/corporate-responsibility/documents/2018/morrisons_modern_slavery_act_2019_final.pdf (accessed 25 June 2019).

footprint, to help business prevent and address their involvement in modern slavery.

In the year 2018, for example, **Rio Tinto** supported the **Australian Modern Slavery Act**, publicly endorsing the introduction of the draft legislation as well as its final passage by the Australian Parliament. **Rio Tinto's** support included signing a multi-stakeholder letter to the Prime Minister, alongside several leading civil society organisations, investors and business associations, calling for the bill to pass without delay.

Rio Tinto also hosted the first meeting, and are a member, of the Global Compact Network Australia's business led Modern Slavery Community of Practice, which helps Australian businesses share learning and progress implementation of the **Australian Modern Slavery Act** and broader modern slavery risk management.

In the year 2018, **Rio Tinto** also participated in multi-stakeholder forums to discuss human rights issues, including modern slavery, such as:

– International Council on Mining & Metals

– UN Global Compact (including the Australian and UK local networks)

– Business for Social Responsibility Human Rights Working Group

– UN Annual Forum on Business and Human Rights.[91]

---

[91] RioTinto (2018), 'Respecting Human Rights: Our Statement on Modern Slavery', Available at:

CASE STUDY 4.4: COLLABORATIVE TRAINING AND TOOLS FOR IDENTIFYING ISSUES

J Sainsbury, PLC., engages in a number of collaborations in their quest to raise the awareness and the capabilities of its suppliers. In 2014, **J Sainsbury** established a ground-breaking partnership with the UK's foremost investigator of labour exploitation, the Gangmasters and Labour Abuse Authority (GLAA), to deliver bespoke and first of its kind training for its suppliers and farmers.

J Sainsbury is also made up of the founding members and funders of Stronger Together, a collaborative programme designed to raise awareness, gain commitment, and provide tools for responsible businesses to proactively prevent and address modern slavery in their own operations and supply chains. **J Sainsbury** further supports Stronger Together through its role on the Consumer Goods Steering Group.[92]

4.5 WHISTLEBLOWING

Employees, sub-contractors or suppliers who become aware of possible improper, unethical or even illegal behaviour should be allowed to raise the matter with their manager or alternatively refer the matter to a confidential and independent telephone number.

British American Tobacco encourages anyone working for, or with, the Group to raise concerns or grievances through their Speak Up channels. These independently managed channels are available online, by text and telephone hotlines, 24 hours a day,

https://www.riotinto.com/documents/RT_Slavery_and_human_trafficking_statement_2018.pdf (accessed 26 June 2019).

[92] J Sainsbury PLC. (2016/17), 'Modern Slavery Statement', Available at: http://www.j-sainsbury.co.uk/-/media/Files/S/Sainsburys/documents/Sainsburys_Modern_Slavery_Statement_2016_17.pdf (accessed 26 June 2019).

seven days a week and in multiple local languages. They can be used in confidence (and anonymously, if they prefer to do so), without fear of reprisal. **British American Tobacco** promotes Speak Up through regular staff training and communications, and details are communicated to suppliers via **British American Tobacco's** supplier Code of Conduct.

British American Tobacco thoroughly investigates all reported issues and allegations and strong action is taken where required. Information on compliance and reported incidents is gathered at a global level and reported through the year to the relevant regional audit and CSR committees (RACCs), and quarterly to the Board Audit Committee.

In 2018, **British American Tobacco** also ran an informal, targeted Speak Up survey, which showed strong employee awareness – over 92% believed that reported Standards of Business Conduct (SoBC) breaches are investigated fully and objectively, and almost all respondents indicated they felt able to raise concerns without fear of reprisals.[93]

Unilever offers both internal and external channels for raising concerns confidentially via their 24/7 hotline or their online reporting tool. External parties, including their suppliers and their workers, can also use their global Code Breach Process.[94]

---

[93] British American Tobacco (2018), 'Human Rights and Modern Slavery Act: Respecting and Recognising Fundamental Freedoms', Available at: https://www.bat.com/msa (accessed 25 June 2019).

[94] Unilever (2018), 'Modern Slavery and Human Trafficking Statement', Available at: https://www.unilever.com/Images/unilever-slavery-and-human-trafficking-statement-2018_tcm244-521391_en.pdf (accessed 26 June 2019).

CHAPTER 5

RISK CONTROL MEASURES FOR FINANCIAL INSTITUTIONS DEALING WITH PROCEEDS OF MODERN SLAVERY

Banks or financial institutions may be involved in facilitating financing from or supporting cases of modern slavery and bonded labour in operations or supply chains or through money laundering.[95] Where legal vehicles and structures are used, it is important for banks to establish that their use is genuine and to be able to follow any chain of title to know who the beneficial owner is.[96]

---

[95] Money laundering can be defined as the process of converting "black money" obtained from illicit sources such as narcotic trafficking, extortion, smuggling and the flesh trade, into legal money. Here, the original source of the money is concealed from the authorities. For more on the definition of money laundering see Thanasegaran, H. and Shanmugam, B. (2007), 'International trade- based money laundering: the Malaysian perspective', Journal of Money Laundering Control, 10 (4), pp. 429-437; see also the following cases: R v. Nabil Zekari, [2010] EWCA Crim 1649, [2011] 1 Cr App R (S) 59 which is to the effect that: hiding proceeds of crime in your car comes within the meaning of concealing criminal property; Regina v. Fazal [2009] EWCA Crim 1697, [2010] 1 WLR 694 [22] which is to the effect that: where a person allows his account to be deposited and withdrawn with proceeds of fraud, such constitutes converting criminal property; R v. Christopher Smale and Ann Smale [2008] EWCA Crim 1235, [2009] 1 Cr App R (S) 25 which is to the effect that: entering into an arrangement could be by agreeing with someone to conceal money; Dare v. Crown Prosecution Service [2012] EWHC 2074 (Admin) (2013) 177 JP 37, [2012] Lloyd's Rep FC 718; Regina v. John Middleton, Veronica, Patricia Rourke [2008] EWCA Crim 233 which is to the effect that: holding a certain amount could amount to possessing criminal property.

[96] United Kingdom' Joint Money Laundering Steering Group: Prevention of Money Laundering/Combating Terrorist Financing 2017 Revised Version: Guidance for the UK Financial Sector Part II: Sectoral Guidance, paragraph 5.2.

Shell companies, particularly non-listed shell companies, for example, have been known to be exploited by corrupt politically exposed persons (PEPs) to launder their corruption proceeds under the guise of legitimate business transactions and to hide their involvement in the transactions.[97]

Banks should have sufficient processes in place to prevent the layering of illicit funds. Such processes involve a host of anti-money laundering/countering the financing of terrorism (AML/CFT) measures, including customer due diligence, enhanced due diligence, recordkeeping, account monitoring and suspicious activity reporting, all of which can help flag illicit funds before such proceeds are fully integrated back into the system as clean money.

BOX 5.1: SHELL COMPANIES

Shell companies can be used to mask the beneficial ownership of account assets and can make the tracking of funds movements more difficult for law enforcement and tax officials. The term "shell company," as used herein, refers to non-publicly traded corporations, limited liability companies (LLCs), and trusts that typically have no physical presence (other than a mailing address) and generate little to no independent economic value.[98]

---

[97] Otusanya, OJ. and Lauwo, S. (2012), 'The role of offshore financial centres in elite money laundering practices: evidence from Nigeria', Journal of Money Laundering Control, 15(3), pp. 336-361.

[98] Department of the Treasury (2005), 'US Money Laundering Threat Assessment', Available at: https://www.treasury.gov/resource-center/terrorist-illicit-finance/Documents/mlta.pdf (accessed 26 December 2017). See also Department of the Treasury (2015), 'National Money Laundering Risk Assessment', Available at: https://www.treasury.gov/resource-center/terrorist-illicit-finance/Documents/National%20Money%20Laundering%20Risk%20Assessment%20%E2%80%93%2006-12-2015.pdf (accessed 26 December 2017).

The Financial Crimes Enforcement Network (FinCEN) has identified the following as common money laundering red flags associated with shell companies:

- **Payments have no stated purpose, do not reference goods or services, or identify only a contractor invoice number;**
- **A company's purported goods and services do not match the company's profile based on information previously provided to the financial institution;**
- **Transacting businesses share the same address, provide only a registered agent's address, or raise other address-related inconsistencies;**
- **An unusually large number and variety of beneficiaries receive wire transfers from one company;**
- **Frequent involvement of beneficiaries located in high-risk, offshore financial centers; and**
- **Multiple high-value payments or transfers with no apparent legitimate business purpose.**[99]

Financial institutions must develop sufficient policies and procedures to address the anti-money laundering (AML) risks associated with providing financial services to shell companies, including the potential for straw ownership and risks related to the commingling of funds.

The bank's customer identification program should detail the identification requirements for opening an account for a business entity. When opening an account for a customer that is not an individual, banks should obtain information about the

[99] Financial Crimes Enforcement Network (2006), 'Potential Money Laundering Risks Related to Shell Companies', Available at: https://www.sec.gov/about/offices/ocie/aml2007/fin-2006-g014.pdf (accessed 23 July, 2019).

individuals who have authority and control over such accounts in order to verify the customer's identity (the customer being the business entity). Required account opening information may include articles of incorporation, a corporate resolution by the directors authorizing the opening of the account, or the appointment of a person to act as a signatory for the entity on the account. Particular attention should be paid to articles of association that allow for nominee shareholders, board members, and bearer shares.

Risk assessments may include a review of the domestic or international jurisdiction where the business entity was established, the type of account (or accounts) and expected versus actual transaction activities, the types of products used, and whether the business entity was created in-house or externally.[100]

Ongoing account monitoring is critical to ensure that the accounts are reviewed for unusual and suspicious activity. The bank should be aware of higher-risk transactions in these accounts, such as activity that has no business or apparent lawful purpose, funds transfer activity to and from higher-risk jurisdictions, currency intensive transactions, and frequent changes in the ownership or control of the nonpublic business entity.[101]

Banks must ensure that their automated monitoring system captures not only the amount and date of a transaction but also

---

[100] United States' Federal Financial Institutions Examination Council (2014), 'Bank Secrecy Act/Anti-Money Laundering Examination Manual', Available at: https://www.occ.treas.gov/publications/publications-by-type/other-publications-reports/ffiec-bsa-aml-examination-manual.pdf (accessed 10 January 2017).

[101] United States' Federal Financial Institutions Examination Council (2014), 'Bank Secrecy Act/Anti-Money Laundering Examination Manual', Available at: https://www.occ.treas.gov/publications/publications-by-type/other-publications-reports/ffiec-bsa-aml-examination-manual.pdf (accessed 10 January 2017).

the identity or geographic location of the persons sending or receiving the wires. Failure to do this may lead to a situation where the Bank is unable to identify and investigate potentially suspicious transactions based on the presence of important risk factors, such as jurisdiction and the potential involvement of politically-exposed persons (PEPs).

BOX 5.2: DUE DILIGENCE ON CORRESPONDENT ACCOUNTS FOR FOREIGN FINANCIAL INSTITUTIONS

A "correspondent account" is an account established by a bank for a foreign bank to receive deposits from, or to make payments or other disbursements on behalf of the foreign bank, or to handle other financial transactions related to the foreign bank. An "account" means any formal banking or business relationship established to provide regular services, dealings, and other financial transactions. It includes a demand deposit, savings deposit, or other transaction or asset account and a credit account or other extension of credit.

Financial institutions must develop risk-based policies, procedures, and controls that are reasonably designed to (a) gather all relevant due diligence information concerning such foreign correspondent accounts, (b) employ this due diligence information to determine whether an account is subject to enhanced due diligence, (c) conduct assessments of money laundering risks for each account, including a periodic review of the correspondent account activity to determine consistency with information obtained about the type, purpose, and anticipated

activity of the account, and (d) comply with suspicious activity reporting requirements.[102]

Credit institutions and financial institutions must not enter into, or continue, a correspondent relationship with a shell bank.[103] A "shell bank" means a credit institution or financial institution, or an institution engaged in equivalent activities to those carried out by credit institutions or financial institutions, incorporated in a jurisdiction in which it has no physical presence involving meaningful decision-making and management, and which is not part of a financial conglomerate or third-country financial conglomerate.[104] "financial conglomerate" and "third-country financial conglomerate" have the meanings given by regulations 1(2) and 7(1) respectively of the Financial Conglomerates and Other Financial Groups Regulations 2004(a).

Credit institutions and financial institutions must take appropriate enhanced measures to ensure that they do not enter into, or continue, a correspondent relationship with a credit institution or financial institution which is known to allow its accounts to be used by a shell bank.[105]

5.1 CUSTOMER DUE DILIGENCE

Effective account opening policies and procedures are fundamental risk controls for customer relationships. Effective procedures include the proper identification of the owners of the account,

[102] For more on the enhanced due diligence measures for foreign correspondent accounts, see regulation 34(1) of the UK Money Laundering, Terrorist Financing and Transfer of Funds (Information on the Payer) Regulations 2017.

[103] The UK Money Laundering, Terrorist Financing and Transfer of Funds (Information on the Payer) Regulations 2017, regulation 34(2).

[104] The UK Money Laundering, Terrorist Financing and Transfer of Funds (Information on the Payer) Regulations 2017, regulation 34(4)(b).

[105] The UK Money Laundering, Terrorist Financing and Transfer of Funds (Information on the Payer) Regulations 2017, regulation 34(3).

including the beneficial owners, the sources of their wealth and their normal and expected transactions.[106]

The type of information that would normally be needed to perform this function would be:

- Legal name and any other names used (such as maiden name);
- Permanent address (full address shall be obtained and the use of a post office box number only, is not sufficient);
- Telephone number, fax number, and email address;
- Date and place of birth;
- Nationality
- Occupation, public position held and name of employer;
- An official personal identification number or other unique identifier contained in an unexpired official document such as passport, identification card, residence permit, social security records or drivers' licence that bears a photograph of the customer;
- Type of account and nature of the banking relationship; and
- Signature.[107]

---

[106] Financial Action Task Force (2006), 'Report on New Payment Methods', Available at: http://www.fatf-gafi.org/media/fatf/documents/reports/Report%20on%20New%20Payment%20Methods.pdf (accessed 21 January 2017); The United Kingdom's Money Laundering, Terrorist Financing and Transfer of Funds (Information on the Payer) Regulations 2017, regulations 27 and 28.

[107]Australia's Anti-Money Laundering and Counter-Terrorism Financing Rules Instrument 2007 (as amended), paragraph 4.2.3-4.2.5, Officer of the Superintendent of Financial Institutions Canada Guideline: Deterring and Detecting Money Laundering and Terrorist Financing 2008, 20, CBN (Anti-Money Laundering and Combating the Financing of Terrorism in Banks and Other Financial Institutions in Nigeria) Regulations, 2013, Schedule II Paragraph 1 (1). See also South Africa's Money Laundering and Terrorist Financial Control Regulations, 2002 (as amended), Regulation 3, See United States Federal Financial Institutions Examination Council: Bank Secrecy Act/Anti-Money Laundering Examination Manual 2014, 48-49.

An AML/CTF program must include a procedure for the reporting entity to verify, at a minimum, the following Customer Due Diligence (CDD) information about a customer:

- the customer's full name; and
- either:
  - the customer's date of birth; or
  - the customer's residential address.

A financial Institution shall verify the information referred to above, by at least one of the following methods –

- Confirming the full name and date of birth from an official document (such as birth certificate, passport, identity card, social security records);
- Confirming the permanent address (such as utility bill, tax assessment, bank statement, a letter from a public authority);
- Contacting the customer by telephone, by letter or by e-mail to confirm the information supplied after an account has been opened (such as a disconnected phone, returned mail, or incorrect e-mail address shall warrant further investigation);
- Confirming the validity of the official documentation provided through certification by an authorized person such as embassy official, notary public.[108]

[108]Australia's Anti-Money Laundering and Counter-Terrorism Financing Rules Instrument 2007 (as amended), paragraphs 4.2.6 - 4.2.13, Officer of the Superintendent of Financial

When using an electronic/digital source to verify a customer's identity, financial institutions should ensure that they are able to demonstrate that they have both verified that the customer exists, and satisfied themselves that the individual seeking the business relationship is, in fact, that customer (or beneficial owner).[109]

Electronic verification may be carried out by the financial institution either direct, using as its basis the customer's full name, address and date of birth, or through an organisation which meets the criteria in paragraphs 5.3.51 and 5.3.52 of the The Joint Money Laundering Steering Group (JMLSG) Guidance for the UK financial sector Part I, June 2017 (Amended December 2017).[110]

A number of commercial agencies which access many data sources are accessible online by firms, and may provide financial institutions with a composite and comprehensive level of electronic verification through a single interface. Such agencies use databases of both positive and negative information, and many also access high-risk alerts that utilise specific data sources to identify high-risk conditions, for example, known identity

---

Institutions Canada Guideline: Deterring and Detecting Money Laundering and Terrorist Financing 2008, 21, Central Bank of Nigeria (Anti-Money Laundering and Combating the Financing of Terrorism in Banks and Other Financial Institutions in Nigeria) Regulations, 2013, Schedule II Paragraph 1 (2), See also South Africa's Money Laundering and Terrorist Financial Control Regulations, 2002 (as amended), Regulation 4, See United States Federal Financial Institutions Examination Council: Bank Secrecy Act/Anti-Money Laundering Examination Manual 2014, 49-50

[109] The Joint Money Laundering Steering Group JMLSG, *Prevention of money laundering/combating terrorist financing* 2017 Revised Version, Guidance for the UK financial sector Part I, June 2017 (Amended December 2017), para. 5.3.79

[110] The Joint Money Laundering Steering Group JMLSG, *Prevention of money laundering/combating terrorist financing* 2017 Revised Version, Guidance for the UK financial sector Part I, June 2017 (Amended December 2017), para. 5.3.80

frauds or inclusion on a sanctions list. Some of these sources are, however, only available to closed user groups.[111]

Positive information (relating to full name, current address, date of birth) can prove that an individual exists, but some can offer a higher degree of confidence than others. Such information should include data from more robust sources - where an individual has to prove their identity, or address, in some way in order to be included, as opposed to others, where no such proof is required.[112]

Negative information includes lists of individuals known to have committed fraud, including identity fraud, and registers of deceased persons. Checking against such information may be necessary to mitigate against impersonation fraud.[113]

For an electronic check to provide satisfactory evidence of identity on its own, it must use data from multiple sources, and across time, or incorporate qualitative checks that assess the strength of the information supplied. An electronic check that accesses data from a single source (e.g., a single check against the Electoral Roll) is not normally enough on its own to verify identity.[114]

Before using a commercial agency for electronic verification, financial institutions should be satisfied that information supplied by the data provider is considered to be sufficiently

---

[111] The Joint Money Laundering Steering Group JMLSG, *Prevention of money laundering/combating terrorist financing* 2017 Revised Version, Guidance for the UK financial sector Part I, June 2017 (Amended December 2017), para. 5.3.46

[112] The Joint Money Laundering Steering Group JMLSG, *Prevention of money laundering/combating terrorist financing* 2017 Revised Version, Guidance for the UK financial sector Part I, June 2017 (Amended December 2017), para. 5.3.47

[113] The Joint Money Laundering Steering Group JMLSG, *Prevention of money laundering/combating terrorist financing* 2017 Revised Version, Guidance for the UK financial sector Part I, June 2017 (Amended December 2017), para. 5.3.49

[114] The Joint Money Laundering Steering Group JMLSG, *Prevention of money laundering/combating terrorist financing* 2017 Revised Version, Guidance for the UK financial sector Part I, June 2017 (Amended December 2017), para. 5.3.50

extensive, reliable and accurate. This judgement may be assisted by considering whether the provider meets all the following criteria:

- **It is recognised, through registration with the Information Commissioner's Office, to store personal data;**
- **It uses a range of positive information sources that can be called upon to link an applicant to both current and previous circumstances;**
- **It accesses negative information sources, such as databases relating to identity fraud and deceased persons;**
- **It accesses a wide range of alert data sources; and**
- **It has transparent processes that enable the telecommunications company to know what checks were carried out, what the results of these checks were, and what they mean in terms of how much certainty they give as to the identity of the subject.**[115]

In addition, a commercial agency should have processes that allow the enquirer to capture and store the information they used to verify an identity.[116]

Where the client is a company, a financial Institution will understand the structure of the company sufficiently to determine the provider of funds, the beneficial owner(s) of the assets held by the company and those with the power to give direction to the directors of the company. This principle applies regardless of whether the share capital is in registered or bearer form.[117]

[115] The Joint Money Laundering Steering Group JMLSG, *Prevention of money laundering/combating terrorist financing* 2017 Revised Version, Guidance for the UK financial sector Part I, June 2017 (Amended December 2017), para. 5.3.52

[116] The Joint Money Laundering Steering Group JMLSG, *Prevention of money laundering/combating terrorist financing* 2017 Revised Version, Guidance for the UK financial sector Part I, June 2017 (Amended December 2017), para. 5.3.53.

[117]The Wolfsberg Group: Wolfsberg Anti-Money Laundering Principles for Private Banking (2012), paragraph 1.2.3.

The type of information that would normally be needed to perform this function would be:

- Name of the institution
- Principal place of the institution's business operations;
- Mailing address of the institution;
- Contact telephone and fax numbers;
- Some form of official identification number, if available such as tax identification number;
- The original or certified copy of the certificate of incorporation and memorandum and articles of association;
- The resolution of the board of directors to open an account and identification of those who have authority to operate the account; and
- Nature and purpose of business and its legitimacy.[118]

A financial Institution shall verify the information above, by at least one of the following methods:

- For established corporate entities, reviewing a copy of the latest report and audited accounts, if available;
- Conducting an enquiry by a business information service or an undertaking from a reputable and known firm of lawyers or accountants confirming the documents submitted;
- Undertaking a company search and/or other commercial enquiries to see that the institution has not been, or is not

---

[118]Australia's Anti-Money Laundering and Counter-Terrorism Financing Rules Instrument 2007 (as amended), paragraph 4.3.1-4.3.4, Officer of the Superintendent of Financial Institutions Canada Guideline: Deterring and Detecting Money Laundering and Terrorist Financing 2008, 21, Central Bank of Nigeria (Anti-Money Laundering and Combating the Financing of Terrorism in Banks and Other Financial Institutions in Nigeria) Regulations, 2013, schedule II paragraph 3(1). See also South Africa's Money Laundering and Terrorist Financial Control Regulations, 2002 (as amended), regulation 7.

in the process of being dissolved, struck off, wound up or terminated;

- Utilising an independent information verification process, such as accessing public and private databases;
- Obtaining prior bank references;
- Visiting the corporate entity; and
- Contacting the corporate entity by telephone, mail or e-mail.[119]

Financial institutions shall also take reasonable steps to verify the identity and reputation of any agent that opens an account on behalf of a corporate customer, if that agent is not an officer of the corporate customer.[120]

In each of the above cases, a financial institution will make a reasonable judgment as to the need for further due diligence. This would be explained in more detail in the next section.

5.2 ENHANCED CUSTOMER DUE DILIGENCE

A financial institution shall make an initial assessment of a customer's risk profile from the information provided and verified at the standard due diligence stage and particular attention shall be focused on those customers identified as having a higher risk

[119]Australia's Anti-Money Laundering and Counter-Terrorism Financing Rules Instrument 2007 (as amended), paragraph 4.3.5-4.3.13; Officer of the Superintendent of Financial Institutions Canada Guideline: Deterring and Detecting Money Laundering and Terrorist Financing 2008, 21-22; Central Bank of Nigeria (Anti-Money Laundering and Combating the Financing of Terrorism in Banks and Other Financial Institutions in Nigeria) Regulations, 2013, schedule II paragraph 3 (2), See also South Africa's Money Laundering and Terrorist Financial Control Regulations, 2002 (as amended), regulation 8.

[120]Australia's Anti-Money Laundering and Counter-Terrorism Financing Rules Instrument 2007 (as amended), paragraph 4.3.5; Central Bank of Nigeria (Anti-Money Laundering and Combating the Financing of Terrorism in Banks and Other Financial Institutions in Nigeria) Regulations, 2013, schedule II paragraph 3(3).

profile and any additional inquiries made or information obtained in respect of those customers shall include:

i. Evidence of an individual's permanent address sought through a credit reference agency search, or through independent verification by home visits;

ii. Personal reference by an existing customer of the same institution;

iii. Prior bank reference and contact with the bank regarding the customer;

iv. Source of wealth; and

v. Verification of employment and public position held where appropriate.[121]

Customers that pose higher money laundering or terrorist financing risks present increased exposure to financial institutions; due diligence policies, procedures, and processes should be enhanced as a result. Enhanced due diligence (EDD) for higher-risk customers like politically exposed persons is especially critical in understanding their anticipated transactions and implementing a suspicious activity monitoring system that reduces the firm's reputation, compliance, and transaction risks. Higher-risk customers and their transactions should be reviewed more closely at account opening and more frequently throughout the term of their relationship with the firm.[122]

[121] The United Kingdom's Money Laundering, Terrorist Financing and Transfer of Funds (Information on the Payer) Regulations 2017, regulation 33.

[122] The United Kingdom's Money Laundering, Terrorist Financing and Transfer of Funds (Information on the Payer) Regulations 2017, regulations 33 and 34.

The firm may determine that a customer poses a higher risk because of the customer's business activity, ownership structure, anticipated or actual volume and types of transactions, including those transactions involving higher-risk jurisdictions. If so, the firm should consider obtaining, both at account opening and throughout the relationship, the following information on the customer:

- Purpose of the account;
- Source of funds and wealth;
- Individuals with ownership or control over the account, such as beneficial owners, signatories or guarantors;
- Occupation or type of business (of customer or other individuals with ownership or control over the account);
- Financial statements;
- Banking references;
- Domicile (where the business is organized);
- Proximity of the customer's residence, place of employment, or place of business to the firm;
- Description of the customer's primary trade area and whether international transactions are expected to be routine;
- Description of the business operations, the anticipated volume of currency and total sales, and a list of major customers and suppliers;
- Explanations for changes in account activity.[123]

[123] United States' Federal Financial Institutions Examination Council (2014), 'Bank Secrecy Act/Anti-Money Laundering Examination Manual', Available at: https://www.occ.treas.gov/publications/publications-by-type/other-publications-reports/ffiec-bsa-aml-examination-manual.pdf (accessed 10 January 2017).

5.3 ACCOUNT MONITORING

The type of monitoring framework implemented will depend on a financial institution's risk assessment and so will vary between institutions and even between business units within a financial services group. Based on this risk assessment, the development of an appropriate monitoring framework will depend both on the products and services being supported, the size and nature of the institution's operations and, where appropriate, the adoption of a risk-based approach. The results of this assessment will determine whether an institution opts for a single approach to monitoring or deploys a combination of monitoring activities.[124]

The most appropriate and effective overall monitoring framework may contain one or more of the following elements - A dedicated automated transaction monitoring system - System-generated exception reports - Manual "line of business" incident reports - Scheduled periodic reviews/sampling - Event-driven reviews (e.g., following issuance of new typologies) In all cases the objective is to try and focus monitoring resource on the most unusual and potentially suspicious transactions and patterns of activity whilst reducing, as far as possible, the "false/positive" rate.[125]

Monitoring criteria should cover all relevant indicators. Relevant indicators could include:

---

[124] The Wolfsberg Group (2009), 'Wolfsberg Statement on AML Screening, Monitoring and Searching', Available at: https://www.cbr.ru/StaticHtml/File/36883/Wolfsberg_Nov_9_2009.pdf (accessed 6 July 2019).

[125] The Wolfsberg Group (2009), 'Wolfsberg Statement on AML Screening, Monitoring and Searching', Available at: https://www.cbr.ru/StaticHtml/File/36883/Wolfsberg_Nov_9_2009.pdf (accessed 6 July 2019).

- Frequent and unexplained movement of accounts to different financial institutions;
- Frequent and unexplained movement of funds between different financial institutions in various geographic locations;
- A client wishes to have credit and debit cards sent to destinations other than his or her address;
- A client has numerous accounts and makes or receives cash deposits in each of them amounting to a large aggregated amount;
- A client frequently exchanges currencies;
- A client wishes to have unusual access to safe deposit facilities;
- A client's account shows virtually no normal business related activities, but are used to receive or disburse large sums;
- A client has accounts that have a large volume of deposits in bank cheques, postal orders or electronic funds transfers;
- A client is reluctant to provide complete information regarding the client's activities;
- A client's financial statements differ noticeably from those of similar businesses;
- A business client's representatives avoid contact with the branch;

- A client's deposits to, or withdrawals from, a corporate account are primarily in cash, rather than in the form of debit and credit normally associated with commercial operations;
- A client maintains a number of trustee accounts or client subaccounts;
- A client makes a large volume of seemingly unrelated deposits to several accounts and frequently transfers a major portion of the balances to a single account at the same bank or elsewhere.
- A client makes a large volume of cash deposits from a business that is not normally cash intensive;
- A small business in one location makes deposits on the same day at different branches;
- There is a remarkable transaction volume and a significant change in a client's account balance;
- A client's account shows substantial increase in deposits of cash or negotiable instruments by a company offering professional advisory services;
- A client's account shows a sudden and inconsistent change in transactions or patterns.

The examples referred to above may be legitimate features of certain categories of businesses, or may make business sense if viewed in the context of the client's business activities. However, it is equally possible that these features would be unexpected in relation to certain categories of businesses, or would have no apparent business purpose, given a particular client's business activities. The purpose of obtaining additional information concerning certain clients in these circumstances is to assist the financial institution/designated non-financial institution to more accurately identify truly suspicious behaviour or relationships and transactions that pose a risk of money laundering, on the basis of a broader profile of the client than the mere client identification particulars.

The information that a financial institution must obtain in such circumstances must be adequate to reasonably enable a financial institution to determine whether transactions involving a client are consistent with a financial institution's knowledge of that client and that client's business activities and must include particulars concerning:

- the source of that client's income; and
- the source of the funds that the particular client expects to use in concluding the single transaction or transactions in the course of the business relationship.[126]

BOX 5.3: NEED FOR FINANCIAL INSTITUTIONS TO UPDATE INFORMATION ON CUSTOMERS IN ORDER TO MAINTAIN A HIGH STANDARD OF MONITORING

Occasionally customers may seek to deliberately build up a degree of trust before they use their account for criminal or/and terrorist financing purposes. Customers may be involved in money laundering and terrorist financing, therefore any product or service offered by the financial institution is a potential medium for either activity.

---

[126] South Africa' Financial Intelligence Centre Guidance Note 3A Guidance for accountable institutions on client identification and verification and related matters 2013, paragraph 4.

The nature of business must be recorded when the account is opened and that is the initial yardstick by which staff will measure whether the account is being conducted in line with the expectations or whether suspicious transactions are being passed through. It is the early period of a new customer relationship that represents the greatest vulnerability and warrants close attention.

It is also vital that financial institutions accept every opportunity to update information on customers in order to maintain a high standard of monitoring. Attention should also be given to ensuring that documentation is reviewed on a regular basis and is automatically updated when events such as change of address or change of signatories occurs.

Identification of any of the types of transaction does not automatically establish suspicion, but should arouse prompt enquiry and consideration of the circumstance. Hence, there is need for good Know Your Customer (KYC)/Know Your Customer's Business (KYCB) knowledge and records.

Whereas the primary responsibility for identifying suspicious transactions lies with the staff processing or checking items, financial institutions, as an additional safeguard, should deploy appropriate software/technology that will generate report for suspicious transactions that are scrutinized by the money laundering reporting officer.

On risk assessment basis, customer information must be updated during general communication with customers. This information must include but is not limited to the names of current directors (if applicable), type of business and volume to be expected over the account. It also gives the customer the opportunity to inform the financial institution of any new areas of business intended.

Consequently, the financial institution will be able to see if there are any material changes to the organization. Such information is an integral part of the KYC process and must be kept up to date.

BOX 5.4: ADJUSTING A CUSTOMER'S RISK RATING WHERE THERE IS A DEVIATION IN THE CUSTOMER'S ACTIVITY

When a financial institution detects a deviation in a customer's activity from the anticipated activity identified at account opening, it should change the customer's risk rating and not the anticipated activity in the account. The practice of not changing the customer's risk rating but rather the anticipated activity in the account will undermine the purpose of conducting risk ratings and cause the financial institution to apply insufficient transaction monitoring to accounts it should have identified as high-risk, and limit the institution's ability to detect red flags of suspicious activity.

5.4 RECORD KEEPING

Financial institutions should keep all records of the identification data obtained through the customer due diligence process (*e.g.*, copies or records of official identification documents such as passports, identity cards, driver's licenses and similar documents, account files and business correspondence, including the results of any analysis undertaken such as inquiries to establish the background and purpose of complex and unusual large transactions), for at least five years after the business relationship is ended, or after the date of the occasional transaction. This measure is in line with the **Financial Action Task Force Recommendations (Recommendation 11)** and the United Kingdom **Money Laundering, Terrorist Financing and Transfer of Funds (Information on the Payer) Regulations 2017 (Regulation 40).**

The rationale for record keeping is to facilitate the reconstruction of individual transactions and provide, if necessary, evidence for the prosecution of criminal activity.[127]

5.4.1 PRESERVATION OF RECORDS

The records related to the transactions discussed below must be retained by a financial institution for at least five years. However, as noted below, the records related to the identity of a financial institution's customer must be maintained for five years after the account (e.g., loan, deposit or trust) is closed. Additionally, on a case-by-case basis, a financial institution may be ordered or requested to maintain some of these records for longer periods.

1. International Transactions in Excess of the Designated Threshold

Financial institutions are required to maintain records of requests made or instructions received or given regarding transfers of currency or other monetary instruments, cheques, funds, investment securities or credit greater than the designated threshold to or from any person, account or place outside the country concerned.

2. Signature Cards

Financial institutions are required to keep records of each grant of signature authority over each deposit account.

3. Account Statements

Financial institutions are also required to keep statements, ledger cards or other records on each deposit account showing each transaction in or with respect to that account.

---

[127] Financial Action Task Force (2011), 'FATF GUIDANCE: Anti-Money Laundering and Terrorist Financing Measures and Financial Inclusion', Available at: http://www.fatf-gafi.org/media/fatf/content/images/AML%20CFT%20measures%20and%20financial%20inclusion.pdf (accessed 13 January 2017).

4. Cheques

Each cheque, draft or money order drawn on the telecommunications company or issued and payable by it must be kept.

5. Deposits

Each deposit slip or credit ticket reflecting a transaction, record for direct deposit or other funds transfer deposit transactions are required to be kept. The slip or ticket must record the amount of any currency involved.

6. Records to Reconstruct Demand Deposit Accounts

To be kept are the records prepared or received by the financial institution in the ordinary course of business which would be needed to reconstruct a transaction account and to trace a cheque deposited in a demand deposit account through its domestic processing system or to supply a description of a deposited cheque.

7. Certificates of Deposit Purchased or Presented

This record which contained the following will be kept:

(i) Name of customer (purchaser or presenter).

(ii) Address of customer.

(iii) Tax Identification Number (TIN) of customer.

(iv) Description of the certificate of deposit.

(v) Notation of the method of payment if purchased.

(vi) Date of transaction.

8. Purchase of Monetary Instruments

A financial institution must maintain records of each of its cheques/draft, cashier's cheque, money order or traveler's cheque.

If the purchaser has a deposit account with the financial institution, this record shall contain:

(i) Name of purchaser.

(ii) Date of purchase

(iii) Type(s) of instrument purchased.

(iv) Amount of each of the instrument(s) purchased.

(v) Serial number(s) of the instrument(s) purchased.

If the purchaser does not have a deposit account with the financial institution, this record shall contain:

(i) Name of purchaser.

(ii) Address of purchasers.

(iii) Social security number of purchaser or alien identification number.

(iv) Date of birth of purchaser.

(v) Date of purchase

(vi) Type(s) of instrument purchased.

(vii) Amount of each of the instrument(s) purchased.

(viii) Serial number(s) of the instrument(s) purchased.

(ix) Description of document or method used to verify the name and address of the purchaser (e.g., state of issuance and number driver's licence).

9. Funds Transfers

A financial institution's AML/CFT record-keeping requirements with respect to funds transfer vary based upon its role with respect to the funds transfer.

10. Financial institution acting as an originator

For each payment order that the financial institution accepts as the originator, it must obtain and retain records of the following information:

(i) Name and address of originator.

(ii) Amount of the payment order.

(iii) Execution date of the payment order.

(iv) Any payment instruction received from the originator with the payment order.

(v) Identity of the beneficiary's financial institution.

(vi) As many of the following items as are received with the payment order:

(a) Name and address of the beneficiary

(b) Account number of the beneficiary.

(c) Any other specific identifier of the beneficiary.

(d) For each payment order that a financial institution accepts for an originator that is not its established customer, it (in addition to the information listed above) must obtain appropriate extra information as may be required.

11. A financial institution acting as an intermediary or a beneficiary's bank

For each payment order that a financial institution accepts as an intermediary bank or a beneficiary's financial institution, it must retain a record of the payment order.

For each payment order that a financial institution accepts for a beneficiary that is not its established customer, the institution must also obtain additional information as required.

12. Tax Identification Number (TIN)

The institution is required to keep the record of the TIN of any customer opening an account.

In cases of joint accounts, information on a person with a financial interest must be maintained.

13. Exceptions in respect of TIN

A financial institution does not need to maintain TIN for accounts or transactions with the following:

(i) Agencies and instrumentalities of federal, state, local or foreign governments.

(ii) Judges, public officials or clerks of courts of record as custodians of funds in controversy or under the control of the court.

(iii) Certain aliens.

(iv) Certain tax-exempt organizations and units of tax-exempt organizations.

(v) A person under 18 years of age with respect to an account opened as a part of a school thrift savings Programme.

14. Suspicious Transaction Report and Supporting Documentation

A financial institution must maintain a record of any suspicious transaction report (STR) filed and the original or business record equivalent of any supporting documentation for a period of five years from the date of filing.

15. Currency Transaction Report

A financial institution must maintain a record of all Currency Transaction Reports (CTR) for a period of five years from the date of filing.

16. Customer Identification Programme

A financial institution must maintain a record of all information it obtains under its procedures for implementing its customer identification programme (CIP). At a minimum, these records must include the following:

(i) All identifying information about a customer (e.g., name, date of birth, address and TIN).

(ii) A description of the document that the financial institution relied upon to identity of the customer.

(iii) A description of the non-documentary methods and results of any measures the financial institution took to verify the identity of the customer.

(iv) A description of the financial institution's resolution of any substantive discrepancy discovered when verifying the identifying information obtained.

A financial institution must retain the identifying information about a customer for a period of five years after the date the account is closed or in the case of credit card accounts, five years after the account becomes closed or dormant.

A financial institution must retain the information relied on, methods used to verify identity and resolution of discrepancies for a period of five years after the record is made.

These AML/CFT record-keeping requirements are independent of and in addition to requirements to file and retain reports imposed by other laws.[128]

5.5. REPORTING MEASURES

Reporting measures are key to anti-money laundering/countering the financing of terrorism (AML/CFT) efforts and support law enforcement investigations.[129] These measures can be used by financial institutions to curb money laundering. The transaction record of a payment or funds transfer should be used to monitor the activities of the customer's account for suspicious activities. If a financial institution suspects or has reasonable grounds to suspect that funds are being paid to the wrong person, it should report promptly its suspicions to the police. This measure is in line with the **Financial Action Task Force Recommendations (Recommendation 20)** and the **UK Proceeds of Crime Act 2002 (as amended) (Section 331).**

5.5.1 WHAT TO FILE

A firm's nominated officer must report any transaction or activity that, after his evaluation, he knows or suspects, or has reasonable grounds to know or suspect, may be linked to money laundering

[128] Esoimeme, E.E. (2015), 'The Risk-Based Approach to Combating Money Laundering and Terrorist Financing', Eric Press; Available on Amazon: https://www.amazon.co.uk/Risk-Based-Combating-Laundering-Terrorist-Financing/dp/9789486030/ref=sr_1_2?ie=UTF8&qid=1437508453&sr=8-2&keywords=ehi+eric+esoimeme (accessed 16th April, 2019).

[129] Financial Action Task Force (2013), 'GUIDANCE FOR A RISK BASED-APPROACH: PREPAID CARDS, MOBILE PAYMENTS AND INTERNET-BASED PAYMENT SERVICES', Available at: http://www.fatf-gafi.org/media/fatf/documents/recommendations/Guidance-RBA-NPPS.pdf (accessed 12 January 2017).

or terrorist financing, or to attempted money laundering or terrorist financing.[130] Such report is called a Suspicious Activity Report (SAR).[131]

Having knowledge means actually knowing something to be true. In a criminal court, it must be proved that the individual in fact knew that a person was engaged in money laundering. That said, knowledge can be inferred from the surrounding circumstances; so, for example, a failure to ask obvious questions may be relied upon by a jury to imply knowledge. The knowledge must, however, have come to the firm (or to the member of staff) in the course of business, or (in the case of a nominated officer) as a consequence of a disclosure under **Section 330 of the Proceeds of Crime Act (POCA) or Section 21A of the Terrorism Act.** Information that comes to the firm or staff member in other circumstances does not come within the scope of the regulated sector obligation to make a report. This does not preclude a report being made should staff choose to do so, or are obligated to do so by other parts of these Acts.[132]

Suspicion is more subjective and falls short of proof based on firm evidence. Suspicion has been defined by the courts as being beyond mere speculation and based on some foundation, for example:

---

[130] The UK Proceeds of Crime Act 2002 (as amended), s. 331; the Joint Money Laundering Steering Group JMLSG, *Prevention of money laundering/combating terrorist financing,* 2017 Revised Version, Guidance for the UK financial sector Part I June 2017 (Amended December 2017), para. 6.33.

[131] Joint Money Laundering Steering Group JMLSG, *Prevention of money laundering/combating terrorist financing,* 2017 Revised Version, Guidance for the UK financial sector Part I June 2017 (Amended December 2017), Chapter 6, See also Lilley, P. (2006), *Dirty Dealing: The Untold Truth About Global Money Laundering, International Crime and Terrorism,* Kogan Page Limited, United Kingdom.

[132] Joint Money Laundering Steering Group JMLSG, *Prevention of money laundering/combating terrorist financing,* 2017 Revised Version, Guidance for the UK financial sector Part I June 2017 (Amended December 2017), para. 6.10.

"A degree of satisfaction and not necessarily amounting to belief but at least extending beyond speculation as to whether an event has occurred or not"; and

"Although the creation of suspicion requires a lesser factual basis than the creation of a belief, it must nonetheless be built upon some foundation."[133]

A transaction which appears unusual is not necessarily suspicious. Even customers with a stable and predictable transactions profile will have periodic transactions that are unusual for them. Many customers will, for perfectly good reasons, have an erratic pattern of transactions or account activity. So, the unusual is, in the first instance, only a basis for further enquiry, which may in turn require judgement as to whether it is suspicious. A transaction or activity may not be suspicious at the time, but if suspicions are raised later, an obligation to report then arises.[134]

A member of staff, including the nominated officer, who considers a transaction or activity to be suspicious, would not necessarily be expected either to know or to establish the exact nature of any underlying criminal offence, or that the particular funds or property were definitely those arising from a crime or terrorist financing.[135]

Transactions, or proposed transactions, such as '419' scams, are attempted advance fee frauds, and not money laundering; they are therefore not reportable under POCA or the Terrorism Act, unless

[133] Joint Money Laundering Steering Group JMLSG, *Prevention of money laundering/combating terrorist financing,* 2017 Revised Version, Guidance for the UK financial sector Part I, para. 6.11.

[134] Joint Money Laundering Steering Group JMLSG, *Prevention of money laundering/combating terrorist financing,* 2017 Revised Version, Guidance for the UK financial sector Part I, para. 6.12.

[135] Joint Money Laundering Steering Group JMLSG, *Prevention of money laundering/combating terrorist financing,* 2017 Revised Version, Guidance for the UK financial sector Part I, para. 6.13.

the fraud is successful, and the firm is aware of resulting criminal property.[136]

The objective test of suspicion would likely be met when there are demonstrated to be facts or circumstances, known to the member of staff, from which a reasonable person engaged in a business subject to the Money Laundering Regulations would have inferred knowledge, or formed the suspicion, that another person was engaged in money laundering or terrorist financing.[137]

To defend themselves against a charge that they failed to meet the objective test of suspicion, staff within financial sector firms would need to be able to demonstrate that they took reasonable steps in the particular circumstances, in the context of a risk-based approach, to know the customer and the rationale for the transaction, activity or instruction. It is important to bear in mind that, in practice, members of a jury may decide, with the benefit of hindsight, whether the objective test has been met.[138]

Depending on the circumstances, a firm being served with a court order in relation to a customer may give rise to reasonable grounds for suspicion in relation to that customer. In such an event, firms should review the information it holds about that customer across the firm, in order to determine whether or not such grounds exist.[139]

---

[136] Joint Money Laundering Steering Group JMLSG, *Prevention of money laundering/combating terrorist financing,* 2017 Revised Version, Guidance for the UK financial sector Part I, para. 6.14.

[137] Joint Money Laundering Steering Group JMLSG, *Prevention of money laundering/combating terrorist financing,* 2017 Revised Version, Guidance for the UK financial sector Part I, para. 6.15.

[138] Joint Money Laundering Steering Group JMLSG, *Prevention of money laundering/combating terrorist financing,* 2017 Revised Version, Guidance for the UK financial sector Part I, para. 6.16.

[139] Joint Money Laundering Steering Group JMLSG, *Prevention of money laundering/combating terrorist financing,* 2017 Revised Version, Guidance for the UK financial sector Part I, para. 6.17.

5.5.2 WHERE TO FILE

To avoid committing a failure to report offence, nominated officers must make their disclosures to the National Crime Agency (NCA). The national reception point for disclosure of suspicions, and for seeking consent to continue to proceed with the transaction or activity, is the UK Financial Intelligence Unit (FIU) within the NCA.[140]

5.5.3 WHEN TO FILE

Such reports must be made as soon as is reasonably practicable after the information comes to the nominated officer.[141]

The SARs consent regime has the practical effect of preventing an activity from going ahead for an initial notice period of 7 days,[142] and where appropriate, for a period of 31 days known as the 'moratorium period'.[143] The moratorium period allows law enforcement agencies to gather evidence to determine whether further action, such as restraint of the funds, should take place.

There are times when law enforcement agents may not have sufficient time to gather evidence related to particularly complex activities, which are linked to overseas grand corruption or other serious crime. The provisions in the **United Kingdom Criminal Finances Act 2017** provide for the extension of the moratorium period by a court, for up to 31 days. This can be repeated up to 186 days (approximately 6 months), from the end of the initial 31-day moratorium period. The process will have judicial oversight

---

[140] Joint Money Laundering Steering Group JMLSG, *Prevention of money laundering/combating terrorist financing,* 2017 Revised Version, Guidance for the UK financial sector Part I, para. 6.40.

[141] Joint Money Laundering Steering Group JMLSG, *Prevention of money laundering/combating terrorist financing,* 2017 Revised Version, Guidance for the UK financial sector Part I June 2017 (Amended December 2017), para. 6.33.

[142] The UK Proceeds of Crime Act 2002 (as amended), s. 335 (5), s. 336 (7).

[143] The UK Proceeds of Crime Act 2002 (as amended), s. 335 (6), s. 336 (8).

and the interested party will be notified that an application has been made to extend the moratorium period.[144]

5.5.4 CONFIDENTIALITY OF SARS/TIPPING OFF (GENERAL RULE)

A person is not to disclose a SAR if such disclosure is likely to prejudice any investigation that might be conducted following the disclosure and the information on which the disclosure is based came to the person in the course of a business in the regulated sector.[145]

5.5.5 CONFIDENTIALITY OF SARS/TIPPING OFF (EXCEPTION)

i. An employee, officer or partner of an undertaking does not commit an offence if the disclosure is to an employee, officer or partner of the same undertaking.[146]

ii. A person does not commit an offence in respect of a disclosure by a credit institution or a financial institution if—

   a. The disclosure is to a credit institution or a financial institution,

   b. The institution to whom the disclosure is made is situated in an European Economic Area (EEA) State or in a country or territory imposing equivalent money laundering requirements, and

   c. Both the institution making the disclosure and the institution to which it is made belong to the same group.[147]

---

[144] The UK Criminal Finances Act 2017, s. 10.

[145] The UK Proceeds of Crime Act 2002 (as amended), s. 333A (1).

[146] The UK Proceeds of Crime Act 2002 (as amended), s. 333B (1).

[147] The UK Proceeds of Crime Act 2002 (as amended), s. 333B (2).

iii. A professional legal adviser or a relevant professional adviser does not commit an offence under section 333A if—

(a) The disclosure is to professional legal adviser or a relevant professional adviser,

(b) both the person making the disclosure and the person to whom it is made carry on business in an EEA State or in a country or territory imposing equivalent money laundering requirements, and

(c) Those persons perform their professional activities within different undertakings that share common ownership, management or control.[148]

5.5.6 PENALTIES

5.5.6.1 TIPPING OFF

A person guilty of the offence of tipping off is liable on summary conviction to imprisonment for a term not exceeding 3 months or to a fine not exceeding level 5 on the standard scale or to both[149] and on conviction on indictment, to imprisonment for a term not exceeding two years, or to a fine, or to both.[150]

5.5.6.2 FAILURE TO FILE A SAR

A person guilty of not filing a SAR is liable on summary conviction for a term not exceeding 6 months or to a fine not exceeding the statutory maximum or to both,[151] and on conviction on

[148] The UK Proceeds of Crime Act 2002 (as amended), s. 333B (4), See also the UK Proceeds of Crime Act 2002 (as amended), s. 333C and D for more exceptions.

[149] The UK Proceeds of Crime Act 2002 (as amended), s. 333A(4)(a).

[150] The UK Proceeds of Crime Act 2002 (as amended), s. 333A(4)(b).

[151] The UK Proceeds of Crime Act 2002 (as amended), s. 334(2)(a).

indictment, to imprisonment for a term not exceeding five years or to a fine or to both.[152]

CASE STUDY 5.1: FAILURE TO FILE TIMELY AND COMPLETE SUSPICIOUS ACTIVITY REPORTS

Case 5.1.1: Financial Crimes Enforcement Network v. Great Eastern Bank of Florida No. 2002-02

During the relevant time period, Great Eastern failed to file Suspicious Activity Reports (SARs) on transactions for at least six customers that it "knew, suspected, or had reason to suspect" were reportable as suspicious under the **Bank Secrecy Act (BSA).** For example, Great Eastern failed to file a SAR on a customer that engaged in suspicious wire transfer activity in one Great Eastern account. The account received over nine hundred thousand dollars in 29 wire transfers from a foreign company, most of which was wired out the following day to the customer's account at another bank. The activity could not be supported by the normal operations of the customer's business. Indeed, this same customer engaged in nearly identical activity in another account at Great Eastern, and Great Eastern did file a SAR on the customer's activity in the other account, thus demonstrating that it did in fact recognize such behavior as suspicious.

In addition, Great Eastern failed to file a timely SAR for a customer that had millions of dollars of incoming and outgoing wires transfers, many from the same source. Great Eastern only analyzed the transaction after it was specifically required to do so by the Federal Deposit Insurance Corporation (FDIC) in 1999, and only then determined that there was no apparent business reason for the large amounts of wire transfer activity for this customer and filed a SAR. The information available to Great Eastern when it finally

[152] The UK Proceeds of Crime Act 2002 (as amended), s. 334(2)(b).

filed the SAR two years after the fact was the same information available to it at the time of the transaction. Great Eastern should have detected this transaction and have filed a SAR before being required to do so by the FDIC, two years after the transaction occurred.

1. Failure to File Complete SARs

For at least 14 other customer transactions, Great Eastern filed SARs, but in these SARs the Bank failed to include required information about the suspicious activity that it had in its files at the time it filed the SAR. For example, during the relevant time period, as noted above Great Eastern filed a SAR on a customer identifying wire transfers totaling over nine hundred thousand dollars that were wired out of the account almost immediately, but did not file a SAR on identical transactions engaged in by the same customer in another Great Eastern account. As an alternative to filing a second SAR, Great Eastern could have included this activity in the SAR that was filed, but it failed to do so, thus understating the scope of the suspicious activity by one-half.

During the relevant time period, Great Eastern filed a SAR which merely stated that a customer made a seventy-one thousand two hundred and fifty dollars deposit to an account that had minimal activity prior to that time. The report did not adequately describe the alleged suspicious activity and, therefore, the SAR failed to include important required information that was readily available to Great Eastern – that is, why it was filing the SAR. The SAR failed to report that six of the checks in the deposit were sequentially numbered checks from a single account in even thousand-dollar amounts. Furthermore, the SAR failed to report that the traveler's check portion of the deposit was comprised of 236 checks from 10 banks. The SAR failed to report that wire transfers shortly after the deposit transferred the majority of the funds out of the account. This failure to indicate on the form why the Bank thought the transaction was suspicious undermines the utility of the SAR in alerting law enforcement to transactions that deserve investigation.

Similarly, Great Eastern filed a SAR that simply reported a fifty thousand dollars deposit of money orders. The SAR did not describe the monetary instruments by denomination, issuer, or place of origin as explicitly required by the instructions to the SAR form. The SAR did not state that there was little activity in the account but for the deposit and did not indicate that the customer withdrew the funds soon after the deposit. Again, the SAR did not provide law enforcement with important information about the transaction and why it believed the transaction was suspicious based on information that was readily available to the bank.

In addition, Great Eastern failed to maintain sufficient documentation to support the filing of numerous SARs. With respect to SARs filed on 14 customers, the files contained only a portion of the necessary documentation required by the SAR regulations. In some cases, documents included in the file as supporting documentation were not legible. Supporting documentation is an important means of preserving evidence and enabling law enforcement to follow up on a SAR. Therefore, Great Eastern failed to file SARs that were timely and complete in accordance with **31 U.S.C. §5318(g)** and **31 CFR §1010.320.**[153]

---

[153] United States of America Department of the Treasury Financial Crimes Enforcement Network (2002), 'IN THE MATTER OF GREAT EASTERN BANK OF FLORIDA MIAMI FLORIDA', Available at: https://www.fincen.gov/sites/default/files/enforcement_action/geassessfinal.pdf (accessed 2 April 2017).

Case 5.1.2: Financial Crimes Enforcement Network v. Korea Exchange Bank No. 2003-04

Financial Crimes Enforcement Network (FinCEN) determined that between March 1998 and May 2001, the Broadway Branch of the Korea Exchange Bank failed to file approximately thirty-nine (39) suspicious activity reports ("SARs") involving nearly thirty-two million dollars in suspicious transactions, in a timely manner in violation of **31 U.S.C. §5318(g)** and **31 CFR §1010.320**.

A bank must report any transaction involving or aggregating to at least five thousand dollars that it "knows, suspects, or has reason to suspect" (i) involves funds derived from illegal activities or is conducted to disguise funds derived from illegal activities, (ii) is designed to evade the reporting or recordkeeping requirements of the BSA (e.g., structuring transactions to avoid currency transaction reporting) or (iii) "has no business or apparent lawful purpose or is not the sort in which the particular customer would normally be expected to engage, and the bank knows of no reasonable explanation for the transaction after examining the available facts, including the background and possible purpose of the transaction." **31 USC §5318(g)** and **31 CFR §1010.320**.

As an FDIC-supervised bank, the Broadway Branch was on notice of the SAR requirements and the need to have policies and procedures in place to ensure these requirements are met. **Section 326.8(b) of the FDIC's regulations** requires a bank to develop and administer a program to assure compliance with the BSA. According to the FDIC, at a minimum, the bank's system of internal controls must be designed to "identify reportable transactions at a point where all of the information necessary to properly complete the required reporting forms can be obtained." See, FDIC Manual of Exam Policies, Financial Recordkeeping and

Reporting Regulations, Section 9.4. The system must also "ensure that all required reports are completed accurately."

Information in the reports of examination of the Broadway Branch by the FDIC shows that the Branch knew, suspected or had reason to suspect that certain transactions were "suspicious" within the meaning of the BSA but failed to file SARs for these transactions. In its March 31, 1999 examination report, the FDIC specifically cited the Branch for the failure to establish or implement an adequate system of internal controls for the identification, investigation, documentation, and reporting of suspicious transactions. The FDIC also found inadequate BSA and SAR compliance in the October 18, 1999 and March 31, 2001 examinations of the Branch.

To comply with the SAR rule, a financial institution must be able to determine whether transactions are in fact reportable. Therefore, a financial institution is required to have in place systems to identify the kinds of transactions that may be a high risk for money laundering or that exhibit indicia of suspicious activity, taking into account the type of products and services it offers and the nature of its customers. Otherwise, a financial institution cannot assure that it is in fact reporting suspicious transactions as required by the BSA. In this case, the record shows that during the relevant time period, the Broadway Branch had information about its customers and their transactions that caused it to "know, suspect, or have reason to suspect" that many transactions were reportable suspicious transactions, yet the Branch failed to report these transactions because its procedures to identify, analyze, document, or report suspicious activity were not properly implemented. As a result, the Broadway Branch violated the SAR requirements of **31 U.S.C. §5318(g)** and **31 CFR §1010.320**.

1. Frequent Large Cash Deposits

The Broadway Branch's review of cash deposits in large amounts was inadequate for the identification of suspicious patterns of activity. As a result, the Branch failed to timely file SARs regarding suspicious transactions by at least five (5) customers in violation of **31 U.S.C. §5318(g)** and **31 CFR §1010.320.**

For example, in a span of two months thirty-seven cash deposits in excess of ten thousand dollars, totaling almost one million two hundred thousand dollars, were made to the account of a company that imported wigs for wholesale sales. Despite the unusual cash deposit activity on the customer's account that lacked any apparent legal or business purpose, the Branch failed to detect and report the suspicious pattern of transactions. The FDIC noted in its March 31, 1999 report of examination that, because the customer had such an exceptionally high volume of cash deposits over the past year, the FDIC was unable to review more than two months of activity in the account. In June 1999, the Branch filed a SAR in response to the FDIC's citation of the Branch in its examination findings for SAR filing violations.

2. Frequent Large Cash Deposits Followed by Wire Transfers

The Broadway Branch failed to implement adequate procedures to detect suspicious patterns of activity involving numerous cash deposits in large amounts followed by outgoing wire transfers. As a result, the Branch failed to timely file at least eleven (11) SARs for suspicious transactions by at least five (5) customers in violation of **31 U.S.C. §5318(g)** and **31 CFR §1010.320**.

For example, one customer, an individual who imported wigs and purported to be a business partner of the company discussed above, made numerous cash deposits in amounts over ten thousand dollars to his accounts at the Bank that aggregated to over thirteen million dollars from 1986 through 1999 and to his account at the Branch that aggregated to over three million eight hundred thousand dollars from May 1998 through February 1999. The Branch did not know or make an attempt to verify the business relationship between the two businesses or to determine the actual origin of these funds. Most of the currency placed in the account that the individual opened at the Branch in May 1998 was wired out shortly after its deposit. Withdrawals on this account included over seventy (70) wire transfers, through foreign banks, to a number of beneficiaries primarily located in Korea and Japan. The Branch did not attempt to determine the actual business of the majority of the beneficiaries of these transfers and all of the requests for transfer were submitted by facsimile from the company rather than the individual customer. In June 1999, the Branch filed a SAR on these transactions in response to the FDIC's examination findings.

3. Wire Transfers Structured to Avoid Recordkeeping Requirements

The Broadway Branch's review of its inward and outward wire remittance was inadequate for the identification of suspicious patterns of activity designed to evade the regulations promulgated under the BSA. As a result, FinCEN determined that the Branch failed to file SARs for suspicious transactions by at least four (4) non-customers and two (2) customers in violation of **31 U.S.C. §5318(g)** and **31 CFR §1010.320**.

For example, in one instance, the FDIC noted sixty-five (65) wire transfers, all but two of which were between two thousand nine hundred and fifty dollars and two thousand nine hundred and eighty dollars, from the same group of non-bank customers to the same group of beneficiaries. These transactions, all of which were conducted in cash, appear to have been structured to circumvent the recordkeeping requirements for funds transfers of three thousand dollars or more appearing in **31 CFR §1010.410(e)**. In its March 31, 2001 report of examination, the FDIC concluded that the Branch should have filed SARs regarding these transactions, given the volume, frequency, and commonality of the customers involved.

4. Cash Deposits Structured to Avoid CTR Reporting Requirements

While the Broadway Branch identified successive cash deposits of just under ten thousand dollars by certain customers as potentially suspicious activity that warranted investigation, the Branch did not undertake the due diligence necessary to make an informed decision or meaningful analysis of whether the activity was actually suspicious and whether a SAR should be filed. The Branch's process for documenting client profiles and investigating suspicious activity was inadequate. As a result, the Branch failed to timely file SARs for suspicious transactions by at least three (3) customers in violation of **31 U.S.C. §5318(g)** and **31 CFR §1010.320**.

For example, the Branch identified the high volume of cash transaction activity within the business checking account of one customer as potentially suspicious and included the activity on the Branch Suspicious Activity Investigation Log for investigation. For a period of 15 months, the customer made one hundred fifty-five (155) cash deposits to the account, aggregating seven hundred and sixty-six dollars. Of these transactions, twenty-nine were in amounts ranging from eight thousand dollars to ten thousand dollars, including five at exactly ten thousand dollars. None of the deposits was over the currency transaction report (CTR) threshold of ten thousand dollars. These transactions appeared to have been structured to circumvent the Branch's obligation to report any cash deposit over ten thousand dollars on a CTR as described in **31 CFR §1010.330**.

The Branch did not file a SAR regarding these transactions because the U.S. Compliance Officer concluded that the cash activity appeared normal and that there was no indication of suspicious activity. During its March 31, 2001 examination of the Branch, the FDIC noted that the Branch could not produce any analysis or documentation to support the U.S. Compliance Officer's assertion that the cash activity appeared normal. If an investigation and analysis was performed by the Branch, it was not documented. The FDIC concluded that the Branch should have filed SARs regarding these transactions.[154]

CASE STUDY 5.2: FAILURE TO FILE TIMELY CURRENCY TRANSACTION REPORTS

CASE 5.2.1: FINANCIAL CRIMES ENFORCEMENT NETWORK V. SOVEREIGN BANK NO. 2002-01

FinCEN determined that from June 1998, through May 2001, Sovereign failed to file timely approximately 2000 Currency Transaction Report ("CTR") forms for currency transactions in amounts greater than ten thousand dollars as required by **31 CFR §1010.330**, promulgated under **§5313 of the Bank Secrecy Act**.

FinCEN had determined that Sovereign's failures to file CTRs were willful. Over a two-year period, Sovereign had experienced a number of extraordinary events, including several mergers and acquisitions and systems conversions. These events strained Sovereign's compliance systems, leading to the failure to file CTRs

[154] United States of America Department of the Treasury Financial Crimes Enforcement Network (2003), 'IN THE MATTER OF KOREA EXCHANGE BANK NEW YORK', Available at: https://www.fincen.gov/sites/default/files/enforcement_action/koreaexchangeassessment.pdf (accessed 3 May 2017).

primarily for new cash management customers in Pennsylvania and New Jersey that had been acquired through the mergers and acquisitions. While Sovereign BSA compliance personnel or its internal auditors ultimately identified each of these problems, the recurring nature of the problems should have alerted Sovereign and particularly the group responsible for arranging cash pickups and deliveries for these new customers ("Group"), to the need to more fully evaluate its BSA compliance procedures and systems completely and thoroughly at an earlier time.

In particular, Sovereign relied on third party vendors without adequate internal controls to assure BSA compliance. First, for a year after it acquired the cash management business, Sovereign believed that its outside vendors, several armored car services that picked up and delivered cash to and from the Bank's customers, prepared and filed the necessary CTRs for the pick-ups and deliveries for these customers.

However, Sovereign did not have sufficient internal controls in place to verify this belief and did not monitor or test the vendors' performance of this function. In fact, the vendors did not prepare or file the CTRs for these customers. As a result, from June 1998 though March 1999, Sovereign failed to file about 1155 CTRs.

Second, when Sovereign discovered that neither the outside vendors nor the Bank's branches had filed the required CTRs, the Group assumed responsibility for preparing and filing CTRs. The Group obtained a list from the vendors of the customers taking advantage of the cash pick-up and delivery service but did not verify that the list was complete. Because some of these customers were not on the vendors' lists, Sovereign failed to file timely an additional approximately 241 CTRs for a five-month period between March and August 1999 for reportable cash transactions by customers missing from the list.

Lastly, from July 1999 through May 2001, the Group relied on a third-party currency handling service to prepare reports of the currency orders by the Bank's customers who received cash from or delivered cash to these third-party vendors. The Group would identify reportable transactions from the information in the vendor's reports and prepare and file the necessary CTRs. The BSA Compliance Department, in turn, would compare the CTRs prepared by the Group to the same vendor's report. Beginning in July 1999, however, the report provided by the vendor did not list all the transactions.

The Bank did not test the accuracy of the vendor's reports against the Bank's own records of such currency transactions by these customers and did not monitor or test the accuracy of the resulting CTRs. Because of undetected inaccuracies in the vendor's reports, Sovereign failed to file over about 578 additional CTRs between July 1999 and May 2001.

FinCEN had determined that Sovereign failed to implement sufficient internal controls and testing to ensure that it filed accurate and timely CTRs, even after it was on notice that there were significant deficiencies in its BSA compliance. Therefore, FinCEN had concluded that Sovereign's failures to file CTRs constitute willful violations of the BSA.[155]

[155] United States of America Department of the Treasury Financial Crimes Enforcement Network (2002), 'IN THE MATTER OF SOVERIGN BANK', Available at: https://www.fincen.gov/sites/default/files/enforcement_action/sovereignbank.pdf (accessed 28 April, 2017).

5.6. TRAINING FOR ANTI-MONEY LAUNDERING COMPLIANCE

Financial institutions are recommended to train all appropriate personnel with respect to their responsibilities to comply with the requirements of due diligence, record keeping and reporting. Sufficient training will need to be given to all relevant employees to enable them to recognise when a transaction is unusual or suspicious, or when they should have reasonable grounds to know or suspect that fraud or money laundering is taking place.[156]

A financial institution's training program should provide relevant examples of money laundering in financial institutions and should discuss AML/CFT policies and procedures, liability issues and regulatory requirements. In addition, the training program should provide for regular updates to ensure employees are kept current in AML policies and regulatory changes. This measure is in line with the **Financial Action Task Force Recommendations (Recommendation 18)** and **the United Kingdom Money Laundering, Terrorist Financing and Transfer of Funds (Information on the Payer) Regulations 2017 (Regulation 24).**

The money laundering reporting officer (MLRO) shall ensure adequate training of staff on AML/CFT compliance issues and act as a contact point within the financial institution to provide answers to compliance queries from respondent financial institutions and staff members. The MLRO shall also help in establishing written guidance for staff on the appropriate compliance with laws, rules and standards through policies and procedures and other documents such as compliance manuals, codes of conduct and practice guidelines.

[156] The Joint Money Laundering Steering Group JMLSG, *Prevention of Money Laundering/Combating Terrorist Financing* (2017) revised version, Guidance for the United Kingdom Financial Sector Part I, June 2017 [Amended December 2017], para. 7.32.

At a minimum, all new employees must receive formal training within 60 days of their joining the firm. This training should cover the relevant anti-money laundering laws, anti- Money Laundering Policy and Procedures, and recognizing and reporting Suspicious Transactions (employee responsibilities and examples of suspicious activity, "red flags").

The AML/CFT Compliance Office must maintain a record of all formal training, to include the names and positions of the participants, for at least 5 years. Annually all staff are targeted to attend AML refresher training to update them of all new developments including information on current money laundering and the financing of terrorism (ML/ FT) techniques, methods and trends; ML red flags; KYC requirements; customer transaction monitoring and suspicious transaction reporting; new changes in the Global AML world and local regulations.[157]

There is no single solution when determining how to deliver training; a mix of training techniques may be appropriate. On-line learning systems can often provide an adequate solution for many employees, but there will be classes of employees for whom such an approach is not suitable. Focused classroom training for higher risk or minority areas can be more effective. Relevant videos always stimulate interest, but continually re-showing the same video may produce diminishing returns.[158]

---

[157] Central Bank of Nigeria' Anti-Money Laundering/Combating the Financing of Terrorism (AML/CFT) Policy and Procedure Manual' 2018, para. 32.0.

[158] The Joint Money Laundering Steering Group JMLSG, *Prevention of Money Laundering/Combating Terrorist Financing* (2017) revised version, Guidance for the United Kingdom Financial Sector Part I, June 2017 [Amended December 2017], para. 7.42.

5.7. AUDIT FOR COMPLIANCE WITH ANTI-MONEY LAUNDERING MEASURES

An important component of an anti-money laundering (AML) Program is an independent test or audit of the program. The independent test requirement must be performed, either internally or externally, by parties independent of the creation of the business' AML procedures. In most cases, this testing is performed by Internal Audit Department. To supplement this independent test, there are several other internal controls to be performed by the AML/CFT Compliance Office. The scope and breadth of the activities of the AML/CFT compliance function shall be subject to periodic review by the internal audit function. An audit programme which covers the adequacy and effectiveness of the financial institution's compliance function should be established, including testing of controls commensurate with the perceived level of risk.[159] Audit programs should focus on high-risk accounts and should include comprehensive transaction testing. This measure is in line with the **Financial Action Task Force Recommendations (Recommendation 18)** and **the United Kingdom Money Laundering, Terrorist Financing and Transfer of Funds (Information on the Payer) Regulations 2017 (Regulation 21(1)(c)).**

While the frequency of audit is not specifically defined in any statute, a sound practice is for the financial institution to conduct independent testing generally every 12 to 18 months or commensurate with the Money Laundering/Financing of Terrorism ML/FT risk profile of the institution.

Financial institutions that do not employ outside auditors, consultants or have internal audit departments may comply with

[159] Central Bank of Nigeria' Anti-Money Laundering/Combating the Financing of Terrorism (AML/CFT) Policy and Procedure Manual' 2018, para. 33.0.

this requirement by using qualified persons who are not involved in the function that is tested.

The persons conducting the AML/CFT testing should report directly to the board of directors or to a designated board committee consisting primarily or completely of outside directors.

Those persons responsible for conducting an objective independent evaluation of the written AML/CFT Compliance Programme should perform testing for specific compliance with the FATF Recommendations (Recommendation 1). They are required to also evaluate pertinent management information systems (MIS). The audit has to be risk-based and must evaluate the quality of risk management for all the financial institution's operations, departments and subsidiaries.

Independent testing should (at a minimum) include:

- **The evaluation of the overall adequacy and effectiveness of the AML/CFT Compliance Programme, including policies, procedures and processes.** This evaluation will contain an explicit statement about the AML/CFT compliance programme's overall adequacy and effectiveness and compliance with applicable regulatory requirements. At the very least, the audit should contain sufficient information for the reviewer (e.g. an Examiner, review auditor or Financial Intelligence Unit officer) to reach a conclusion about the overall quality of the AML/CFT Compliance Programme;

- A review of the financial institution's risk assessment for reasonableness given the institution's risk profile (products, services, customers, entities and geographic locations);

- Appropriate risk-based transaction testing to verify the financial institution's adherence to the Financial Action Task Force record keeping and rendition of returns requirements on Politically Exposed Persons (PEPs), STRs and CTRs information sharing requests;

- An evaluation of management's efforts to resolve violations and deficiencies noted in previous audits and regulatory examinations, including progress in addressing outstanding supervisory actions (if applicable);

- A review of staff training for adequacy, accuracy and completeness;

- A review of the effectiveness of the suspicious transaction monitoring systems (are they manual, automated or a combination?) used for AML/CFT compliance. Related reports may include, but are not limited to:

    - ❖ Suspicious transaction monitoring reports;
    - ❖ Large currency aggregation reports;
    - ❖ Monetary instrument records;
    - ❖ Funds transfer records;
    - ❖ Non-sufficient funds (NSF) reports;
    - ❖ Large balance fluctuation reports;
    - ❖ Account relationship reports;

- An assessment of the overall process for identifying and reporting suspicious transaction, including a review of filed or prepared STRs to determine their accuracy, timeliness, completeness and effectiveness of the institution's policy; and

- An assessment of the integrity and accuracy of MIS used in the AML/CFT Compliance Programme. MIS includes reports used to identify and extract data on the large currency transactions, aggregate daily currency transactions, funds-transfer transactions, monetary instrument sales transactions and analytical and trend reports.

The auditors' reports should include their documentation on the scope of the audit, procedures performed, transaction testing completed and findings of the review.

All audit documentation and work-papers should be made available for the Examiner to review. Any violations, policy and/or procedures exceptions or other deficiencies noted during the audit should be included in the audit report and reported to the board of directors or its designated committee in a timely manner.

The board or designated committee and the audit staff are required to track the deficiencies observed in the auditors' report and document the corrective actions recommended and taken.[160]

[160]Central Bank of Nigeria's Anti-Money Laundering/Combating the Financing of Terrorism (AML/CFT) Risk Based Supervision (RBS) Framework, 2011, para. 5.1.

5.8. KNOW YOUR EMPLOYEE PROGRAM

Knowing your employees is as important as knowing your customers. An insider can pose the same fraud/money laundering threat as a customer, and a criminally co-opted financial institution's employee might facilitate fraud and money laundering.[161]

A Know Your Employee (KYE) program means that the financial institution has a program in place that allows it to understand an employee's background, conflicts of interest and susceptibility to fraud/money laundering complicity. Policies, procedures, internal controls, job descriptions, code of conduct/ethics, levels of authority, compliance with personnel laws and regulations, accountability, dual control, and other deterrents should be firmly in place.

5.8.1 BACKGROUND SCREENING OF PROSPECTIVE AND CURRENT EMPLOYEES

Background screening of prospective and current employees, especially for criminal history, is essential to keeping out unwanted employees and identifying those to be removed. While some foresee legal requirements for mandatory background screening by employers, it is still a matter of employer discretion in most industries.

KYE information such as background information should be obtained prior to job interview, during job interview and just before offer of employment. Any serious gap observed must be documented and should form part of the basis for offer of employment. After acceptance of offer, but before confirmation;

[161] SSA ZAIDI (2015), 'Banks need to follow Know Your Employees norms for robust internal AML control systems', Available at: https://www.moneylife.in/article/banks-need-to-follow-know-your-employees-norms-for-robust-internal-aml-control-systems/44095.html (accessed 15 February 2018).

background screening checks must be conducted to verify the identity of employees. All information supplied by prospective employees must be verified during probation. Any change in such information, including marital status and additional qualifications obtained during the period must be verified against appropriate documents and issuing institutions.[162]

The pre-employment background screening process can be an effective risk-management tool by providing management with a degree of certainty that the information provided by the applicant is true and correct, and that the potential employee does not have a criminal record. Used effectively, the pre-employment background screening process may reduce turnover by verifying that the potential employee has the requisite skills, certification, license or degree for the position; deter theft and embezzlement; and prevent litigation over hiring practices. Financial institutions should verify that contractors are subject to screening procedures similar to those used by financial institutions in the United Kingdom.

There are costs associated with developing and implementing an effective screening process. However, absent an effective screening process, a financial institution may incur significant expenses from recruiting, hiring and training unqualified individuals based upon their skill sets or backgrounds. These individuals may have to be replaced due to an inability to perform assigned duties or for other reasons.

The Federal Deposit Insurance Corporation (FDIC), a U.S. regulator, has provided guidance on employee screening in its paper "Pre-Employment Background Screening: Guidance on

---

[162] FCMB (2013), 'FCMB Enterprise Risk Management (Compliance Risk Management) Know Your Customer, Anti-Money Laundering and Countering Financing of Terrorism and Proliferation Manual', Available at: http://www.fcmb.com/sites/default/files/NEW-AML-POLICY-1.pdf (accessed 15 February 2018).

Developing an Effective Pre-Employment Background Screening Process".

According to the FDIC, Management should develop a risk-focused approach to determining when pre-employment background screening is considered appropriate or when the level of screening should be increased, based upon the position and responsibilities associated with a particular position. The sensitivity of the position or the access level of an individual staff member may warrant additional background screening, which should include verification of references, experience, education and professional qualifications. Furthermore, management should verify the applicant's identity. An on-going approach to screening should be considered for specific positions, as circumstances change, or for a comprehensive review of departmental staff over a period of time. Management should also have a policy that addresses appropriate actions when a pre-employment or subsequent screening detects information contrary to what the applicant or employee provided.

Section 19 of the Federal Deposit Insurance Act prohibits any person who has been convicted of any criminal offence involving dishonesty or a breach of trust or money laundering, or has agreed to enter into a pretrial diversion or similar program in connection with a prosecution, from becoming or continuing as an institution-affiliated party; owning or controlling, directly or indirectly, an insured institution; or otherwise participating, directly or indirectly, in the conduct of the affairs of an insured institution without the prior written consent of the FDIC. Note that consultants who participate in the conduct of the affairs of an insured institution may be subject to **Section 19**. Therefore, a pre-employment background screening process should be established by all financial institutions that, at a minimum, uncovers information regarding a job applicant's convictions and program entries to ensure that only appropriate persons are employed.

5.8.2 MONITORING OF EMPLOYEES

Once a business relationship has been established with an employee, financial institutions must conduct ongoing monitoring of the business relationship in accordance with the assessed level of risk. Financial institutions must ensure that employees are subject to effective systems for monitoring. Tools like modern employee monitoring software are a new implementation.

Financial institutions may monitor their employees for suspicious activity. The following examples are red flags that, when encountered, may warrant additional scrutiny. The mere presence of a red flag is not by itself evidence of criminal activity. Closer scrutiny should help to determine whether the activity is suspicious or one for which there does not appear to be a reasonable business or legal purpose:

i. Employee exhibits a lavish lifestyle that cannot be supported by his or her salary;

ii. Employee fails to conform to recognized policies, procedures and processes, particularly in private banking;

iii. Employee is reluctant to take a vacation;

iv. Employee exaggerates the credentials, background or financial ability and resources of a customer in written reports the bank requires;

v. Employee frequently overrides internal controls or established approval authority or circumvents policy;

vi. Employee uses company resources to further private interests;

vii. Employee assists transactions where the identity of the ultimate beneficiary or counter party is undisclosed.[163]

[163] Esoimeme, E.E. (2015), 'The Risk-Based Approach to Combating Money Laundering and Terrorist Financing', Eric Press; Available on Amazon: https://www.amazon.co.uk/Risk-Based-Combating-Laundering-Terrorist-Financing/dp/9789486030/ref=sr_1_2?ie=UTF8&qid=1437508453&sr=8-2&keywords=ehi+eric+esoimeme

CHAPTER 6

MEASURING THE EFFECTIVENESS OF RISK CONTROL MEASURES

Business enterprises should make particular efforts to track the effectiveness of their responses to impacts on individuals from groups or populations that may be at heightened risk of vulnerability or marginalization.[164]

Tracking should be integrated into relevant internal reporting processes. Business enterprises might employ tools they already use in relation to other issues. This could include performance contracts and reviews as well as surveys and audits, using gender-disaggregated data where relevant.[165] Operational-level grievance mechanisms can also provide important feedback on the effectiveness of the business enterprise's human rights due diligence from those directly affected.[166]

To assist tracking in their extended supply chain, in 2017 **Unilever** created an Integrated Social Sustainability Dashboard giving the number of non-conformances for each fundamental principle of the Responsible Sourcing Policy (RSP), broken down by cluster, category and portfolio. **Unilever** uses this dashboard to capture information on salient issue hotspots, allowing them to prioritise,

---

[164] United Nations (UN) 'Guiding Principles on Business and Human Rights' 2011, Principle 20 Commentary.

[165] United Nations (UN) 'Guiding Principles on Business and Human Rights' 2011, Principle 20 Commentary.

[166] United Nations (UN) 'Guiding Principles on Business and Human Rights' 2011, Principle 29.

build guidance, produce webinars, and support regions and portfolios where the need is greatest.

Dashboard results are shared with all procurement Vice Presidents, Directors and Managers. In those regions at highest risk, **Unilever** ask their auditors to focus on the identification of forced labour, emphasising this during their regular meetings with them and providing guidance on the retention of documents and other items of value. **Unilever** also provide guidance for Unilever Procurement in order to drive awareness and understanding of this issue, and to present best practices to avoid issues leading to modern slavery and forced labour.[167]

BOX 6.1: RISK-BASED AUDIT PROGRAMMES

Senior management will need to have a means of independently validating the development and operation of the risk assessment and management processes and related internal controls, and obtaining appropriate comfort that the adopted risk-based methodology reflects the risk profile of the company. This independent testing and reporting should be conducted by, for example, the internal audit department, external auditors, specialist consultants or other qualified parties who are not involved in the implementation or operation of the company's anti-modern slavery (AMS) compliance programme.

Independent testing should assess the commercial organisation's risk assessment for reasonableness given the institution's risk profile (products, services, suppliers, entities and geographic locations). External auditors should be allowed to carry out a review of staff training measures for adequacy, accuracy and completeness. An assessment of the overall process for identifying and reporting slavery like practices in the supply chain, including

[167] Unilever (2018), 'Modern Slavery and Human Trafficking Statement', Available at: https://www.unilever.com/Images/unilever-slavery-and-human-trafficking-statement-2018_tcm244-521391_en.pdf (accessed 29 June 2019).

a review of the whistleblowing reports to determine their accuracy, timeliness, completeness and effectiveness should be carried out by external auditors, specialist consultants or other qualified parties who are not involved in the implementation or operation of the company's AMS compliance programme.

Independent testing should be risk-based (focusing attention on higher-risk suppliers, products and services); should evaluate the adequacy of the commercial organisation's overall AMS programme and the quality of risk management for the commercial organisation's operations, departments and subsidiaries; include comprehensive procedures and testing; and cover all activities.

While the frequency of audit is not specifically defined in any statute, a sound practice is for the company to conduct independent testing generally every 12 to 18 months or commensurate with the modern slavery/human rights risk profile of the institution.

The persons conducting the AMS testing should report directly to the board of directors or to a designated board committee consisting primarily or completely of outside directors.

It should be noted that the risk-based auditing will enable the board of directors and auditors to use the institution's risk assessment to focus its scope of audit on the areas of greatest concern. The testing should assist the board of directors and management in identifying areas of weakness or areas where there is a need for enhancements or stronger controls.

The board or designated committee and the audit staff are required to track the deficiencies observed in the auditors' report and document the corrective actions recommended and taken.

6.1 MONITORING EFFECTIVENESS OF RISK CONTROL MEASURES USING KEY PERFORMANCE INDICATORS

Performance indicators are important in driving the performance of a business and shaping the way it operates. They can also affect how exposed the business is to the risk of modern slavery.

The direction and focus of particular performance incentives (such as that Sourcing Directors should buy the lowest cost products, that can be shipped in the fastest time) may influence and create a modern slavery risk if not managed carefully. This should be considered when improving internal management performance indicators and should be linked to the organisation's risk assessment.

For example, a business could set targets for:

— Training and capacity building of staff about modern slavery issues, measuring changes in awareness of risk; appropriate decision-making and swift action, as appropriate;

— Grievance procedures and whistle-blowing procedures for workers and employees if cases are suspected or found;

— Visibility, leverage and oversight of suppliers in relevant goods and services supply chains.

Carefully designed Key Performance Indicators (KPIs) could help a business to demonstrate as clearly as possible if they are making progress over time in preventing modern slavery in their business or supply chains.[168]

[168] Home Office (2015 but Updated in 2018), 'Transparency in Supply Chains etc. A practical guide', Available at:
https://assets.publishing.service.gov.uk/government/uploads/system/uploads/attachment_data/

Kingfisher PLC., monitor the effectiveness of their ethical audit programme for production sites supplying goods for resale using a number of indicators.

These include:

— Percentage of sites according to audit grades;

— Number of sites that failed to comply with **Kingfisher PLC's** minimum standards and the number of these which have been remedied;

— Top non-conformances identified by category.[169]

In line with their first two statements **Wm Morrison Supermarkets PLC.,** continue to measure their performance based on four indicators:

• Reported incidences of modern slavery in their supply chains and their response;

• Third party ethical audits undertaken on their own brand and exclusive sites;

• Colleagues and suppliers who have undertaken modern slavery awareness training; and

• Collaborative improvement action undertaken in specific areas of their supply chain.[170]

---

file/649906/Transparency_in_Supply_Chains_A_Practical_Guide_2017.pdf (accessed 25 June 2019).

[169] Kingfisher (2018/19), 'Modern Slavery Act Transparency Statement', Available at: https://www.kingfisher.com/content/dam/kingfisher/Corporate/Documents/Sustainability/2019/Kingfisher%20MSA%20Statement%202018%2019.pdf.downloadasset.pdf (accessed 29 June 2019).

[170] Wm Morrison Supermarkets PLC. (2018/2019), 'Modern Slavery Act Statement', Available at: https://www.morrisons-corporate.com/globalassets/corporatesite/corporate-

National Grid PLC., measure the effectiveness of their internal ethics programme through their Employee Engagement Survey by asking a series of questions, including how aware employees are of their procedures and how confident individuals feel about speaking up and that their concerns will be acted upon. **National Grid PLC.,** survey results are good and continue to improve. Within their business **National Grid PLC.,** Ethics Champions use the survey results to develop action plans to improve on areas highlighted by the survey.[171]

British American Tobacco had made a considerable effort in 2017 to improve the robustness of their approach, including their strengthened Standards of Business Conduct (SoBC) compliance procedures and training, launch of their *Speak Up* website and hotlines and their new human rights e-learning course.

British American Tobacco's key performance indicators include:

— Reported incidents and results of investigations into suspected improper conduct contrary to their Standards;

— Number, and results, of reviews and audits conducted as part of their due diligence processes for their suppliers and business operations;

— Number of employees who have completed their annual compliance sign-off for their SoBC; and

responsibility/documents/2018/morrisons_modern_slavery_act_2019_final.pdf (accessed 29 June 2019).

[171] National Grid (2018), 'Our statement on slavery and human trafficking', Available at: https://www.nationalgrideso.com/sites/eso/files/documents/14842_NG_Modern_Slavery_A4_AW08_INT1%20%281%29.pdf (accessed 29 June 2019).

— Number of farmers who have received training and communications on human rights and forced labour issues.[172]

Business enterprises should review their policies and procedures on an ongoing basis to ensure they remain effective and identify opportunities to further enhance and strengthen their approach. This includes regular monitoring by their Board Audit Committee, as well as by the regional audit and Corporate Social Responsibility (CSR) committees, Operations Sustainability Forum, chaired by its Group Operations Director, and Supply Chain Due Diligence Governance Committee.[173]

British Telecommunications PLC., check how they are measuring up against their business standards – including The Way they Work – in a number of ways. **British Telecommunications PLC's** Line of Business Audit and Risk Committees and Regional Governance Committees monitor how many people complete their mandatory training at least quarterly against their targets. Mandatory training reports (which include The Way We Work course) go to their Operating Committee and to other parts of their business each month.

British Telecommunications PLC., Human Rights Steering Group monitors their approach to human rights; they regularly update their Operating Committee and Board. They have set up a cross-functional team to look at how they address modern slavery and human trafficking. It's made up of people from legal,

[172] British American Tobacco (2017), 'Modern Slavery Act Statement', Available at: https://www.bat.com/group/sites/uk__9d9kcy.nsf/vwPagesWebLive/DOAK8P7C/$FILE/medMDAWUNCY.pdf?openelement (accessed 29 June 2019); British American Tobacco (2018), 'Modern Slavery Statement', Available at: https://www.bat.com/group/sites/uk__9d9kcy.nsf/vwPagesWebLive/DOAK8P7C/$FILE/medMDBA3JHG.pdf?openelement (accessed 29 June 2019).

[173] Burberry Group PLC. (2018/19), 'Transparency in the Supply Chain and Modern Slavery Statement', Available at: https://www.burberryplc.com/en/site-services/transparency-in-the-supply-chain-and-modern-slavery-statement.html (accessed 29 June 2019).

governance, compliance, policy, human resources and procurement.

Every year they report publicly on their ethical procurement key performance indicator. It tracks how effective **British Telecommunications PLC.,** are doing in following up responses to their Sourcing with Human Dignity questionnaire from high and medium risk suppliers. **British Telecommunications PLC.,** also track the number of Speak Up reports every year and their measures of employees' awareness of ethical issues.[174]

[174] British Telecommunications PLC. (2017/18), 'Modern Slavery Act Transparency Statement', Available at: https://www.btplc.com/Thegroup/Ourcompany/Ourvalues/ModernSlaveryAct/Modern-Slavery-Act-Statement-2018.pdf (accessed 29 June 2019).

APPENDIX 1

THE 2018 GLOBAL SLAVERY INDEX

The 2018 Global Slavery Index provides a country by country ranking of the number of people in modern slavery, an analysis of the actions governments are taking to respond, and the factors that make people vulnerable.

OVERVIEW

It is a confronting reality that even in the present day, men, women and children all over the world remain victims of modern slavery. They are bought and sold in public markets, forced to marry against their will and provide labour under the guise of "marriage," forced to work inside clandestine factories on the promise of a salary that is often withheld, or on fishing boats where men and boys toil under threats of violence. They are forced to work on construction sites, in stores, on farms, or in homes as maids. Labour extracted through force, coercion, or threats produces some of the food we eat, the clothes we wear, and the footballs we kick. The minerals that men, women, and children have been made to extract from mines find their way into cosmetics, electronics, and cars, among many other products.

This is modern slavery. It is widespread and pervasive, often unacknowledged, and its extent was previously believed to be unknowable. In 2017, the **Walk Free Foundation** and the **International Labour Organization (ILO)**, together with the **International Organization for Migration (IOM)**, developed the Global Estimates of Modern Slavery, which provides the best available data and information about the scale and regional distribution of modern slavery. These estimates provide the starting point for this report, the Global Slavery Index. The national estimates presented here were calculated by the Walk Free Foundation on the basis of a predictive model that accounted for individual and country-level risk factors and resulting prevalence estimates were then adjusted to ensure regional totals were aligned with the regional totals in the Global Estimates of Modern Slavery.

An analysis of the national estimates in this Global Slavery Index confirms that modern slavery is a crime that affects all countries globally, including, perhaps surprisingly, highly developed countries. While an understanding of prevalence is critical to formulating sound policy responses to modern slavery, equally important is building our understanding of what is driving prevalence. For this reason, the national prevalence estimates are analysed in the context of results of the Vulnerability Model, which provides important context for understanding the national results.

In this chapter, we also consider the important issue of government responses to modern slavery. The Government Response Index provides a comparable measure of the steps being taken by 181 countries across 104 indicators of good practice. An analysis of these findings confirms that while there has been important progress made since the publication of the last Global Slavery Index in 2016, there are still critical gaps and responses to them need to be developed.

Overall, our findings confirm that modern slavery remains a critical issue for all countries. Just as responding to environmental concerns cannot be the task of one country alone, responding to modern slavery is a challenge that requires commitment and effort from all countries.

WHAT DOES THE DATA TELL US ABOUT MODERN SLAVERY?

It is widely acknowledged that measuring modern slavery is a difficult undertaking, not least because no single source provides suitable and reliable data on all forms of modern slavery. In developing the Global Estimates of Modern Slavery, the Walk Free Foundation and the ILO adopted a methodology that combined survey research involving face-to-face interviews with more than 71,000 people in 53 local languages with administrative data on victims of trafficking who had been assisted by the IOM. An estimate of forced labour imposed by state authorities was derived from validated sources and systematic review of comments from the ILO supervisory bodies with regard to the ILO Conventions on forced labour.

An estimated 40.3 million men, women, and children were victims of modern slavery on any given day in 2016. Of these, 24.9 million people were in forced labour and 15.4 million people were living in a forced marriage. Women and girls are vastly over-represented, making up 71 percent of victims. Modern slavery is most prevalent in Africa, followed by the Asia and the Pacific region.

Although these are the most reliable estimates of modern slavery to date, we know they are conservative as significant gaps in data remain. The current Global Estimates do not cover all forms of modern slavery; for example, organ trafficking, child soldiers, or child marriage that could also constitute forced marriage are not able to be adequately measured at this time. Further, at a broad regional level there is high confidence in the estimates in all but one of the five regions. Estimates of modern slavery in the Arab States are affected by substantial gaps in the available data. Given this is a region that hosts 17.6 million migrant workers, representing more than one-tenth of all migrant workers in the world and one in three workers in the Arab States, and one in which forced marriage is reportedly widespread, the current estimate is undoubtedly a significant underestimate.

NOTE ON RECRUITMENT OF CHILDREN BY ARMED FORCES AND ORGAN TRAFFICKING

Conceptually, the practices of recruiting child soldiers and trafficking persons for removal of their organs fall under the concept of modern slavery. Recruitment of children by armed forces and groups is expressly prohibited by various treaties, while the UN Trafficking Protocol specifically designates organ removal as a form of exploitation associated with the crime of trafficking in persons. Unfortunately, due to the limits of existing data, it was not possible for the Global Estimates of Modern Slavery to measure and include the scale of trafficking for organ removal or the recruitment child soldiers. Accordingly, the estimates in this Global Slavery Index do not capture these practices.

This, however, should not be taken as an indication of diminished importance of these forms of modern slavery. The following sections provide a brief overview of the existing state of knowledge on both trafficking for organ removal and recruitment of child soldiers.

TRAFFICKING IN PERSONS FOR ORGAN REMOVAL

While there is only limited information compiled globally on trafficking persons for the purpose of organ removal, it is possible to get some insight by looking at the broader statistics on organ transplants. An estimated 126,670 solid organ transplants were performed worldwide in 2015. The **World Health Organization (WHO)** conservatively estimates that the illegal organ trade comprises approximately 10 percent of global transplant activity. Revenue from the illegal trade is estimated to range between US$840 million and US$1.7 billion. The black-market organ trade has been documented in countries as diverse as India, Pakistan, Kosovo, and the Philippines. What is unclear is the extent to which coercion is being applied, and in what circumstances. It is, however, certain that unscrupulous traffickers and brokers target vulnerable people, including irregular migrants and refugees on the move.

It appears from the limited number of cases that have been investigated and prosecuted that international brokers are pivotal to the series of transactions involved in this crime, particularly in terms of receiving the highest profits. It is usually these brokers who fix the price for the illegal transplant, as well as the "fee" for the organ supplier, dependent on the broker's insight into the "market" and the circumstances of the recipients.

Poverty and corruption are two of the principal underlying factors in organ trafficking. Sellers give up their organs out of economic necessity and, for most buyers, who may have been waiting on legitimate transplant lists for months, desperation and frustration usually push them to commit the illegal act. In some parts of India, poor people use their kidneys as collateral for money lenders.

Researchers have documented instances of Kidneys sourced from the "kidney belt" region of southern India are sold to clients in Sri Lanka, the Gulf States, the UK, and the US.

Developed countries such as the US, Canada, Australia, and the UK receive organs from most of the world's developing countries, including India, China, the Philippines, and Pakistan. Organ transplants tend to be carried out more in wealthy countries due to their better economic conditions and technological capabilities. Sale of organs is illegal in many developing countries, with the exception of Iran where paid donation is permitted but strictly regulated.

RECRUITMENT OF CHILDREN BY ARMED FORCES

The use of children in armed conflicts is clearly and directly linked to the trafficking and sale of children and is therefore globally recognised as a form of modern slavery. Due to the hidden nature of this crime, scholars have argued in the past that "the total number of child soldiers in each country, let alone the global figure, is not only unknown, but unknowable." Similarly, it is noted in the Global Estimates of Modern Slavery that some forms of modern slavery which did not involve elements of forced labour (such as organ trafficking) are not captured due to a lack of reliable data.

One obvious but often overlooked prerequisite for the involvement of children in armed conflicts is the presence and extent of conflict around the world. That is, when conflicts persist along with the presence of armed groups open to child involvement, then there continue to be child soldiers. Additionally, the extraordinary complexity surrounding the world's current conflicts has reportedly contributed to an increase in the number of children at risk.

Beyond those necessary conditions, children may become involved in armed conflicts for a host of interrelated reasons. Some of the specific factors that influence child involvement in conflict include physical and food security, family and peer networks (children may be heavily influenced by pre-existing networks, such as where other family members have joined armed forces), financial incentives, coercion, status, and cultural and religious identity.

Although there are no reliable estimates on the number of children involved in armed conflicts, the UN provides some information on documented cases of children involved in armed conflict. In 2016, there were globally at least 4,000 instances of children recruited and used in armed conflict by government forces and more than 11,500 such instances by non-state armed groups, notably in Africa, Asia, and Latin America. This reflects cases recorded in Afghanistan, the Central African Republic, Colombia, Democratic Republic of the Congo (DRC), Iraq, Lebanon, Libya, Mali, Myanmar, Nigeria, Somalia, Sudan, Syria and the Philippines.

Notwithstanding these critical data gaps, the 2018 Global Slavery Index presents national-level estimates for 167 countries based on the proportion of the population that is estimated to be in some form of modern slavery.

The 10 countries with the highest prevalence of modern slavery are

1. **North Korea**
2. **Eritrea**
3. **Burundi**

4. **the Central African Republic**
5. **Afghanistan**
6. **Mauritania**
7. **South Sudan**
8. **Pakistan**
9. **Cambodia**
10. **Iran**

An analysis of the ten countries with highest prevalence indicates a connection between modern slavery and two major external drivers- highly repressive regimes and conflict. As the data in this Global Slavery Index confirm, several of the countries with the highest prevalence of modern slavery – the Central African Republic, Afghanistan, South Sudan, and Pakistan – also score above 90 percent in the Vulnerability Model, which measures systemic, individual, and environmental risk factors in 167 countries. The interplay between modern slavery and risk factors is discussed further below.

Despite a change in methodology, Mauritania and Cambodia remained in the top 10 in 2018. Mauritania continues to host a high proportion of people living in modern slavery. The national survey confirmed the existence of forced marriage and forced labour. Forced labour was found to occur in different sectors, to both males and females across different age groups and geographic regions. The practice is entrenched in Mauritanian society with slave status being inherited, and deeply rooted in social castes and the wider social system. Those owned by masters often have no freedom to own land, cannot claim dowries from their marriages nor inherit property or possessions from their families. Despite improvements to legislation in 2015, which strengthens the provisions on slavery, allows third parties to bring cases on behalf of slavery victims, and establishes special tribunals to investigate slavery crimes, progress in Mauritania remains slow. There are reports that police and the judiciary are reluctant to implement the new legislation and that several cases of slavery have been reclassified as lesser crimes, although the ILO Committee of Experts notes some positive steps in recent times. In Cambodia, men, women, and children are known to be exploited in various forms of modern slavery – including forced labour, debt bondage and forced marriage. While the prevalence of forced sexual exploitation and forced begging in the country has been reported previously, the national survey also pointed to forced labour in manufacturing, farming, construction and domestic work. In Cambodia, the government has been slow to improve their response to modern slavery.

KEY TRENDS

Three main trends emerge from the national estimates of modern slavery.

First:

Many of the countries with the highest estimated levels of prevalence are marked by conflict – Eritrea, Burundi, Central African Republic, Afghanistan, South Sudan, and Pakistan all appear among the 10 countries with highest prevalence. The role that conflict plays in compounding vulnerability to slavery is widely recognised and finds support in an assessment of vulnerability at the national level. In the Walk Free Foundation's assessment of vulnerability across five dimensions – governance issues, lack of basic needs, inequality, disenfranchised groups, and effects of conflict – countries with high vulnerability due to effects of conflict generally have higher vulnerability scores across the remaining four dimensions. This is not surprising given the disruption to, and often complete dismantling of, the rule of law, as well as damage to critical infrastructure and limited access to education, health care, and food and water as a result of conflict. Similarly, the Walk Free Foundation's government response data highlight the disruption caused by conflict to government functions. Eritrea, Central African Republic, Pakistan, and Iran all score lowly on government responses, while Afghanistan and South Sudan were excluded from the government response assessment this year due to significant ongoing conflict.

Second:

The improved measurement of state-imposed forced labour reveals the substantial impact this form of slavery has on populations. **The three countries with highest prevalence – North Korea, Eritrea, and Burundi – stand out has having a very high prevalence of state-imposed forced labour**. State-imposed forced labour includes citizens recruited by their state authorities to participate in agriculture or construction work for purposes of economic development, young military conscripts forced to perform work that is not of military nature, those forced to perform communal services that were not decided upon at the community level and do not benefit them, or prisoners forced to work against their will. In North Korea, one in 10 people are in modern slavery with the vast majority being forced to work by the state. See "Spotlight: Forced Labour in North Korea" on this page for further analysis.

Governments that regularly impose forced labour on their citizens perform poorly across other measures of vulnerability. For example, they tend to be more autocratic, are believed to have lower quality policy and regulations, perform below the global average in ensuring access to necessities such as food and water and health care, and typically do not protect the rights of highly discriminated groups in the broader population. **More specifically, the presence of state-imposed forced labour undermines at best, and at worst renders meaningless, any government response to modern slavery.** North Korea has the weakest response to modern slavery globally due to the state's role in forced labour both within North Korea and of North Koreans abroad. The abuse of civic duties in Burundi and conscription in Eritrea also threatens any concrete actions these governments may be taking.

Third:

The prevalence of modern slavery in highly developed, high-income countries is higher than previously understood. This learning reflects improvements in the methodology, in particular, the ability to systematically count cases at the point of exploitation which was made possible with a substantially larger number of surveys. For example, if an Indian man reported being exploited in the construction sector in the United Arab Emirates (UAE), that case was attributed to UAE. In the five-year reference period for the estimates, while surveys were conducted in 48 countries, men, women, and children were reported to have been exploited in 79 countries. This results in higher estimates in countries such as the United States, Australia, United Kingdom, Germany, France, the Netherlands, and several other European nations.

While these findings emphasise the responsibility of highly developed countries to act, the estimates reveal only part of the picture. **It is important to note that the governments in several of**

these countries - the Netherlands, the United Kingdom, the United States, Sweden, Belgium, Croatia, Spain, Norway, Portugal, and Montenegro – are also taking the most action to respond to modern slavery. These countries also tend to have lower vulnerability scores across all measures, which reflects effective governance across a broad range of areas and, in particular, a strong capacity to provide protections for vulnerable subgroups and ensure access to necessities such as food and water. Collectively, these factors mitigate risks of enslavement for citizens. However, higher prevalence of modern slavery among these countries suggests that critical gaps remain around the implementation of existing legislation and policies and in tackling the root causes of exploitation. It is very likely that this reflects the reality that, even in countries with seemingly strong systems, there are gaps in protections, with certain groups such as irregular migrants, the homeless, or minorities subject to intense and widespread discrimination and typically less able to access protection. In Europe, which has had a very strong response to modern slavery, there has been a tightening of migration policy and a reduction in the protections available to migrants in recent years. While in part this is a response to the current refugee and migrant crisis, this also renders these individuals more vulnerable to modern slavery. Similar approaches have also been adopted in the US and Australia.

On the other hand, when our assessment of government responses is correlated against GDP (PPP) per capita, we find that some highly developed, high-income countries have taken limited action to respond to modern slavery. Countries including Qatar, Singapore, Saudi Arabia, and the UAE have taken limited action despite high levels of resources. These countries tend to perform relatively well in comparison with other countries in the region on overall vulnerability scores given their greater capacity to address areas of critical need for citizens. However, there remain gaps in protections for migrant populations, often the most vulnerable groups to modern slavery in these countries. Even a seemingly strong response is undermined where there are subgroups of people who suffer high levels of discrimination, as they are likely to be "left behind" where responses to slavery are concerned. This can be linked to a lack of legal status in a country, for example, women in Saudi Arabia, domestic workers who fall outside the protection of labour laws in most Gulf countries, or the stateless hill tribes of Thailand and the Rohingya people of Myanmar, the latter of whom are at the center of the world's fastest growing refugee crisis.

The 10 countries with the largest estimated absolute numbers of people in modern slavery include some of the world's most populous. Collectively, these 10 countries – India, China, Pakistan, North Korea, Nigeria, Iran, Indonesia, Democratic Republic of the Congo, Russia, and the Philippines – account for 60 percent of people living in modern slavery and over half the world's population.

DATA LIMITATIONS

While regional estimates were presented in the Global Estimates of Modern Slavery, critical gaps in available data were noted. These are particularly problematic in the Arab States, where only two national surveys were undertaken, none of which were in the Gulf Cooperation Council (GCC) countries, despite the incidence of forced labour reported there by various sources in such sectors as domestic work and construction. Further, measurement of forced marriage among residents of countries within the region is almost impossible where there are no surveys at all. Taken together, these gaps point to a significant underestimate of the extent of modern slavery in this region.

Similarly, it is typically not possible to survey in countries that are experiencing profound and current conflict, such as Syria, Iraq, Yemen, Libya, South Sudan, and parts of Nigeria and Pakistan. Yet it is known that conflict is a significant risk factor for modern slavery – the breakdown of the rule of law, the loss of social supports, and the disruption that occurs with conflict all increase risk of both forced labour and forced marriage. The lack of data from countries experiencing conflict means that modern slavery estimates in regions in which conflict countries are situated will understate the problem. While drawing on vulnerability data goes some way towards mitigating the impact of this gap, the need for better data in conflict countries remains an urgent research priority.

COMPARABILITY OF THE PREVALENCE ESTIMATES TO THE PREVIOUS GLOBAL SLAVERY INDEX

Due to substantial differences in scope, methodologies, and expanded data sources, prevalence estimates in the 2018 Global Slavery Index (GSI) are not directly comparable to the previous edition. Since 2014, nationally representative household surveys have formed the core element of the Walk Free Foundation's approach to measuring modern slavery. In 2016, our estimates were based on results of surveys in 25 countries through the Gallup World Poll, the results of which were extrapolated to countries with an equivalent risk profile. Although this represented the best data available at the time, measurements of forced sexual exploitation and children in modern slavery were identified as critical data gaps to address in future estimations.

In 2017, these gaps were addressed by adopting a combined methodological approach when developing the Global Estimates of Modern Slavery with the ILO and the IOM. This involved drawing on three sources of data: (1) The existing survey program was expanded to cover 48 surveys in 54 countries. To date, more than 71,000 people have been interviewed and the countries surveyed represent over half of the world's population. It is the most extensive survey program on modern slavery ever undertaken and forms the central component of the Global Estimates of Modern Slavery. (2) Administrative data from IOM's databases of assisted victims of trafficking. And (3) data derived from validated secondary sources and a systematic review of comments from the ILO supervisory bodies regarding ILO Conventions on forced labour. The Global Slavery Index 2018 uses the same data sources and regional and global estimates as its starting point.

As an example of the impact of changes in methodology on the comparability between the previous and current prevalence estimates, the 2016 Index estimated that around 18.3 million people were in modern slavery in India, whereas the 2018 Index estimates that there are around 8 million people living in modern slavery. This difference reflects the presentation of the number who experienced modern slavery on any given day in 2016 (a "stock" figure) as opposed to the number of people in slavery over a five-year period (a "flow" figure), as was presented in 2016. The present estimates also reflect the addition of forced sexual exploitation and children in modern slavery. For a fuller list of the changes to the methodology, refer to Appendix 2: Part B.

SPOTLIGHT: FORCED LABOUR IN NORTH KOREA

In 2017, the Walk Free Foundation partnered with researchers at the Leiden Asia Centre and the **Database Center for North Korean Human Rights (NKDB)** in an effort to learn more about the hidden reality regarding forced labour and other forms of modern slavery inside North Korea. As it is not possible to directly survey or otherwise collect data within North Korea, the research involved undertaking interviews with 50 defectors from North Korea who are living in South Korea.

Of the 50 people interviewed, all but one described situations they had been subjected to while living in North Korea that meet the international legal definition of "forced labour." In this sample, three key typologies of modern slavery emerged. First, repeated mobilisation by the government of children, and later adults, through mandatory, unpaid "communal labour" in agriculture, road building, and construction.

For children, this might involve daily work in agriculture, or a month of work at harvest time. The schools, and not the children, received payment for the work. If children did not participate, they would later be punished and criticised within the school itself. Participation could be avoided through paying bribes.

For adults, communal labour involved being mobilised for "battles" in which workers are sent to work for 70 or 100 days in a row. The penalty for refusal is a cut in food rations or the assessment of taxes.

For children, the forced mobilisation started at an early age and ranged from light agricultural duties to longer periods of hard labour, all of which was without pay:

When I was a teenager in the Youth League, I had to participate in the speed battles as part of the shock brigade at least once. I was mobilised to do construction on the Pyongyang Highway for six months. Respondent No. 7, female, adult

From the age of 13, every student is mobilised for farm work without exception. It lasts 40 days for the spring mobilisation and 30 days for the autumn one. Respondent No .10, male, adult

One adult male respondent described his experience with mobilisation as follows:

You cannot refuse. If the work unit leader orders you to go to work, you have to do it. If you don't, then your food rations are cut off. Respondent No .1, male, adult

The second typology was forced labour of the general population by the state. Almost all respondents in this sample indicated they had either not been paid for their work other than through provision of rations (which themselves can be refused or withheld as punishment) or, if they had been theoretically paid, wages were in fact withheld due to official donation drives and other deductions. As some workplaces exist but have no actual production, workers reported having to procure on their own the goods their workplaces are supposed to be producing so that the employer could show some output. Others paid fees to be registered as employees (to avoid being classified as unemployed and thereby risk being sent to a labour camp) but actually worked elsewhere (the so-called "8/3 workers"). To survive and cover the cost of holding their jobs, they would trade or otherwise sell their labour on the black market. All but one respondent noted that it was impossible to refuse or leave a job without permission, and any attempt to do this would result initially in loss of rations and then internment in a labour camp.

Respondents gave examples of some of the absurd situations they found themselves in as a result of both having to pay to work and pay to prop up the broken system:

On paper I was a labourer but in reality I did not work as one. It was a place that raised pigs to support the People's Army and shock brigades. It was supposed to raise pigs. But no one actually raised pigs there. There was no space to raise pigs there and no feed for them either. Since the labourers cannot work, they are required to pay a certain amount of money instead. Every month the labourers must give 2kg of pork to the management office. Respondent No. 23, female, adult

Compliance was backed up by the need to be employed, at risk of being sent to a labour camp. Respondents noted for example:

If you quit without receiving approval, you will be detained at a labour training camp. Respondent No. 30, male, adult

If I'd quit, I would be caught. And if I didn't go to work for more than two months and was caught as unemployed, I would be investigated by the police office and would be detained in a labour training camp. Usually, the period of detainment was six months. Respondent No. 38, male, adult

I couldn't quit my job. If I didn't go to work, I would be sent to a labour training camp. Respondent No. 44, male, adult

Finally, respondents also described forced labour inside labour camps. One respondent noted the following experience:

The work was hard. Gathering beans in the autumn was fine because I had done this kind of work, but because it was done in the labour camp and I did not have any freedom, that was the difficult part. It was difficult to work under surveillance. […] I couldn't use the toilet whenever I wanted, I had to ask for permission before using it. […] I got up at six in the morning and went to bed at ten in the evening. In the morning, I got up and cleaned the yard, then washed my face. They lined us up in the morning. The line-up officer talked with the head of the camp and distributed our work tasks. Respondent No. 8, female, adult

The sample for this research included two defectors who had worked both inside North Korea and for the North Korean government overseas. Both explained that their wages were withheld and, at most, some portion was paid to them (after three years, one received the equivalent of $55 for each month he worked; the second worked for three years to earn sufficient funds to live in North Korea for about three months). While being physically located overseas, they described their workplaces as exported North Korean environments in which the hierarchical structures and ideological sessions travelled with them.

While the study did not seek to examine the situation of North Korean women who have been forced to marry in China, one respondent (a member of the Workers Party of Korea with a well-positioned job in North Korea) did share the following experience that is relevant to understanding the complexities of this issue:

I didn't come to [South] Korea because I wanted to. I sent one person across the border. She was with her friend. She directly came to Korea but the broker sold her friend to a farm owner (in China) who was 20 years older than her. So she often pleaded to the broker to send her to South Korea and paid him for that. But all nine people who set out were caught in China and were repatriated back to North Korea. They mentioned my name when they were investigated about their escape route and helpers at Cheongjin police holding camp. After this, I had no choice but to leave North Korea so I left in a hurry. It was unimaginable that the arrested woman wouldn't divulge my name during the interrogation process and torture at the police holding camp, so I left right away. They put most serious responsibility and penalty for assisting people with their escape to South Korea. So there was much possibility that I could have been buried alive so I left. Respondent No. 27, Male, adult

To understand the experiences of these 50 men and women, it is necessary to understand the operating environment inside North Korea. Following the famine in the late 1990s and the collapse of the Public Distribution System for all but a minority of citizens, North Korean daily life has become a perverse mix of socialist rhetoric (in which the Supreme Leader and the state provide for its people) and market-based realities (in which the general population supports and funds the Supreme Leader and the State). As noted in interviews, key features that impact on degrees of freedom in working life inside North Korea include the following:

- All officially recognised work is centrally organised.
- Social class determines the nature of the employment you receive (along with your housing, access to education, and

other benefits). There are three main classes: the core class (the elite, party cadres, and their families), the wavering class (average North Koreans), and lastly the hostile class (including descendants of landlords or capitalists). Status can be and is inherited.

- The punishment for being unemployed or failing to attend work is internment in a labour camp.
- Workers are provided with rations for food and other necessities of life, which can also be withheld as punishment.
- While in theory all work involves a salary, in reality most wages remain unpaid. Respondents noted many cases where they had to in fact pay both to keep their job (to avoid being formally unemployed and then sent to a labour camp) and to cover the costs of production (when quotas or were not met or the workplace actually had no materials or production). To maintain their "employment" and to survive, they reported working on the black market, trading or selling whatever they could.
- Obtaining a job, keeping it, or switching jobs normally involves payment of bribes to officials.

As one defector explained that, while forced mobilisation is compulsory, it is equally possible to avoid mobilisation through bribery:

There is a certain mobilisation campaign that people should work for three years. There is mobilisation to Mt. Baekdu for making grass fields. People from the government would come to a certain region and mobilise residents for joint work for a large-scale construction project such as paving highways. I did not participate in such mobilisation. I paid money instead. I paid 50 North Korean won in 2008. Why should I work when I have money? Working there is extremely hard and people escape from there. Respondent No. 39, male, adult

The picture that emerges is as disturbing as it is perhaps unique. While gaining access to a wider sample of workers across North Korea itself is simply not possible, there is no reason to doubt that the first-hand experiences related this group reflect the brutal reality of modern slavery perpetrated by the state. They also described a broader system that they saw operating around them that not only involves state-sponsored forced labour, but also depends on these practices for its very survival. To read the report in full, see Pervasive, Punitive, and Predetermined: Understanding Modern Slavery in North Korea.

WHAT ARE GOVERNMENTS DOING TO ADDRESS MODERN SLAVERY?

Globally, governments have taken important strides in the fight against modern slavery since the publication of the 2016 Global Slavery Index. Overall, the Government Response Index suggests that national legal, policy, and programmatic responses to modern slavery are improving, with an increasing number of countries with a BBB and BB rating in 2018 over 2016, and fewer CCC and CC ratings. However, there are some responses that appear to be going backwards, with a small increase in the number of countries that were rated C or D in 2018 compared to 2016.

In 2018, 122 countries have criminalised human trafficking in line with the UN Trafficking Protocol, while only 38 countries have criminalised forced marriage. There are now 154 countries that provide services for victims, compared to 150 in 2016, although important gaps remain. Eighty-two countries report gaps in the provision of services to either migrants, men, and children, or a combination of these. More countries are now coordinating their responses, with a three percent increase in the number of countries implementing National Action Plans covering some, if not all, aspects of a modern slavery response. One of the more striking findings in 2018 is the growing government engagement with business and the increasing political interest in the investigation of government procurement, with 36 countries taking steps to investigate forced labour in private or public supply chains. This is a significant increase from the four governments identified in 2016.

This year, we have for the first time included data on all 53 Commonwealth countries in our government response database, bringing the total number of countries included in our assessment to 181. As data for the smaller island nations of the Commonwealth are limited, we have not provided an overall rating for these individual countries. However, taking these countries into account in our global analysis of key indicators does reveal an encouraging narrative: when including all Commonwealth countries, the number of countries criminalising human trafficking increases to 135, with 164 countries providing services to victims of modern slavery. Due to the ongoing conflict and extreme disruption to government, we have not included ratings for Afghanistan, Iraq, South Sudan, Syria, and Yemen this edition.

In 2018, the governments taking the most action to respond to modern slavery are:

1. The Netherlands

2. United States

3. United Kingdom

4. Sweden

5. Belgium

6. Croatia

7. Spain

8. Norway

9. Portugal

10. Montenegro.

These countries are characterised by strong political will, high levels of resources, and a strong civil society that holds these governments to account for their actions to respond to modern slavery. These results are similar to 2016, but with some slight shifts in the positioning of Australia downwards as Belgium moves upwards. While the positive conclusion of the Australian inquiry into an Australian Modern Slavery Act is to be commended, we strongly encourage the government to pass legislation that incorporates an Independent Commissioner. On the other hand, we welcome the issuance of public procurement guidelines in 2017 in Belgium which incorporate suggestions on how to implement ILO Conventions, including the abolition of forced labour and the pilot initiative looking at the application of ILO standards in the personal protective equipment sector in Ghent.

It is not just governments at the top of the table that are taking positive action to respond to modern slavery. Other countries are taking notable action, as well. Morocco and Côte d'Ivoire passed comprehensive trafficking legislation in 2016, which has resulted in improved ratings from CC to CCC and from CCC to B respectively. Chile has improved its victim protection mechanisms by launching the Blue Campaign, a website to help improve identification of victims, establishing guidelines to help first responders identify and refer victims, and supporting the implementation of the National Referral Mechanism. As a result, Chile has moved from a B to BBB rating.

As with the 2016 findings, when correlated against GDP (PPP) per capita, some countries stand out as taking relatively strong action when compared with those that have stronger economies. Countries including Georgia, Moldova, Senegal, Sierra Leone and Mozambique are taking positive steps to respond to this issue relative to their wealth. Sierra Leone's coordination body, the Inter-Agency Human Trafficking Task Force, resumed activities in 2015 and approved the 2015-2020 National Action Plan. In Georgia, the government adopted a victim-centred approach by establishing victim witness coordinators from the initial stages of investigations through the end of court proceedings.

Since the 2016 Index, more countries have proactively implemented reporting requirements for businesses to detail actions taken to investigate their supply chains for labour violations, including forced labour. Twenty-seven EU member states have fully transposed the EU non-financial reporting Directive **(Directive 2014/95/EU)** into domestic legislation. The Directive requires large companies to disclose certain information on the way they operate and manage social and environment challenges. Although not specific to forced labour, the Directive offers an opportunity for more businesses to demonstrate action taken to combat forced labour beyond those already reporting under the UK government's Modern Slavery Act. The first non-financial statements will be included in businesses' annual reports from 2018 onward.

Governments are beginning to recognise that public procurement is also at high risk of modern slavery. The United States leads the way with **Executive Orders 13627 (2012)** and **13126 (1999)**, which require mandatory reporting and due diligence from all federal government contractors and subcontractors. Guidelines and training on forced labour are provided to all government procurement officials, while the closure of a loophole in the **1930 Tariff Act (19 U.S.C. § 1307)** has meant that goods are regularly seized and inspected if they are believed to be produced with forced or child labour. In Europe, **Article 57 of Directive 2014/24/EU** allows for the exclusion of contractors from public procurement where there has been a conviction of human trafficking or child labour. At the time of writing, these have been transposed into domestic legislation of all European countries apart from Luxembourg and Austria. Interestingly, there is also evidence that the Chinese government has investigated incidents where subcontractors in government contracts have failed to pay wages and the Paraguayan National Secretariat for Children and Adolescents has an inter-institutional agreement with the National Bureau for Public Contracts to ensure that any goods or services procured by the government are not produced through child labour. Across **Organisation for Economic Co-operation and Development (OECD)** countries, general government procurement spending equalled nearly 12 percent of GDP in 2015. Tackling government supply chains to reduce instances of forced labour therefore has enormous potential to reduce the number of people in modern slavery.

Governments are increasingly collaborating with businesses to eradicate modern slavery. In 2017, the Bali Process launched the Bali Process Business and Government Forum (BPGBF), which is a subsidiary body to the existing intergovernmental Bali Process. The BPGBF is a cooperative initiative to combat modern slavery and human trafficking in the Indo-Pacific region. The Forum brings together government representatives from 45 countries, three United Nations organisations, and the private sector. The initial meeting provided a unique opportunity for information sharing and implementing partnerships with the joint goal of ending modern slavery. Looking ahead, the Forum is expected to have the joint outcome of promoting good business practices across the private sector while also encouraging legislative changes by government.

Countries have taken steps to strengthen criminal justice responses to modern slavery. As of 15th June 2018, **the 2014 Forced Labour Protocol** is in force in 17 countries, with an additional seven ratifications coming into force in the next 12 months. This is important as the **Forced Labour Protocol** brings the framework created by the **1930 Convention** on Forced Labour into the 21stcentury. The Indian government has taken recent action to reduce the worst forms of child labour by ratifying the **ILO Convention 182 on the Worst Forms of Child Labour**. In line with the Optional Protocols to the Convention on the Rights of the Child, 56 countries have criminalised the buying and selling of children for sex or sexual services, and 27 have criminalised the use of children in armed conflict. Despite these promising steps, in 64 countries penalties for modern slavery crimes remain disproportionate to their severity, as perpetrators can be penalised with a relatively small fine or conversely penalised with corporal punishment (itself a breach of international human rights standards).

The existence of legislation is not in itself enough to deter modern slavery crimes and in many cases the lack of effective implementation of legislation indicates a significant gap in a government response. While 145 countries have provided at least one training session since 2012 for their front-line police officers on identification of victims and investigation of modern slavery crimes, 11 of these did not subsequently identify any victims, suggesting poor execution or low quality of the training provided. Fewer countries have provided training to judges and prosecutors, with 108 and 109 governments respectively providing training for these groups since 2012. Regular training was provided to judges and prosecutors in South Africa, Bolivia, Jordan, and Serbia, among others, however there are reports that this has not resulted in the most stringent of sentences for identified traffickers and exploiters, with some evidence of suspended sentences or conviction for lesser crimes.

Access to justice and protection for identified victims has improved in some countries. For example, despite an overall poor response in Hong Kong, children and vulnerable witnesses may now give testimony via video conference. In Indonesia, the government has opened a child-friendly integrated public space in East Jakarta where child and adult victims of trafficking can report trafficking crimes to trained counsellors. Fifty-eight countries have a National Referral Mechanism for victims of modern slavery. In Albania, the establishment of a National Referral Mechanism has been supplemented by Standard Operating Procedures, that are used by regulatory and non-regulatory bodies that may come into contact with victims, including those covering teachers, doctors, and people working in the tourism sector. Since 2016, 118 governments have provided funding to shelters or victim support services. Longer-term reintegration services are less frequent, with 97 governments offering measures for foreign victims to remain within the country and 71 governments providing longer term support. Of those 97 countries, only 37 governments offered visas on humanitarian or other grounds not tied to participation in a court case.

While many positive actions were taken by governments around the world in 2018, those taking the least action to combat modern slavery are:

1. North Korea

2. Libya

3. Eritrea

4. Central African Republic

5. Iran

6. Equatorial Guinea

7. Burundi

8. Congo

9. Sudan

10. Mauritania.

Those countries with weaker responses to modern slavery are characterised by government complicity (as is the case in North Korea), low levels of political will (as is the case in Iran), fewer available resources (as is the case in Equatorial Guinea), or high levels of conflict (as is the case in Libya).

These results are broadly similar to our 2016 assessment, with some small improvements in Papua New Guinea, Guinea, Democratic Republic of the Congo, and Hong Kong. Following the launch of the 2016 Global Slavery Index, the Hong Kong government began to take some steps to recognise that modern slavery is a problem by training front-line police and establishing a specialised police force. The fact that the government is starting to respond is to be commended, however, more remains to be done, including criminalising of modern slavery offences and providing those exploited within Hong Kong with alternative options to deportation.

Responses in certain countries have worsened since 2016. Protection measures for identified victims of modern slavery in Pakistan are limited, with evidence that victims are detained in prison-like shelters where traffickers are able to enter and force inmates into prostitution. Services for men, including victims of bonded labour, are also lacking. Progress remains slow in Mauritania despite improvements in 2015 to legislation, such as allowing third parties to bring cases on behalf of slavery victims and establishing special tribunals to investigate slavery crimes. There are reports that police and the judiciary are reluctant to implement the new legislation and that several cases of slavery have been reclassified as lesser crimes. In Nepal, the government lessened protections for refugees, a cohort highly vulnerable to abuse and exploitation. In Nepal, refugees from Pakistan, Myanmar, Afghanistan, and Sri Lanka, among others, are required to pay prohibitive fines of up to US$5 a day and a penalty of US$500 to obtain an exit permit. These refugees also lacked legal access to education and the right to work.

Despite these countries taking fewer actions due to limited resources or ongoing conflict, there are wealthier, more stable countries that have taken little relative action when it comes to combatting modern slavery; when correlated against GDP (PPP) per capita Qatar, Singapore, Kuwait, Brunei, Hong Kong, and Saudi Arabia stand out as countries taking relatively limited action despite the size of the problem and resources at their disposal.

Corruption continues to be a serious impediment to any effective response to modern slavery. Almost every country in the Global Slavery Index has criminalised corruption, including bribery of officials, however around 68 countries have conducted limited, if any, investigations into alleged cases of government complicity in modern slavery cases. This ranges from alleged complicity of police and border officials in Madagascar in trafficking of Malagasy citizens overseas through to the alleged complicity of high-ranking government officials in El Salvador in child sex trafficking cases. Diplomatic officials from the Philippines, Bangladesh, Benin, Saudi Arabia, and Eritrea are also alleged to have been complicit in modern slavery cases.

In 2017, the Global Estimates of Modern Slavery produced the first robust measure and typology of state-imposed forced labour. For the Global Slavery Index 2018, we have updated our assessment of state-imposed forced labour to identify those governments that meet these criteria by using ILO Committee of

Experts comments and observations in combination with recent reports of exploitation at the hands of the government. As a result, 20 countries in 2016 and 2017 showed evidence of forcing their population or sub-populations to work under threat of menace or penalty. This includes concerning allegations of forced labour in privately-run administrative detention centres in the United States and Belarus and compulsory prison labour in public and private prisons in Russia. In Vietnam and China we found evidence of forced labour in drug rehabilitation centres where inmates are forced to work as part of their recuperation. In Belarus, we found abuse of civic duties in the practice of *Subbotniks,* which requires government employees to work weekends and donate their earnings to finance government projects under the intimidation or threat of fines by state employers. Abuse of civic duties also occurs in Burundi, Myanmar, Rwanda, and in Swaziland, where there is evidence of the continuing practice of *Kuhlehla*, under which the community is forced to render services or work for the King or local chief. Forced labour for economic development occurs in Uzbekistan and Turkmenistan, where the practice of forcing parts of the population to work in the annual cotton harvest is well documented. In Venezuela, Resolution No. 9855 of 19 July 2016 establishes a system of transition labour that is compulsory for all work entities, public and private. The resolution allows the government to transfer workers to entities in the agro-food sector, which requires additional support to increase production. These entities are also able to request additional workers, thus creating a system of forced recruitment to reinforce agro-food production to ensure food security. As noted, there is strong evidence, including recent interviews with defectors undertaken by the Walk Free

Foundation, of the prevalence of forced labour imposed by the North Korean state.

Abuse of conscription becomes state-imposed forced labour in cases where conscripts are forced to perform work of a non-military nature. We find evidence of this in Colombia, Egypt, Madagascar, Mongolia, and Mali and perhaps most significantly in Eritrea. Under the pretext of "defending the integrity of the state and ensuring its self-sufficiency," the Eritrean government has developed a system of national service in which conscripts are exploited and forced to labour for indefinite periods of time. These forced labourers are required to build infrastructure and work in other projects for economic development that help to prop up the Eritrean government. Also, in 2016 there were wide reports of slave markets in Libya, where migrant men, women, and children are sold off to the highest bidder. Alongside this, there are reports of state involvement from the Libyan Coast Guard and the Department for Combating Irregular Migration forcing people who are in migrant detention into forced labour.

Source: Walk Free Foundation (2018), 'Global Slavery Index 2018', Available at: https://www.globalslaveryindex.org/2018/findings/global-findings/ (accessed 30 June 2019).

APPENDIX 2
INTERNATIONAL TRADE UNION CONFEDERATION Global Rights Index 2019: AN OVERVIEW

The International Trade Union Confederation (ITUC) Global Rights Index 2019 ranks 145 countries against 97 internationally recognised indicators to assess where workers' rights are best protected in law and in practice.

The report's key findings include:

• 85% of countries have violated the right to strike.

• 80% of countries deny some or all workers collective bargaining.

• The number of countries which exclude workers from the right to establish or join a trade union increased from 92 in 2018 to 107 in 2019.

• Workers had no or restricted access to justice in 72% of countries.

• The number of countries where workers are arrested and detained increased from 59 in 2018 to 64 in 2019.

• Out of 145 countries surveyed, 54 deny or constrain free speech and freedom of assembly.

• Authorities impeded the registration of unions in 59% of countries.

• Workers experienced violence in 52 countries.

• Trade unionists were murdered in ten countries - **Bangladesh, Brazil, Colombia, Guatemala, Honduras, Italy, Pakistan, the Philippines, Turkey and Zimbabwe**.

The report ranks the ten worst countries for workers' rights in 2019 as **Algeria, Bangladesh, Brazil, Colombia, Guatemala, Kazakhstan, the Philippines, Saudi Arabia, Turkey and Zimbabwe**.

Brazil and Zimbabwe entered the ten worst countries for the first time with the adoption of regressive laws, violent repression of strikes and protest, and threats and intimidation of union leaders.

Belgium, Brazil, Eswatini, Iraq, Sierra Leone, Thailand and Vietnam have all seen their rankings worsen in 2019 with a rise in attacks on workers' rights in law and practice.

The **Middle East and North Africa** was again the worst region for treatment of workers, with the kafala system continuing to exclude migrants, the overwhelming majority of the workforce, from any labour protection, leaving 90% of the workforce unable to access their rights to form or join a trade union. The absolute denial of basic workers' rights remained in place in **Saudi Arabia** where an Indonesian worker was secretly executed.

Conditions in **Asia-Pacific** deteriorated more than any other region with an increase in violence, criminalisation of the right to the strike and violent attacks on workers. Ten trade unionists were murdered in the Philippines in 2018.

In Africa, workers were arrested or detained in 49% of countries. Attacks on workers reached unprecedented levels in **Cameroon, Nigeria, Chad, Ghana, Eswatini and Zimbabwe** as security forces fired live ammunition at protesting workers.

The Americas remain plagued by the pervasive climate of extreme violence and repression against workers and union members; in **Colombia** alone, 34 trade unionists were murdered in 2018 – a dramatic rise from 15 in the previous year.

In **Europe**, workers were arrested and detained in 25% of countries. Trade union leaders were murdered in Turkey and Italy.

The ITUC has been collecting data on violations of workers' rights to trade union membership and collective bargaining around the world for more than 30 years. This is the sixth year the ITUC has presented its findings through the Global Rights Index, putting a unique and comprehensive spotlight on how government laws and business practices have deteriorated or improved in the last 12 months.

The three global trends for workers' rights identified in the 2019 Global Rights Index show that democracy is in crisis, governments are attempting to silence the age of anger through brutal repression, but legislative successes for workers' rights are still being won.

The 2019 ITUC Global Rights Index rates countries according to 97 indicators, with an overall score placing countries in rankings of one to five plus:

1 Sporadic violations of rights: 12 countries including Iceland and Sweden.

2 Repeated violations of rights: 24 countries including Belgium and Republic of Congo.

3 Regular violations of rights: 26 countries including Canada and Rwanda.

4 Systematic violations of rights: 39 countries including Chile and Nigeria.

5 No guarantee of rights: 35 countries including Brazil and Eritrea.

5+ No guarantee of rights due to breakdown of the rule of law: 9 countries including, Palestine, Sudan, Syria and Yemen.[175]

[175] International Trade Union Confederation (2019), 'ITUC Global Rights Index 2019: Democracy in crisis as brutal repression used to silence age of anger', Available at: https://www.ituc-csi.org/ituc-global-rights-index-2019 (accessed 2 July 2019).

APPENDIX 3

VERISK MAPLECROFT HUMAN RIGHTS RISK DATA AND INDICES

Screening for exposure to human rights violations is essential for organisations seeking to understand the environment in which they're operating. Companies and investors face an increasing array of legal, ethical and reputational challenges around the world, and a deteriorating human rights environment can provide a telling signal about related issues such as political risk and levels of good governance. High-quality data can help companies to uncover unseen risks in their operations, and prioritise mitigation efforts.[176]

Recognised as the most robust and accurate in the market today, Verisk Maplecroft's data gives companies an unparalleled 360° perspective of their global risk exposure and the issues impacting the long-term value of their investments, the security of their assets and personnel, and the sustainability of their operations and supply chains.[177]

Verisk Maplecroft' human rights dataset consists of 31 indices assessing key elements of the human rights and development environment, including labour rights, civil and political rights, human security, poverty, education and health.[178] Verisk Maplecroft risk indices cover areas including:

- Air Quality

---

[176] Verisk Maplecroft (2019), 'Human rights risk data & indices', Available at: https://www.maplecroft.com/risk-indices/human-rights-risk/ (accessed 30 June 2019).
[177] Verisk Maplecroft (2019), 'Risk indices: Forecast dynamic shifts in your operating environment with our unparalleled data', Available at: https://www.maplecroft.com/risk-indices/ (accessed 30 June 2019).
[178] Verisk Maplecroft (2019), 'Human rights risk data & indices', Available at: https://www.maplecroft.com/risk-indices/human-rights-risk/ (accessed 30 June 2019).

- Child and Forced Labour
- Civil and Political Rights
- Civil Unrest
- Climate Change Exposure
- Corruption
- Deforestation
- Environmental Regulations
- Government Stability
- Political Risk
- Terrorism
- Water Stress
- Working Conditions[179]

AIR QUALITY

Verisk Maplecroft's Air Quality Index in 2019 Q1 shows Europe is home to a fifth of the 1,211 world cities where annual fine particulate matter (PM2.5) levels exceed the World Health Organization (WHO) safe levels.

In Asia, where the urban air pollution crisis is worst, the risk picture is confused. Coal plants continue to be built across the continent as a cheap energy source, but continued public outcry over the health impacts of air pollution means we expect more plant shutdowns, snap bans and the stricter enforcement of air pollution regulations that have characterised the past three years.

Spiralling urban populations will leave almost 300 million more people living in polluted areas by 2035 –around 230 million of which will be in China or India – and over a billion worldwide,

[179] Verisk Maplecroft (2019), 'Risk indices: Forecast dynamic shifts in your operating environment with our unparalleled data', Available at: https://www.maplecroft.com/risk-indices/ (accessed 30 June 2019).

raising the prospect of coordinated global restrictions on heavy industry and transportation.[180]

CHILD AND FORCED LABOUR

Despite high levels of economic growth and improvements on poverty and education, progress on child labour has stalled in the manufacturing countries most entwined with global supply chains.

These are the key findings of Verisk Maplecroft's latest annual Child Labour Index, which shows that manufacturing hubs, including China, India, Bangladesh, Vietnam and Cambodia, have registered no tangible improvement in the ranking of 198 countries since 2016.

Nearly 1 billion living in countries where child labour poses an 'extreme risk'

To put the issue of child labour in context, Verisk Maplecroft have identified 27 countries – which account for roughly 12% of the world's total population, or 900 million people – as 'extreme risk.'

The 10 worst performing countries in 2019 are:

1. North Korea (ranked 1st and highest risk globally)

2. Somalia

3. South Sudan

4. Eritrea

[180] Nichols, W. (2019), 'How will regulators respond to the air pollution crisis?', Available at: https://www.maplecroft.com/insights/analysis/how-will-regulators-respond-to-the-air-pollution-crisis/ (accessed 30 June 2019).

5. Central African Republic

6. Sudan

7. Venezuela

8. Papua New Guinea

9. Chad

10. Mozambique

The index, which Verisk Maplecroft developed to enable companies to identify where the risk of association or complicity with child labour is highest in their supply chains, measures the frequency and severity of violations, a country's adoption of laws and international treaties, and its ability and will to enforce them.

With 5 of the 10 highest risk countries, East Africa is the highest risk region.

Child labour still present in manufacturing supply chains

A further 82 countries are categorised as 'high risk' in the index, including Asia's economic giants India (ranked 47th) and China (98). The research shows that despite meteoric economic growth, there has been little or no improvement in their index scores in recent years.

Worryingly for organisations with extended supply chains, this trend is echoed across many manufacturing countries, including Ethiopia (30), Bangladesh (44), Turkey (63) and Vietnam (81), where the high risk of children being exploited or having to work through necessity remains unchanged.

Child labour is still prevalent across many sectors – if countries aren't taking action it is up to companies to make sure it's not happening under their watch.

Red flags for sustainable procurement in China and India

While China and India are categorised as 'high risk' overall, it's important to note that they are scored as 'extreme risk' in the section of the Child Labour Index measuring the frequency and severity of violations. Both have signed up to all relevant international treaties, which improves their position in the ranking, but unlike China, India's domestic laws fall short of ILO standards on the legal working age of 15, and its enforcement capabilities lack significant resources and coverage. These factors ensure that South Asia's largest economy is among the 25% worst performing countries globally.

According to our Industry Risk Data, agriculture, manufacturing, apparel, construction, mining and hospitality all pose high levels of risk in both countries. Trafficking and commercial sexual exploitation of children are also severe issues.

Child labour in Venezuela, Cambodia on the rise

Meanwhile Myanmar shows improvement

The country seeing the highest increase in child labour risks is Venezuela. Continuing political and social instability has seen it fall 80 places in the index since 2016 and it now ranks 7th highest risk globally. Other notable countries seeing an increase in risk include Nigeria and Cambodia, both of which have dropped into the 'extreme risk' category.

On the flipside, 57 countries have registered significant improvements in the index between 2017 and 2019 and feature sourcing locations tied to global supply chains. Liberia has risen 44 places in the index to 58th; Myanmar improved from 3rd highest risk globally in 2018 to 27th this year; while Madagascar has climbed 20 places to 45th since 2017. The index shows that all three countries have increased their enforcement capabilities and commitments towards fighting child labour, but Myanmar has also experienced fewer reported violations.[181]

CIVIL AND POLITICAL RIGHTS, CIVIL UNREST AND POLITICAL RISK

Global operations and investments are exposed to hundreds of political, social, environmental and economic variables that can jeopardise the security of assets and personnel, damage brand reputation and undermine long-term value. While a company's internal teams can track some of these issues, to build a true 360° view of country risk across a large portfolio of developed and emerging markets without external expertise is a huge challenge.

Finding a trusted partner to provide an independent and data driven perspective on an organisation's risk exposure is crucial. Verisk Maplecroft's country risk analysis service combines a forensic understanding of the country-level risks impacting different sectors in markets across the world with the industry's leading and most wide-ranging portfolio of risk analytics. This holistic approach enables companies to anticipate and manage emerging risks, and gives them the confidence they need to make strategic decisions that help protect their people, operations and investments. Learn more about Verisk Maplecroft's risk indices:

---

[181] Verisk Maplecroft (2019), '**Progress on child labour flatlining in world's manufacturing hubs:** Child Labour Index', Available at: https://www.maplecroft.com/insights/analysis/child-labour-in-worlds-manufacturing-hubs/ (accessed 30 June 2019).

- Political risk data
- Economic risk data
- Environmental risk data
- Human rights risk data[182]

CLIMATE CHANGE EXPOSURE

What do 84% of the world's fastest growing cities have in common? Rapid growth, rising temperatures and increasingly severe weather events brought on by climate change are putting companies and investments at risk.

Combining new UN projections on rates of annual population growth in over 1800 cities with subnational data from Verisk Maplecroft's **Climate Change Vulnerability Index (CCVI)**, Verisk Maplecroft's assess the threat from climate change over the next 30 years. Verisk Maplecroft's data reveals that of the 100 fastest growing cities by population, 84 are rated 'extreme risk', with a further 14 in the 'high risk' category.

Europe is a safe zone

Over 95% of the 234 cities most affected by climate change and considered 'extreme risk' in the CCVI are in Africa and Asia, compounding fears that the world's poorest countries with the greatest rates of urbanisation are set to pay the highest price of climate change. The scale of the risk could threaten the capital flows that have streamed into these markets to take advantage of burgeoning economies, emerging consumers and cheap labour.

[182] Verisk Maplecroft (2019), 'Country risk analysis', Available at: https://www.maplecroft.com/solutions/country-risk-analysis/ (accessed 30 June 2019).

At the other end of the spectrum, 86% of the 292 'low risk' cities are located in Europe and the Americas. The five cities considered most insulated from the impacts of climate change in the CCVI, Glasgow, Belfast, Edinburgh, Preston and Middlesbrough, are all located in the UK.

African / Asian cities most affected by climate change

Urban centres in Africa dominate in terms of population growth, with 86 of the 100 fastest growing cities. Significantly, 79 of these are rated 'extreme risk' in the CCVI, including 15 African capitals and many of the continent's key commercial hubs. Among the most at risk of climate change are: Kampala in Uganda, where the annual population is set to grow by 5.1% a year on average between 2018-35; Dar-es-Salaam in Tanzania (4.8%), Abuja (4.5%) and Lagos (3.5%) in Nigeria; Addis Ababa (4.3%) in Ethiopia; and Luanda (3.7%) in Angola.

The relationship between climate change vulnerability and rates of population growth is strong. The highest risk cities already lack adequate healthcare services and disaster mitigation systems and have highly vulnerable populations. The strain on essential services will intensify as populations continue to rise.

Using the latest International Monetary Fund projections, Verisk Maplecroft estimate future exposure of urban GDP under the CCVI to illustrate the levels of financial risk. The 10 cities rated 'extreme risk' in the CCVI with the highest economic exposure to climate change in 2023 include the largest commercial centres of some of the world's key emerging markets: Jakarta, Indonesia – US$233bn; Manila, Philippines – US$166bn; Lagos, Nigeria – US$128.5bn; Baghdad, Iraq – US$88bn; and Addis Ababa, Ethiopia – US$69bn.

Corporates exposed

At the national level, the International Monetary Fund (IMF) estimates that 8 of the top 10 fastest growing economies between 2018 and 2023 will be African countries. As the full effects of urbanisation and climate change unfold, companies investing in these markets could face a set of costly risks. The amount of Gross domestic product (GDP) in African countries exposed to 'extreme risk' in the CCVI will grow from US$895bn in 2018 to US$1397bn in 2023.

This represents 48% of the entire continent's GDP

Damage to infrastructure, property and assets caused by tropical cyclones or flooding are among the more obvious impacts, but the potential disruption caused by the secondary threats of disease and increases in crime and civil unrest are not to be ignored. Drought, crop failure and instability brought on by climate change may also compound the risks by driving even larger numbers of people towards cities through cross-border and rural migration.[183]

COMPLIANCE RISK

The burden of compulsory and voluntary compliance is growing for firms as new legislation emerges, particularly around environmental, social and governance (ESG) issues. This trend places the actions of a company's business under greater scrutiny than ever and it is only set to continue. For many companies, just keeping track of new and ever-changing regulations is a challenge in itself, while dealing with the additional obligations demands a

[183] Verisk Maplecroft (2019), '84% of world's fastest growing cities face 'extreme' climate change risks', Available at: https://www.maplecroft.com/insights/analysis/84-of-worlds-fastest-growing-cities-face-extreme-climate-change-risks/ (accessed 30 June 2019).

lot of time, effort and money that a company's stretched teams and budgets can ill afford.

With Verisk Maplecroft's dedicated teams of subject matter experts and consultants, risk analytics and customised solutions, Verisk Maplecroft help remove some of the burdens of compliance, and can support companies in their public reporting across issues such as modern slavery and human rights. Learn more about Verisk Maplecroft's risk indices:

- Human rights risk data
- Political risk data
- Commodity risk data

The world's largest organisations work with us because they trust our data and analysis. We not only provide the solutions they need to fulfil legal requirements, but the credibility of our research enables them to show leadership on key ethical issues to ever-increasing numbers of ethically minded consumers and investors.[184]

DEFORESTATION, WATER STRESS AND ENVIRONMENTAL REGULATIONS

Significant changes in carbon regulation, shifting public expectations about how organisations manage natural resources, and the growing impacts of climate change mean that companies are having to find new ways to combat environmental risk. Consumers, investors and shareholders are also making increasing demands on business to take a forward-looking approach by

[184] Verisk Maplecroft (2019), 'Compliance risk', Available at: https://www.maplecroft.com/solutions/compliance/ (accessed 30 June 2019).

embedding sustainable practices within their decision-making, operations and supply chains. The costs of inaction will soon outweigh those of implementation.

Verisk Maplecroft's help companies to overcome these unfolding challenges. Using Verisk Maplecroft's internationally recognised risk indices, companies can map global corporate exposure to climate change, natural hazards, water issues and regulatory challenges down to the asset-level. Verisk Maplecroft's team of experienced environmental specialists and consultants use these data-driven insights as the basis to deliver expert analysis and develop risk mitigation strategies that enable companies to understand how and where to focus their resources or to target their investments. Learn more about our risk indices:

- Environmental risk data
- Industry risk data
- Commodity risk data[185]

GOVERNMENT STABILITY

Verisk Maplecroft's Government Stability Index Projection combines analyst forecasts with statistical modelling to generate a probabilistic forecast of its Government Stability Index scores for the period two years ahead. The index assesses the stability of executive authority and the potential for an illegitimate transfer of power, such as a coup.

According to Verisk Maplecroft's Government Stability Index Projection, downside risks will rise in some key investment

[185] Verisk Maplecroft (2019), 'Environmental risk and climate change', Available at: https://www.maplecroft.com/solutions/environment-climate-change/ (accessed 30 June 2019).

destinations. Verisk Maplecroft's expects the worst news to come out of Myanmar and Thailand, where upcoming elections will increase the potential for political upheaval and likely stall much needed industry reforms. But, Malaysia and Papua New Guinea (PNG) could also be in for a bumpy political ride with potential implications for investors.

For investors in Asia Pacific's oil and gas industry, there is a mix of good and bad news if we look ahead over the next couple of years.

On the upside, the region will remain one of the most politically stable in the world, with Indonesia, Australia, China and India – four of the region's biggest capex hotspots – continuing to offer stable political environments in which to operate.[186]

ABOVE-GROUND RISK

For extractive firms, the pursuit of high-return opportunities can go hand-in-hand with high levels of political risk, regulatory uncertainty, social opposition and potential reputational damage from association with human rights violations or environmental impacts. These above-ground risks can, and do, affect the profitability and value of mining and hydrocarbon assets. Anticipating and managing these risks before they manifest is crucial to ensure project return, quarterly performance and shareholder expectations.

Verisk Maplecroft's unique approach enables companies to build an in-depth understanding of how their technical and commercial imperatives interact with above-ground-risks in terms of impact,

---

[186] Hrirbernik, M. (2019), '**Government instability in Asia impacts oil and gas investment:** Myanmar and Thailand top watchlist', Available at: https://www.maplecroft.com/insights/analysis/government-instability-in-asia/ (accessed 30 June 2019).

exposure and consequence. It enables companies to plan and make business-critical decisions based on data they can trust, as well as independent, on-the-ground insight into the strategic issues affecting the company's people, operations and business. Read more about our risk indices:

- Political risk data
- Human rights risk data
- Environmental risk data
- Industry risk data[187]

WORKING CONDITIONS

Does your organisation have full visibility of its global risk exposure across all tiers of the supply chain? Multinational companies can gain an instant picture of the inherent risk within each global supplier and the commodities they source by combining their data with Verisk Maplecroft's proprietary global risk analytics, all from an intuitive online dashboard.

Verisk Maplecroft's sustainable procurement solution combines this crucial intelligence with expert country and commodity analysis to help you understand how human rights, political and environmental risks can impact your reputations and the continuity of goods and raw materials. This holistic approach enables you to streamline responsible sourcing processes; develop

[187] Verisk Maplecroft (2019), '**Above-ground risk:** Oil & Gas, Metals & Mining', Available at: https://www.maplecroft.com/solutions/above-ground-risk/ (accessed 30 June 2019).

data-led audit strategies; and make better, risk-adjusted decisions. Learn more about our risk indices:

- Human rights risk data
- Commodity risk data
- Industry risk data
- Environmental risk data
- Political risk data[188]

---

[188] Verisk Maplecroft (2019), 'Sustainable procurement', Available at: https://www.maplecroft.com/solutions/sustainability/sustainable-procurement/ (accessed 30 June 2019).

APPENDIX 4

U.S. DEPARTMENT OF STATE 2019

Trafficking in Persons Report: an overview

The Trafficking in Persons (TIP) Report is the U.S. Government's principal diplomatic tool to engage foreign governments on human trafficking. It is also the world's most comprehensive resource of governmental anti-trafficking efforts and reflects the U.S. Government's commitment to global leadership on this key human rights and law enforcement issue.

On June 20, at the United States Department of State, Secretary Michael R. Pompeo released the 2019 Trafficking in Persons (TIP) Report, an annual publication documenting the government efforts of 187 countries and territories, including the United States, to combat human trafficking. The theme of this year's TIP Report introduction is "The National Nature of Human Trafficking: Strengthening Government Responses and Dispelling Misperceptions." While not intending to minimize the importance of addressing transnational human trafficking, the report calls on governments to respond to all forms of human trafficking with the most comprehensive and effective measures possible. The report stresses the need for a balanced response that challenges the presumption that human trafficking requires movement or some cross-border element.

The Department of State prepared this Report using information from U.S. embassies, government officials, nongovernmental and international organizations, published reports, news articles, academic studies, research trips to every region of the world, and information submitted to tipreport@state.gov. This email address provides a means by which organizations and individuals can share information with the Department of State on government progress in addressing trafficking.

U.S. diplomatic posts and domestic agencies reported on the trafficking situation and governmental action to fight trafficking based on thorough research that included meetings with a wide variety of government officials, local and international NGO representatives, officials of international organizations, journalists, academics, and survivors. U.S. missions overseas are dedicated to covering human trafficking issues year-round. The 2019 Trafficking in Persons Report covers government efforts undertaken from April 1, 2018 through March 31, 2019.

TIER PLACEMENT

The Department places each country in this Report onto one of four tiers, as mandated by the Trafficking Victims Protection Act (TVPA). This placement is based not on the size of the country's problem but on the extent of governments' efforts to meet the TVPA's minimum standards for the elimination of human trafficking (see page 40-41), which are generally consistent with the Palermo Protocol.

While Tier 1 is the highest ranking, it does not mean that a country has no human trafficking problem or that it is doing enough to address the problem. Rather, a Tier 1 ranking indicates that a government has made efforts to address the problem that meet the TVPA's minimum standards. To maintain a Tier 1 ranking, governments need to demonstrate appreciable progress each year in combating trafficking. Indeed, Tier 1 represents a responsibility rather than a reprieve.

Tier rankings and narratives in the 2019 Trafficking in Persons Report reflect an assessment of the following:

1. Enactment of laws prohibiting severe forms of trafficking in persons, as defined by the TVPA, and provision of criminal punishments for trafficking offenses;

2. Criminal penalties prescribed for human trafficking offenses with a maximum of at least four years' deprivation of liberty, or a more severe penalty;

3. Implementation of human trafficking laws through vigorous prosecution of the prevalent forms of trafficking in the country and sentencing of offenders;

4. Proactive victim identification measures with systematic procedures to guide law enforcement and other government-supported front-line responders in the process of victim identification;

5. Government funding and partnerships with NGOs to provide victims with access to primary health care, counseling, and shelter, allowing them to recount their trafficking experiences to trained social counselors and law enforcement in an environment of minimal pressure;

6. Victim protection efforts that include access to services and shelter without detention and with legal alternatives to removal to countries in which victims would face retribution or hardship;

7. The extent to which a government ensures victims are provided with legal and other assistance and that, consistent with domestic law, proceedings are not prejudicial to victims' rights, dignity, or psychological well-being;

8. The extent to which a government ensures the safe, humane, and to the extent possible, voluntary repatriation and reintegration of victims;

9. Governmental measures to prevent human trafficking, including efforts to curb practices identified as contributing factors to human trafficking, such as employers' confiscation of foreign workers' passports and allowing labor recruiters to charge fees to prospective migrants; and

10. Governmental efforts to reduce the demand for commercial sex acts and international sex tourism.

Tier rankings and narratives are NOT affected by the following:

1. Efforts, however laudable, undertaken exclusively by nongovernmental actors in the country;

2. General public awareness events—government-sponsored or otherwise—lacking concrete ties to the prosecution of traffickers, protection of victims, or prevention of trafficking; and

3. Broad-based law enforcement or developmental initiatives.

A GUIDE TO THE TIERS

Tier 1

Countries whose governments fully meet the TVPA's minimum standards for the elimination of trafficking.

Minimum Standards for the Elimination of Trafficking in Persons - SECTION 108 OF THE TRAFFICKING VICTIMS PROTECTION ACT (TVPA)

(1) The government of the country should prohibit severe forms of trafficking in persons and punish acts of such trafficking.

(2) For the knowing commission of any act of sex trafficking involving force, fraud, coercion, or in which the victim of sex trafficking is a child incapable of giving meaningful consent, or of trafficking which includes rape or kidnapping or which causes a death, the government of the country should prescribe punishment commensurate with that for grave crimes, such as forcible sexual assault.

(3) For the knowing commission of any act of a severe form of trafficking in persons, the government of the country should prescribe punishment that is sufficiently stringent to deter and that adequately reflects the heinous nature of the offense.

(4) The government of the country should make serious and sustained efforts to eliminate severe forms of trafficking in persons.

Indicia of "Serious and Sustained Efforts"

(1) Whether the government of the country vigorously investigates and prosecutes acts of severe forms of trafficking in persons, and convicts and sentences persons responsible for such acts, that take place wholly or partly within the territory of the country, including, as appropriate, requiring incarceration of individuals

convicted of such acts. For purposes of the preceding sentence, suspended or significantly reduced sentences for convictions of principal actors in cases of severe forms of trafficking in persons shall be considered, on a case-by-case basis, whether to be considered as an indicator of serious and sustained efforts to eliminate severe forms of trafficking in persons. After reasonable requests from the Department of State for data regarding investigations, prosecutions, convictions, and sentences, a government which does not provide such data, consistent with the capacity of such government to obtain such data, shall be presumed not to have vigorously investigated, prosecuted, convicted, or sentenced such acts. During the periods prior to the annual report submitted on June 1, 2004, and on June 1, 2005, and the periods afterwards until September 30 of each such year, the Secretary of State may disregard the presumption contained in the preceding sentence if the government has provided some data to the Department of State regarding such acts and the Secretary has determined that the government is making a good faith effort to collect such data.

(2) Whether the government of the country protects victims of severe forms of trafficking in persons and encourages their assistance in the investigation and prosecution of such trafficking, including provisions for legal alternatives to their removal to countries in which they would face retribution or hardship, and ensures that victims are not inappropriately incarcerated, fined, or otherwise penalized solely for unlawful acts as a direct result of being trafficked, including by providing training to law enforcement and immigration officials regarding the identification and treatment of trafficking victims using approaches that focus on the needs of the victims.

(3) Whether the government of the country has adopted measures to prevent severe forms of trafficking in persons, such as measures to inform and educate the public, including potential victims, about the causes and consequences of severe forms of trafficking in persons, measures to establish the identity of local populations, including birth registration, citizenship, and nationality, measures to ensure that its nationals who are deployed abroad as part of a diplomatic, peacekeeping, or other similar mission do not engage in or facilitate severe forms of trafficking in persons or exploit victims of such trafficking, a transparent system for remediating or punishing such public officials as a deterrent, measures to prevent the use of forced labor or child labor in violation of international standards, effective bilateral, multilateral, or regional information sharing and cooperation arrangements with other countries, and effective policies or laws regulating foreign labor recruiters and holding them civilly and criminally liable for fraudulent recruiting.

(4) Whether the government of the country cooperates with other governments in the investigation and prosecution of severe forms of trafficking in persons and has entered into bilateral, multilateral, or regional law enforcement cooperation and coordination arrangements with other countries.

(5) Whether the government of the country extradites persons charged with acts of severe forms of trafficking in persons on substantially the same terms and to substantially the same extent as persons charged with other serious crimes (or, to the extent such extradition would be inconsistent with the laws of such country or with international agreements to which the country is a party, whether the government is taking all appropriate measures to

modify or replace such laws and treaties so as to permit such extradition).

(6) Whether the government of the country monitors immigration and emigration patterns for evidence of severe forms of trafficking in persons and whether law enforcement agencies of the country respond to any such evidence in a manner that is consistent with the vigorous investigation and prosecution of acts of such trafficking, as well as with the protection of human rights of victims and the internationally recognized human right to leave any country, including one's own, and to return to one's own country.

(7) Whether the government of the country vigorously investigates, prosecutes, convicts, and sentences public officials, including diplomats and soldiers, who participate in or facilitate severe forms of trafficking in persons, including nationals of the country who are deployed abroad as part of a diplomatic, peacekeeping, or other similar mission who engage in or facilitate severe forms of trafficking in persons or exploit victims of such trafficking, and takes all appropriate measures against officials who condone such trafficking. A government's failure to appropriately address public allegations against such public officials, especially once such officials have returned to their home countries, shall be considered inaction under these criteria. After reasonable requests from the Department of State for data regarding such investigations, prosecutions, convictions, and sentences, a government which does not provide such data consistent with its resources shall be presumed not to have vigorously investigated, prosecuted, convicted, or sentenced such acts. During the periods prior to the annual report submitted on June 1, 2004, and June 1,

2005, and the periods afterwards until September 30 of each such year, the Secretary of State may disregard the presumption contained in the preceding sentence if the government has provided some data to the Department of State regarding such acts and the Secretary has determined that the government is making a good faith effort to collect such data.

(8) Whether the percentage of victims of severe forms of trafficking in the country that are non-citizens of such countries is insignificant.

(9) Whether the government has entered into effective, transparent partnerships, cooperative arrangements, or agreements that have resulted in concrete and measurable outcomes with

(A) domestic civil society organizations, private sector entities, or international nongovernmental organizations, or into multilateral or regional arrangements or agreements, to assist the government's efforts to prevent trafficking, protect victims, and punish traffickers; or

(B) the United States toward agreed goals and objectives in the collective fight against trafficking.

(10) Whether the government of the country, consistent with the capacity of such government, systematically monitors its efforts to satisfy the criteria described in paragraphs (1) through (8) and makes available publicly a periodic assessment of such efforts.

(11) Whether the government of the country achieves appreciable progress in eliminating severe forms of trafficking when compared to the assessment in the previous year.

(12) Whether the government of the country has made serious and sustained efforts to reduce the demand for

(A) commercial sex acts; and

(B) participation in international sex tourism by nationals of the country.

Tier 2

Countries whose governments do not fully meet the TVPA's minimum standards but are making significant efforts to bring themselves into compliance with those standards.

Tier 2 Watch List

Countries whose governments do not fully meet the TVPA's minimum standards but are making significant efforts to bring themselves into compliance with those standards, and for which:

a) the absolute number of victims of severe forms of trafficking is very significant or is significantly increasing;

b) there is a failure to provide evidence of increasing efforts to combat severe forms of trafficking in persons from the previous year, including increased investigations, prosecution, and convictions of trafficking crimes, increased assistance to victims, and decreasing evidence of complicity in severe forms of trafficking by government officials; or

c) the determination that a country is making significant efforts to bring itself into compliance with minimum standards was based on commitments by the country to take additional steps over the next year.

Tier 3

Countries whose governments do not fully meet the TVPA's minimum standards and are not making significant efforts to do so.

No tier ranking is permanent. Every country, including the United States, can do more. All countries must maintain and continually increase efforts to combat trafficking.

FUNDING RESTRICTIONS FOR TIER 3 COUNTRIES

Pursuant to the TVPA, governments of countries on Tier 3 may be subject to certain restrictions on assistance, whereby the President may determine not to provide U.S. government nonhumanitarian, nontrade-related foreign assistance. In addition, the President may determine to withhold funding for government official or employee participation in educational and cultural exchange programs for certain Tier 3 countries. Consistent with the TVPA, the President may also determine to instruct the U.S. Executive Director of each multilateral development bank and the International Monetary Fund to vote against and use his or her best efforts to deny any loans or other uses of the institutions' funds to a designated Tier 3 country for most purposes (except for humanitarian, trade-related, and certain development-related assistance). Alternatively, the President may waive application of the foregoing restrictions upon a determination that the provision to a Tier 3 country of such assistance would promote the purposes of the TVPA or is otherwise in the national interest of the United States. The TVPA also authorizes the President to waive funding restrictions if necessary to avoid significant adverse effects on vulnerable populations, including women and children.

Applicable funding restrictions apply for the next Fiscal Year, which begins October 1, 2019.[189]

TIER PLACEMENTS

TIER 1

ARGENTINA	FRANCE	SLOVENIA
AUSTRALIA	GEORGIA	SPAIN
AUSTRIA	GUYANA	SWEDEN
THE BAHAMAS	ISRAEL	SWITZERLAND
BAHRAIN	JAPAN	TAIWAN
BELGIUM	KOREA, SOUTH	UNITED KINGDOM
CANADA	LITHUANIA	UNITED STATES OF AMERICA
CHILE	LUXEMBOURG	
COLOMBIA	NETHERLANDS	
CYPRUS	NEW ZEALAND	
CZECH REPUBLIC	NORWAY	
ESTONIA	PHILIPPINES	
FINLAND	PORTUGAL	

TIER 2

ALBANIA	DOMINICAN REPUBLIC	ITALY
ANTIGUA & BARBUDA	ECUADOR	JAMAICA
ARMENIA	EGYPT	JORDAN
ARUBA	EL SALVADOR	KENYA
BENIN	ETHIOPIA	KOSOVO
BOTSWANA	ESWATINI	KUWAIT
BRAZIL	GERMANY	LATVIA
BULGARIA	GHANA	LEBANON
BURKINA FASO	GREECE	MACAU
CABO VERDE	GUATEMALA	MACEDONIA
CAMEROON	GUINEA	MADAGASCAR
CHAD	HAITI	MALI
COSTA RICA	HONDURAS	MALTA
COTE D'IVOIRE	HONG KONG	MAURITIUS
CROATIA	ICELAND	MEXICO
DENMARK	INDIA	MICRONESIA
DJIBOUTI	INDONESIA	MOLDOVA
	IRELAND	MONGOLIA
		MOROCCO

[189] U.S. Department of State (2019), '2019 Trafficking in Persons Report', Available at: https://www.state.gov/wp-content/uploads/2019/06/2019-Trafficking-in-Persons-Report.pdf (accessed 29 June 2019).

- MOZAMBIQUE
- NAMIBIA
- NEPAL
- NIGER
- NIGERIA
- OMAN
- PAKISTAN
- PALAU
- PANAMA
- PARAGUAY
- PERU
- POLAND
- QATAR
- RWANDA
- ST. LUCIA
- ST. MAARTEN
- ST. VINCENT & THE GRENADINES
- SENEGAL
- SERBIA
- SEYCHELLES
- SINGAPORE
- SLOVAKIA
- SOLOMON ISLANDS
- SURINAME
- TAJIKISTAN
- THAILAND
- TIMOR-LESTE
- TOGO
- TONGA
- TRINIDAD & TOBAGO
- TUNISIA
- TURKEY
- UGANDA
- UKRAINE
- UNITED ARAB EMIRATES
- URUGUAY
- ZAMBIA
- ZIMBABWE

TIER 2 WATCH LIST

- ALGERIA
- ANGOLA
- AZERBAIJAN
- BANGLADESH
- BARBADOS
- BELIZE
- BRUNEI
- BOLIVIA
- BOSNIA & HERZEGOVINA
- CAMBODIA
- CENTRAL AFRICAN REPUBLIC
- CONGO, REPUBLIC OF THE
- CURAÇAO
- FIJI
- GABON
- GUINEA-BISSAU
- HUNGARY
- IRAQ
- KAZAKHSTAN
- KYRGYZ REPUBLIC
- LAOS
- LESOTHO
- LIBERIA
- MALAWI
- MALAYSIA
- MALDIVES
- MARSHALL ISLANDS
- MONTENEGRO
- NICARAGUA
- ROMANIA
- SIERRA LEONE
- SOUTH AFRICA
- SRI LANKA
- SUDAN
- TANZANIA
- UZBEKISTAN
- VIETNAM

TIER 3

- BELARUS
- BHUTAN
- BURMA
- BURUNDI
- CHINA (PRC)
- COMOROS
- CONGO, DEMOCRATIC REP. OF THE
- CUBA
- EQUATORIAL GUINEA
- ERITREA
- THE GAMBIA
- IRAN
- KOREA, NORTH
- MAURITANIA

PAPUA NEW GUINEA	SOUTH SUDAN	VENEZUELA
RUSSIA	SYRIA	
SAUDI ARABIA	TURKMENISTAN	

PROMISING PRACTICES IN THE ERADICATION OF TRAFFICKING IN PERSONS: INCREASED FOCUS ON LABOR RECRUITMENT

Combating human trafficking in global supply chains has been an issue of growing importance in the anti-trafficking movement over the last decade. Governments, the private sector, and civil society are increasingly examining human trafficking through this lens as a part of broader anti-trafficking strategies. As labor is a critical part of global supply chains, there has also been an increased focus on labor recruitment as one of the most important pressure points in the global economy for addressing this crime. The past five years have witnessed an exponential growth in initiatives focused on eradicating exploitative labor recruitment practices, developing models for fair recruitment, and changing industry standards in hiring practices.

As globalization increasingly drives markets toward temporary or seasonal contract workers who are mobile and flexible, the importance of the recruitment industry grows. Each year, millions of workers turn to or are approached by labor intermediaries—recruiters, agents, or brokers—who facilitate the movement of labor both within countries and across borders to satisfy global labor demands. A 2018 ILO report estimates there are 164 million migrant workers worldwide, an increase of nine percent since the last estimate in 2015.

Labor intermediaries function as a bridge between workers and employers and, at their best, can provide helpful guidance and assist in matching workers with jobs and in arranging visas and documentation, medical checkups, pre-departure orientation, training, and travel. At their worst, labor recruiters exploit the vulnerability inherent among those migrating for work, often engaging in fraudulent and misleading recruitment practices that can lead to human trafficking.

In particular, low-wage migrant laborers are extremely vulnerable to and at high risk of exploitative practices such as unsafe working conditions, unfair hiring practices, and debt bondage—a form of human trafficking. Some recruiters take advantage of the fact that migrant workers lack information on the hiring process, are unfamiliar with the legal protections they are owed and options for recourse, and often face language barriers. Certain unscrupulous recruitment practices known to facilitate human trafficking include worker-paid recruitment fees, misrepresentation of contract terms, contract switching, and destruction or confiscation of identity documents.

RECRUITMENT INITIATIVES AND NEW RESOURCES

Promising new initiatives focused on recruitment have recently emerged. If governments and other stakeholders can sustain this momentum and work to connect and create areas of collaboration, there is huge potential for progress in improving recruitment practices and protecting workers from human trafficking. Some of the many initiatives can be found below.

International Labor Organization (ILO) General Principles and Operational Guidelines for Fair Recruitment

In 2016, the ILO published a set of non-binding principles and guidelines to "inform the current and future work of the ILO and of other organizations, national legislatures, and the social partners on promoting and ensuring fair recruitment." The principles cover the recruitment of all workers, both within a country and across borders, and in all sectors of the economy. They provide broad tenants for the protection of workers throughout the recruitment process and detail the specific operational responsibilities of governments, the private sector, and public employment services.

ILO Fair Recruitment Initiative

Launched in 2014, the Fair Recruitment Initiative is a multi-stakeholder collaboration aimed at protecting workers from abusive and fraudulent practices during the recruitment process. It focuses on enhancing knowledge of national and international recruitment practices; improving laws, policies, and enforcement mechanisms for fair recruitment; promoting fair business practices; and empowering and protecting workers.

International Recruitment Integrity System (IRIS)

In 2014, the IOM brought together a coalition of stakeholders to develop the IRIS initiative. IRIS is a "social compliance scheme" designed to promote fair labor recruitment. Its primary goal is to identify and support ethical labor recruiters through a variety of tools: establishing a benchmark for ethical recruiting—"the IRIS Standard," establishing a voluntary certification process for recruiters, creating a list of certified recruiters to help employers and workers make informed decisions, and establishing a monitoring and compliance mechanism to ensure standards are lasting. Central to the model is a prohibition on worker-paid recruitment fees or related expenses.

The Issara Institute Ethical Recruitment Program

Through the Ethical Recruitment Program, the Issara Institute brings employers and recruitment agencies together to analyze their current recruitment practices, identify strengths and weaknesses, receive worker voice feedback, and make improvements, so that jobseekers are more protected in the recruitment process. Over a 12-month period, the Issara Institute helps both businesses and recruiters improve their processes by providing an assessment and recommendations, using worker feedback throughout. The program helps participating businesses and recruitment agencies to examine and implement improvements in their contracts and service agreements, cost structures, grievance mechanisms, and capacity building trainings.

Responsible Labor Initiative (RLI)

In 2017, the Responsible Business Alliance or RBA (formerly the Electronic Industry Citizenship Coalition) launched a multi-industry, multi-stakeholder initiative to help companies address the root causes of forced labor. RLI's mission is for its members companies, suppliers, recruitment partners, and stakeholders to "use their collective influence and application of due diligence to drive the transformation of recruitment markets and reduce the risk of forced labor in global supply chains." RBA actively recruits new companies to join RLI and implement forced labor due diligence in their supply chains.

U.S. GOVERNMENT'S FEDERAL ACQUISITION REGULATION DEFINITION OF "RECRUITMENT FEES"

The U.S. government released in December 2018 an official definition of "recruitment fees" that applies to all federal contractors and their subcontractors and gives further meaning to the prohibition on charging workers recruitment fees. While this definition applies only in the context of public procurement by the U.S. government, it represents a model for global efforts to define the types of fees and costs that should no longer be borne by recruited workers to reduce the risk of exploitation and human trafficking.

With an effective date of January 22, 2019, the final rule entitled "Federal Acquisition Regulation: Combating Trafficking in Persons – Definition of "Recruitment Fees" provides the following definition:

Recruitment fees means fees of any type, including charges, costs, assessments, or other financial obligations, that are associated with the recruiting process, regardless of the time, manner, or location of imposition or collection of the fee.

(1) Recruitment fees include, but are not limited to, the following fees (when they are associated with the recruiting process) for—

(i) Soliciting, identifying, considering, interviewing, referring, retaining, transferring, selecting, training, providing orientation to, skills testing, recommending, or placing employees or potential employees;

(ii) Advertising;

(iii) Obtaining permanent or temporary labor certification, including any associated fees;

(iv) Processing applications and petitions;

(v) Acquiring visas, including any associated fees;

(vi) Acquiring photographs and identity or immigration documents, such as passports, including any associated fees;

(vii) Accessing the job opportunity, including required medical examinations and immunizations; background, reference, and security clearance checks and examinations; and additional certifications;

(viii) An employer's recruiters, agents or attorneys, or other notary or legal fees;

(ix) Language interpretation or translation, arranging for or accompanying on travel, or providing other advice to employees or potential employees;

(x) Government-mandated fees, such as border crossing fees, levies, or worker welfare funds;

(xi) Transportation and subsistence costs—

A) While in transit, including, but not limited to, airfare or costs of other modes of transportation, terminal fees, and travel taxes associated with travel from the country of origin to the country of performance and the return journey upon the end of employment; and

(B) From the airport or disembarkation point to the worksite;

(xii) Security deposits, bonds, and insurance; and

(xiii) Equipment charges.

(2) A recruitment fee, as described in the introductory text of this definition, is a recruitment fee, regardless of whether the payment is—

(i) Paid in property or money;

(ii) Deducted from wages;

(iii) Paid back in wage or benefit concessions;

(iv) Paid back as a kickback, bribe, in-kind payment, free labor, tip, or tribute; or

(v) Collected by an employer or a third party, whether licensed or unlicensed, including, but not limited to—

(A) Agents;

(B) Labor brokers;

(C) Recruiters;

(D) Staffing firms (including private employment and placement firms);

(E) Subsidiaries/affiliates of the employer;

(F) Any agent or employee of such entities; and

(G) Subcontractors at all tie[190]

[190] U.S. Department of State (2019), '2019 Trafficking in Persons Report', Available at: https://www.state.gov/wp-content/uploads/2019/06/2019-Trafficking-in-Persons-Report.pdf (accessed 29 June 2019).

APPENDIX 5
U.S. DEPARTMENT OF LABOUR'S 2017 FINDINGS ON THE WORST FORMS OF CHILD LABOUR: AN OVERVIEW

2017 Country Assessments

In 2017, 17 countries received assessments of Significant Advancement, 60 countries received assessments of Moderate Advancement, 42 countries received assessments of Minimal Advancement, 12 countries received assessments of No Advancement, and 1 country received an assessment of No Assessment. The global breakdown of assessment levels for advancement in efforts to eliminate child labor for the 132 countries and territories included in this report is shown in Figure 5.

This year, USDOL developed more stringent criteria by establishing certain basic child labor protections that countries must meet to be eligible to receive an assessment of Significant Advancement. In addition to taking actions suggested in last year's report or making other meaningful efforts during the reporting period in all relevant areas assessed in this report, these countries must have instituted minimally acceptable protections in laws and regulations, coordination mechanisms, and policies and programs to address and prevent the worst forms of child labor. For instance, countries must establish legal prohibitions against forced child labor and a minimum age for work that meets international standards. The U.S. government commends the following governments for receiving an assessment of Significant Advancement, based on their efforts to accelerate the elimination of child labor: Argentina, Brazil, Colombia, Costa Rica, Cote d'Ivoire, Ecuador, Guatemala, Honduras, India, Mauritius, Paraguay, Peru, Rwanda, Serbia, South Africa, Thailand, and Tunisia.

The Department continued implementing the requirement that a country could not receive an assessment level beyond a Minimal Advancement if it continued or established a detrimental law, policy, or practice that delayed its advancement in eliminating the worst forms of child labor. Fourteen countries received an automatic assessment of Minimal Advancement based on this, many due to engaging in a detrimental practice. For example, Mauritania's criminal law enforcement authorities failed to initiate a sufficient number of investigations and prosecutions to combat slavery related to children. The governments of Armenia, Azerbaijan, and the Democratic Republic of the Congo conducted no worksite inspections, while the governments of Azerbaijan and Mongolia did not permit their Labor Inspectorates to conduct unannounced inspections.

In addition, countries could not receive an assessment level beyond No Advancement if they had a policy or demonstrated a practice of being complicit in the use of forced child labor in more than isolated incidents. Three countries—Burma, Eritrea, and South Sudan—received this assessment due to the government's direct or proactive involvement in forced child labor. Burma's national military recruited, sometimes through force, and used children as combatants in armed conflict. The military also forced children to work as porters and cooks in conflict areas. In addition, the Burmese military perpetuated ethnic cleansing and acts of violence against the Rohingya people in Rakhine State, which resulted in children's displacement to refugee camps in Bangladesh, where they are vulnerable to labor exploitation and commercial sexual exploitation.

Several countries received notable changes in assessment levels. After years of receiving an assessment of No Advancement for the forced mobilization of children in the cotton harvest, Uzbekistan is receiving a Moderate Advancement for 2017 (see Box 5 on page 20). This year's assessment reflects the important efforts the country has made to significantly reduce the mobilization of children for the cotton harvest; however, the USDOL continues to call for an end to the mobilization of adult forced labor for this same purpose. The Dominican Republic is also receiving an assessment of Moderate Advancement because, in contrast to previous years in which it received an automatic Minimal Advancement, no cases were reported of children without identity documents being denied access to education. The Dominican government made new efforts to address this unlawful practice, which mainly affected children of Haitian descent. In Eswatini (previously known as Swaziland), there was no evidence in 2017 that local chiefs were forcing children to perform agricultural work or other tasks through kuhlehla, a customary practice that requires residents to carry out communal work, including in chiefs' houses or fields. This resulted in Eswatini's upgrade to an assessment of Minimal Advancement from its previous rating of No Advancement due to government complicity in forced child labor.[191]

[191] Bureau of International Labour Affairs of the U.S. Department of Labour (2017), '2017 Findings on the Worst Forms of Child Labor', Available at: https://www.dol.gov/sites/dolgov/files/ILAB/child_labor_reports/tda2017/ChildLaborReport.pdf (accessed 2 July 2019).

APPENDIX 6

U.S. DEPARTMENT OF LABOUR'S 2018 LIST OF GOODS PRODUCED BY CHILD LABOUR OR FORCED LABOUR

The Bureau of International Labor Affairs (ILAB) maintains a list of goods and their source countries which it has reason to believe are produced by child labor or forced labor in violation of international standards, as required under the **Trafficking Victims Protection Reauthorization Act (TVPRA) of 2005** and subsequent reauthorizations. As of September 20, 2018, the List of Goods Produced by Child Labor or Forced Labor comprises 148 goods from 76 countries.

ILAB maintains the List primarily to raise public awareness about forced labor and child labor around the world and to promote efforts to combat them; it is not intended to be punitive, but rather to serve as a catalyst for more strategic and focused coordination and collaboration among those working to address these problems.

Publication of the List has resulted in new opportunities for ILAB to engage with foreign governments to combat forced labor and child labor. It is also a valuable resource for researchers, advocacy organizations and companies wishing to carry out risk assessments and engage in due diligence on labor rights in their supply chains.[192]

[192] Bureau of International Labour Affairs of the U.S. Department of Labour (2019), 'List of Goods Produced by Child Labor or Forced Labor', Available at: https://www.dol.gov/agencies/ilab/reports/child-labor/list-of-goods (accessed 2 July 2019).

Country	Good	Child Labor	Forced Labor
Afghanistan	Bricks	X	X
Afghanistan	Carpets	X	
Afghanistan	Coal	X	
Afghanistan	Poppies	X	
Afghanistan	Salt	X	
Angola	Diamonds	X	X
Argentina	Blueberries	X	
Argentina	Bricks	X	
Argentina	Cotton	X	
Argentina	Garlic	X	
Argentina	Garments	X	X
Argentina	Grapes	X	
Argentina	Olives	X	
Argentina	Strawberries	X	
Argentina	Tobacco	X	
Argentina	Tomatoes	X	
Argentina	Yerba Mate (stimulant plant)	X	
Azerbaijan	Cotton	X	
Bangladesh	Bidis (hand-rolled cigarettes)	X	
Bangladesh	Bricks	X	
Bangladesh	Dried Fish	X	X
Bangladesh	Footwear	X	
Bangladesh	Furniture (steel)	X	
Bangladesh	Garments	X	
Bangladesh	Glass	X	
Bangladesh	Leather	X	
Bangladesh	Matches	X	
Bangladesh	Poultry	X	
Bangladesh	Salt	X	
Bangladesh	Shrimp	X	
Bangladesh	Soap	X	
Bangladesh	Textiles	X	
Bangladesh	Textiles (jute)	X	
Belize	Bananas	X	
Belize	Citrus Fruits	X	

Belize	Sugarcane	X	
Benin	Cotton	X	X
Benin	Granite (crushed)	X	
Bolivia	Brazil Nuts/Chestnuts	X	X
Bolivia	Bricks	X	
Bolivia	Cattle		X
Bolivia	Corn	X	X
Bolivia	Gold	X	
Bolivia	Peanuts		X
Bolivia	Silver	X	
Bolivia	Sugarcane	X	X
Bolivia	Tin	X	
Bolivia	Zinc	X	
Brazil	Bananas	X	
Brazil	Beef	X	
Brazil	Bricks	X	
Brazil	Cashews	X	
Brazil	Cattle	X	X
Brazil	Ceramics	X	
Brazil	Charcoal	X	X
Brazil	Cocoa	X	
Brazil	Coffee	X	
Brazil	Corn	X	
Brazil	Cotton	X	
Brazil	Fish	X	
Brazil	Footwear	X	
Brazil	Garments		X
Brazil	Hogs	X	
Brazil	Manioc/Cassava	X	
Brazil	Pineapples	X	
Brazil	Poultry	X	
Brazil	Rice	X	
Brazil	Sheep	X	
Brazil	Sisal	X	
Brazil	Sugarcane	X	X
Brazil	Timber		X

Brazil	Tobacco	X	
Burkina Faso	Cotton	X	X
Burkina Faso	Gold	X	X
Burkina Faso	Granite	X	
Burma	Bamboo	X	X
Burma	Beans (green, soy, yellow)	X	X
Burma	Bricks	X	X
Burma	Garments	X	
Burma	Jade	X	X
Burma	Palm Thatch		X
Burma	Rice	X	X
Burma	Rubber	X	X
Burma	Rubies	X	X
Burma	Sesame		X
Burma	Shrimp		X
Burma	Sugarcane	X	X
Burma	Sunflowers		X
Burma	Teak	X	X
Cambodia	Alcoholic Beverages	X	
Cambodia	Bricks	X	
Cambodia	Fish	X	
Cambodia	Manioc/Cassava	X	
Cambodia	Meat	X	
Cambodia	Rubber	X	
Cambodia	Salt	X	
Cambodia	Shrimp	X	
Cambodia	Sugarcane	X	
Cambodia	Textiles	X	
Cambodia	Timber	X	
Cambodia	Tobacco	X	
Cameroon	Cocoa	X	
Central African Republic	Diamonds	X	
Chad	Cattle	X	
China	Artificial Flowers		X
China	Bricks	X	X

China	Christmas Decorations		X
China	Coal		X
China	Cotton	X	X
China	Electronics	X	X
China	Fireworks	X	X
China	Footwear		X
China	Garments		X
China	Nails		X
China	Textiles	X	
China	Toys	X	X
Colombia	Bricks (clay)	X	
Colombia	Coal	X	
Colombia	Coca (stimulant plant)	X	X
Colombia	Coffee	X	
Colombia	Emeralds	X	
Colombia	Gold	X	
Colombia	Pornography	X	
Colombia	Sugarcane	X	
Costa Rica	Cattle	X	
Costa Rica	Coffee	X	
Cote d'Ivoire	Cocoa	X	X
Cote d'Ivoire	Coffee	X	X
Democratic Republic of the Congo	Cobalt ore (heterogenite)	X	
Democratic Republic of the Congo	Copper	X	
Democratic Republic of the Congo	Diamonds	X	
Democratic Republic of the Congo	Gold	X	X
Democratic Republic of the Congo	Tantalum ore (coltan)	X	X
Democratic Republic of the Congo	Tin ore (cassiterite)	X	X
Democratic Republic of the Congo	Tungsten ore (wolframite)	X	X
Dominican Republic	Baked Goods	X	
Dominican Republic	Coffee	X	

Dominican Republic	Rice	X	
Dominican Republic	Sugarcane	X	X
Dominican Republic	Tomatoes	X	
Ecuador	Bananas	X	
Ecuador	Bricks	X	
Ecuador	Flowers	X	
Ecuador	Gold	X	
Egypt	Bricks	X	
Egypt	Cotton	X	
Egypt	Stones (limestone)	X	
El Salvador	Baked Goods	X	
El Salvador	Cattle	X	
El Salvador	Cereal Grains	X	
El Salvador	Coffee	X	
El Salvador	Fireworks	X	
El Salvador	Shellfish	X	
El Salvador	Sugarcane	X	
Eswatini	Bovines	X	
Ethiopia	Cattle	X	
Ethiopia	Gold	X	
Ethiopia	Textiles (hand-woven)	X	X
Ghana	Cocoa	X	
Ghana	Fish	X	X
Ghana	Gold	X	
Ghana	Tilapia (fish)	X	X
Guatemala	Broccoli	X	
Guatemala	Coffee	X	
Guatemala	Corn	X	
Guatemala	Fireworks	X	
Guatemala	Gravel (crushed stones)	X	
Guatemala	Sugarcane	X	
Guinea	Cashews	X	
Guinea	Cocoa	X	
Guinea	Coffee	X	
Guinea	Diamonds	X	
Guinea	Gold	X	

Honduras	Coffee	X	
Honduras	Lobsters	X	
Honduras	Melons	X	
India	Bidis (hand-rolled cigarettes)	X	
India	Brassware	X	
India	Bricks	X	X
India	Carpets	X	X
India	Cottonseed (hybrid)	X	X
India	Embellished Textiles	X	X
India	Fireworks	X	
India	Footwear	X	
India	Garments	X	X
India	Gems	X	
India	Glass Bangles	X	
India	Incense (agarbatti)	X	
India	Leather Goods/Accessories	X	
India	Locks	X	
India	Matches	X	
India	Mica	X	
India	Rice	X	X
India	Silk Fabric	X	
India	Silk Thread	X	
India	Soccer Balls	X	
India	Stones	X	X
India	Sugarcane	X	
India	Thread/Yarn	X	
India	Cotton	X	
Indonesia	Fish	X	X
Indonesia	Footwear (sandals)	X	
Indonesia	Gold	X	
Indonesia	Oil (palm)	X	
Indonesia	Rubber	X	
Indonesia	Tin	X	
Indonesia	Tobacco	X	
Iran	Bricks	X	
Iran	Carpets	X	

Kazakhstan	Cotton	X	X
Kenya	Coffee	X	
Kenya	Fish	X	
Kenya	Miraa (stimulant plant)	X	
Kenya	Rice	X	
Kenya	Sand	X	
Kenya	Sisal	X	
Kenya	Sugarcane	X	
Kenya	Tea	X	
Kenya	Tobacco	X	
Kyrgyz Republic	Cotton	X	
Kyrgyz Republic	Tobacco	X	
Lebanon	Potatoes	X	
Lebanon	Tobacco	X	
Lesotho	Cattle	X	
Liberia	Diamonds	X	
Liberia	Rubber	X	
Madagascar	Sapphires	X	
Madagascar	Stones	X	
Madagascar	Vanilla	X	
Malawi	Tea	X	
Malawi	Tobacco	X	X
Malaysia	Electronics		X
Malaysia	Garments		X
Malaysia	Oil (palm)	X	X
Mali	Cotton	X	
Mali	Gold	X	
Mali	Rice	X	X
Mauritania	Cattle	X	
Mauritania	Goats	X	
Mexico	Beans (green beans)	X	
Mexico	Chile Peppers	X	X
Mexico	Coffee	X	
Mexico	Cucumbers	X	
Mexico	Eggplants	X	
Mexico	Melons	X	

Mexico	Onions	X	
Mexico	Poppies	X	
Mexico	Pornography	X	
Mexico	Sugarcane	X	
Mexico	Tobacco	X	
Mexico	Tomatoes	X	X
Mongolia	Coal	X	
Mongolia	Fluorspar (mineral)	X	
Mongolia	Gold	X	
Mozambique	Tobacco	X	
Namibia	Cattle	X	
Nepal	Bricks	X	X
Nepal	Carpets	X	X
Nepal	Embellished Textiles	X	X
Nepal	Stones	X	X
Nicaragua	Bananas	X	
Nicaragua	Coffee	X	
Nicaragua	Gold	X	
Nicaragua	Gravel (crushed stones)	X	
Nicaragua	Shellfish	X	
Nicaragua	Stones (pumice)	X	
Nicaragua	Tobacco	X	
Niger	Cattle		X
Niger	Gold	X	
Niger	Gypsum (mineral)	X	
Niger	Salt	X	
Niger	Trona (mineral)	X	
Nigeria	Cocoa	X	X
Nigeria	Gold	X	
Nigeria	Granite	X	X
Nigeria	Gravel (crushed stones)	X	X
Nigeria	Manioc/Cassava	X	
Nigeria	Sand	X	
North Korea	Bricks		X
North Korea	Cement		X
North Korea	Coal		X

North Korea	Gold		X
North Korea	Iron		X
North Korea	Textiles		X
North Korea	Timber		X
Pakistan	Bricks	X	X
Pakistan	Carpets	X	X
Pakistan	Coal	X	X
Pakistan	Cotton		X
Pakistan	Glass Bangles	X	
Pakistan	Leather	X	
Pakistan	Sugarcane		X
Pakistan	Surgical Instruments	X	
Pakistan	Wheat		X
Panama	Coffee	X	
Panama	Melons	X	
Paraguay	Beans	X	
Paraguay	Bricks	X	
Paraguay	Cabbages	X	
Paraguay	Carrots	X	
Paraguay	Cattle	X	X
Paraguay	Corn	X	
Paraguay	Fish	X	
Paraguay	Goats	X	
Paraguay	Hogs	X	
Paraguay	Lettuce	X	
Paraguay	Manioc/Cassava	X	
Paraguay	Melons	X	
Paraguay	Onions	X	
Paraguay	Peanuts	X	
Paraguay	Peppers	X	
Paraguay	Pornography	X	
Paraguay	Poultry	X	
Paraguay	Sesame	X	
Paraguay	Sheep	X	
Paraguay	Stones (limestone)	X	
Paraguay	Sugarcane	X	

Paraguay	Sweet Potatoes	X	
Paraguay	Tomatoes	X	
Paraguay	Yerba Mate (stimulant plant)	X	
Peru	Brazil Nuts/Chestnuts		X
Peru	Bricks	X	
Peru	Coca (stimulant plant)	X	
Peru	Fireworks	X	
Peru	Fish	X	
Peru	Gold	X	X
Peru	Timber		X
Philippines	Bananas	X	
Philippines	Coconuts	X	
Philippines	Corn	X	
Philippines	Fashion Accessories	X	
Philippines	Fish	X	
Philippines	Gold	X	
Philippines	Hogs	X	
Philippines	Pornography	X	
Philippines	Pyrotechnics	X	
Philippines	Rice	X	
Philippines	Rubber	X	
Philippines	Sugarcane	X	
Philippines	Tobacco	X	
Russia	Bricks		X
Russia	Pornography	X	X
Russia	Timber		X
Rwanda	Tea	X	
Senegal	Gold	X	
Sierra Leone	Cocoa	X	
Sierra Leone	Coffee	X	
Sierra Leone	Diamonds	X	X
Sierra Leone	Granite	X	
Sierra Leone	Oil (Palm)	X	
South Sudan	Cattle	X	X
Sudan	Gold	X	
Suriname	Gold	X	

Tajikistan	Cotton	X	X
Tanzania	Cloves	X	
Tanzania	Coffee	X	
Tanzania	Nile Perch (fish)	X	
Tanzania	Gold	X	
Tanzania	Sisal	X	
Tanzania	Tanzanite (gems)	X	
Tanzania	Tea	X	
Tanzania	Tobacco	X	
Thailand	Fish		X
Thailand	Garments	X	X
Thailand	Pornography	X	
Thailand	Shrimp	X	X
Thailand	Sugarcane	X	
Turkey	Citrus Fruits	X	
Turkey	Cotton	X	
Turkey	Cumin	X	
Turkey	Footwear	X	
Turkey	Furniture	X	
Turkey	Garments	X	
Turkey	Hazelnuts	X	
Turkey	Peanuts	X	
Turkey	Pulses (legumes)	X	
Turkey	Sugar Beets	X	
Turkmenistan	Cotton	X	X
Uganda	Bricks	X	
Uganda	Cattle	X	
Uganda	Charcoal	X	
Uganda	Coffee	X	
Uganda	Fish	X	
Uganda	Gold	X	
Uganda	Rice	X	
Uganda	Sand	X	
Uganda	Stones	X	
Uganda	Sugarcane	X	
Uganda	Tea	X	

Uganda	Tobacco	X	
Uganda	Vanilla	X	
Ukraine	Amber	X	
Ukraine	Coal	X	
Ukraine	Pornography	X	
Uzbekistan	Cotton		X
Uzbekistan	Silk Cocoons		X
Vietnam	Bricks	X	
Vietnam	Cashews	X	
Vietnam	Coffee	X	
Vietnam	Fish	X	
Vietnam	Footwear	X	
Vietnam	Furniture	X	
Vietnam	Garments	X	X
Vietnam	Leather	X	
Vietnam	Pepper	X	
Vietnam	Rice	X	
Vietnam	Rubber	X	
Vietnam	Sugarcane	X	
Vietnam	Tea	X	
Vietnam	Textiles	X	
Vietnam	Timber	X	
Vietnam	Tobacco	X	
Yemen	Fish	X	
Zambia	Cattle	X	
Zambia	Cotton	X	
Zambia	Gems	X	
Zambia	Stones	X	
Zambia	Tobacco	X	

Source: Bureau of International Labour Affairs of the U.S. Department of Labour (2018), 'List of Goods Produced by Child Labor or Forced Labor', Available at: https://www.dol.gov/sites/dolgov/files/ILAB/ListofGoods.pdf (accessed 2 July 2019).

INDEX

REFERENCES ARE TO PARAGRAPH NUMBERS

P

R

EHI ERIC ESOIMEME'S PUBLICATIONS

BOOKS

- Esoimeme, E.E. (2019), 'Balancing Anti-Money Laundering/Counter-Terrorist Financing Requirements and Financial Inclusion: The Case of Telecommunications Companies', DSC Publications Ltd, Available on Amazon: https://www.amazon.co.uk/Balancing-Anti-Money-Laundering-Counter-Terrorist-Requirements/dp/9782787892/ref=sr_1_1?keywords=esoimeme&qid=1559731958&s=gateway&sr=8-1

- Esoimeme, E.E. (2018), 'Deterring and Detecting Money Laundering and Terrorist Financing: A Comparative Analysis of Anti–Money Laundering and Counterterrorism Financing Strategies', DSC Publications Ltd, Available on Amazon: https://www.amazon.co.uk/Deterring-Detecting-Laundering-Terrorist-Financing/dp/9782787795/ref=sr_1_1?ie=UTF8&qid=1520869556&sr=8-1&keywords=ehi+esoimeme

- Esoimeme, E.E. (2015), 'The Risk-Based Approach to Combating Money Laundering and Terrorist Financing', Eric Press; Available on Amazon: https://www.amazon.co.uk/Risk-Based-Combating-Laundering-Terrorist-

Financing/dp/9789486030/ref=sr_1_2?ie=UTF8&qid=1437508453&sr=8-2&keywords=ehi+eric+esoimeme

- Esoimeme, E.E. (2014), 'A Comparative Study of the Money Laundering Laws/Regulations in Nigeria, the United States and the United Kingdom', Eric Press; Available on Amazon: https://www.amazon.co.uk/Comparative-Laundering-Regulations-Nigeria-Kingdom-ebook/dp/B00OC2X7HK/ref=sr_1_8?s=digital-text&ie=UTF8&qid=1413235091&sr=1-8&keywords=money+laundering

- Onwudiwe, C.C. and Esoimeme, E.E. (2016), 'Banker-Customer Relationship: A Practical Legal Guide', Bank Customers Association of Nigeria.

ARTICLES

- Esoimeme, E.E. (2019), 'Using the Risk-Based Approach to Curb Modern Slavery in the Supply Chain: the Anglo American and Marks & Spencer Example', Journal of Financial Crime, forthcoming.

- Esoimeme E.E. (2019), 'The Abacha Case: How AML Procedures Should Have Flagged $267m Earlier', KYC360 (the global financial crime and compliance knowledge hub powered by RiskScreen), https://www.riskscreen.com/kyc360/article/the-abacha-case-how-aml-procedures-should-have-flagged-267m-earlier/?

- Esoimeme E.E. (2019), 'Enhancing Financial Inclusion: Telecoms and AML in Nigeria', KYC360 (the global financial crime and compliance knowledge hub powered by RiskScreen), https://www.riskscreen.com/kyc360/research-papers/enhancing-financial-inclusion-telecoms-and-aml-in-nigeria/

- Esoimeme E.E. (2019), 'Institutionalising the War Against Corruption: New Approaches to Assets Tracing and Recovery', Journal of Financial Crime, https://papers.ssrn.com/sol3/papers.cfm?abstract_id=3243108, forthcoming (this paper was presented by Ehi Eric Esoimeme at the just concluded Nigerian Bar Association Annual General Conference 2018 in a session titled: Institutionalising the War Against Corruption: New Approaches to Assets Tracing and Recovery).

- Esoimeme E.E. (2019), 'Using Anti-Money Laundering Measures to Curb Pension Fraud in Nigeria', Journal of Financial Crime, forthcoming. The Article version of this research paper has already been published on KYC360 (the global financial crime and compliance knowledge hub powered by RiskScreen), https://www.riskscreen.com/kyc360/research-papers/using-anti-money-laundering-measures-to-curb-pension-fraud-in-nigeria/

- Esoimeme, E.E. (2019), 'Using the Lie Detector Test to Curb Corruption in the Nigerian Police Force', Journal of Financial Crime, forthcoming. The Article version of this research paper has already been published on KYC360 (the global financial crime and compliance knowledge hub powered by RiskScreen), https://kyc360.com/article/using-lie-detector-test-curb-corruption-nigerian-police-force/

- Esoimeme, E.E. (2019), 'A Critical Analysis of the Anti-Corruption Policy of the Federal Executive Council of Nigeria', Journal of Money Laundering Control, Vol. 22 Issue: 2, https://www.emeraldinsight.com/doi/pdfplus/10.1108/JMLC-06-2017-0021

- Esoimeme, E.E. (2019), 'Balancing Anti-money laundering measures and Financial Inclusion: the example of the United Kingdom and Nigeria', Journal of Money Laundering Control, Forthcoming, https://papers.ssrn.com/sol3/papers.cfm?abstract_id=3172081

- Esoimeme, E.E. (2018), 'A Comparative Analysis of the Prepaid Card Laws/Regulations in Nigeria, the United

Kingdom, the United States and India', Journal of Money Laundering Control, Vol. 21 Issue: 4, pp.481-493, https://doi.org/10.1108/JMLC-03-2017-0010

- Esoimeme, E.E. (2018), 'Banking: Curbing employee fraud and corruption with an effective KYE program', KYC360 (the global financial crime and compliance knowledge hub powered by RiskScreen), https://www.riskscreen.com/kyc360/article/banking-curbing-employee-fraud-and-corruption-with-an-effective-kye-program/

- Esoimeme E.E. (2018), 'Fighting Corruption? It's Worth Considering a Preventive Approach to Asset Recovery', KYC360 (the global financial crime and compliance knowledge hub powered by RiskScreen), https://kyc360.com/article/fighting-corruption-its-worth-considering-a-preventive-approach-to-asset-recovery/

- Esoimeme, E.E. (2018), 'A Critical Analysis of the Anti-Corruption Policy of the National Judicial Council of Nigeria', Journal of Money Laundering Control, Vol. 21 Issue: 3, https://www.emeraldinsight.com/doi/pdfplus/10.1108/JMLC-01-2017-0001

- Esoimeme, E.E. (2018), 'The money laundering risks and vulnerabilities associated with MMM Nigeria', Journal of

Money Laundering Control, Vol. 21 Issue: 1, pp.112-119, http://www.emeraldinsight.com/doi/full/10.1108/JMLC-01-2017-0002

- Esoimeme, E.E. (2017), 'A critical analysis of the effects of the Central Bank of Nigeria foreign exchange policy on financial inclusion, anti-money laundering measures and fundamental rights', Journal of Money Laundering Control, Vol. 20 Issue: 4, pp.417-427, https://doi.org/10.1108/JMLC-05-2016-0020

- Esoimeme, E.E. (2017), "The Nigerian Money Laundering (Prevention and Prohibition) Bill, 2016: a critical appraisal", Journal of Money Laundering Control, Vol. 20 Issue: 1, pp.79-88, https://doi.org/10.1108/JMLC-07-2016-0025

- Esoimeme, E.E. (2016), 'Wealth Management, Tax Evasion and Money Laundering: The Panama Papers Case Study', Law Digest Issue 11 Autumn 2016. Available at Law Digest: https://issuu.com/nglawdigest/docs/law_digest_issue_11_autumn_2016

- Esoimeme, E.E. (2016), 'Balancing Anti-Money Laundering/Counter-Terrorist Financing Requirements and Financial Inclusion for Migrants: A Case Study of

Germany', Available at SSRN: https://ssrn.com/abstract=2710097

- Esoimeme, E.E. (2015), 'A Critical Analysis of the Bank Verification Number Project Introduced by the Central Bank of Nigeria', Available at SSRN: https://ssrn.com/abstract=2544934 or http://dx.doi.org/10.2139/ssrn.2544934

- Esoimeme, E.E. (2015), 'A Comparative Study of the Money Laundering Laws/Regulations in Nigeria, the United States and the United Kingdom: Reporting Requirements', Professionals Center for Business Research Volume 2 – June 2015 (06). Available at SSRN: https://ssrn.com/abstract=2441086

- Esoimeme, E.E. (2015), 'The Death Penalty: An Effective Anti-Corruption Mechanism?', Available at SSRN: https://ssrn.com/abstract=2621268

- Esoimeme, E.E. (2015), 'A Critical Analysis of the Anti-Money Laundering Measures Adopted by BitGold Inc', Available at SSRN: https://ssrn.com/abstract=2604721 or http://dx.doi.org/10.2139/ssrn.2604721

- Esoimeme, E.E. (2014), 'Has the Concept of Plea Bargaining Been Abused in Nigeria's Criminal Justice

System?', The Legal Aid Journal Volume 1. Available at SSRN: https://ssrn.com/abstract=2462307

- Esoimeme, E.E. (2014), 'A Comparative Study of the Money Laundering Laws/Regulations in Nigeria, the United States and the United Kingdom: Cash Couriers', The PUNCH, VOL 38 NO. 20,733, 20,739 PAGE 25, 29. Available at SSRN: https://ssrn.com/abstract=2476587

- Esoimeme, E.E. (2013), 'A Critical Analysis of the Effect of the Double Criminality Test on the Investigation Team and the Prosecution's Case', Available at SSRN: https://ssrn.com/abstract=2514719

- Esoimeme, E.E. (2013), 'A Critical Analysis of the Effect of the Double Criminality Test on Nominated Officers and Money Laundering Reporting Officers (MLRO) in the Regulated Sector', Available at SSRN: https://ssrn.com/abstract=2462952

- Esoimeme, E.E. (2013), 'The Importance of Why Firms Dealing with PEPs Must Adopt a Risk-Based Approach to Their Compliance Programmes', Available at SSRN: https://ssrn.com/abstract=2430972

EHI ERIC ESOIMEME HAS EDITED THE FOLLOWING PUBLICATIONS:

- Sasegbon's Judicial Dictionary of Nigerian Law (the first comprehensive judicial dictionary in Nigeria in 7 Volumes), DSC Publications Ltd.

- Sasegbon on Election Petitions, DSC Publications Ltd., Volume 3 Part III and 12 other volumes.

EHI ERIC ESOIMEME HAS ALSO PEER REVIEWED THE FOLLOWING PUBLICATIONS:

- Ross, I. (2015), 'Exposing Fraud: Skills, Process and Practicalities', Wiley Corporate F&A. Available on Amazon: https://www.amazon.co.uk/Exposing-Fraud-Process-Practicalities-Corporate-ebook/dp/B01CJK4Z8Q/ref=sr_1_fkmr0_2?ie=UTF8&qid=1493990138&sr=8-2-fkmr0&keywords=ian+ross+on+fraud

- Nwachukwu, E. (2015), 'Academic Excellence in 21 Days', Partridge Africa. Available on Amazon: https://www.amazon.co.uk/Academic-Excellence-Days-Eric-Nwachukwu/dp/1482826224/ref=sr_1_1?ie=UTF8&qid=1493990393&sr=8-1&keywords=eric+nwachukwu

www.ingramcontent.com/pod-product-compliance
Lightning Source LLC
Chambersburg PA
CBHW072242240926
51846CB00012B/140
* 9 7 8 9 7 8 2 7 8 7 9 1 0 *